THE AFRICAN PRESENCE
IN WORLD AFFAIRS

THE AFRICAN PRESENCE IN WORLD AFFAIRS

National Development and Its Role in Foreign Policy

ARNOLD RIVKIN

The Free Press of Glencoe

Collier-Macmillan Limited, London

A publication in a series of studies on African economic and political development from the Center for International Studies, Massachusetts Institute of Technology

Second Printing October 1964

For information, address:

THE FREE PRESS OF GLENCOE
A Division of The Macmillan Company
The Crowell-Collier Publishing Company
60 Fifth Avenue, New York 11

DESIGNED BY CHRISTIAN OHSER

Library of Congress Catalog Card Number: 63-13542

For
JAY and for
GIGI, MITCH,
and LAURA

FOREWORD

The world is changing at a faster pace than ever before in history. Nowhere is this turbulent mixture of evolution and revolution more dramatically evident than on the continent of Africa. Six years ago, when the studies on which this book is based were first conceived, there were only three independent nations between the Sahara and the Union of South Africa. As I write this a mere six years later there are twenty-six, with several more due for independence in the near future. This abrupt alteration in the political status of millions of Africans is but a symptom of the much more profound social, psychological, and economic changes which characterize the transition from tradition to modernity in emerging societies everywhere.

This explosive change in both the quality of African life and the role of Africa in world affairs poses unusual problems for the United States. In less than a decade a host of issues that we formerly regarded as problems for our European allies have come to rest in our immediate lap, leading in many cases to friction with those same allies. Arnold Rivkin has observed this transition in United States' concerns with Africa from a number of vantage points. During the Marshall Plan period he helped administer aid from Paris and London for what were then called the Dependent Overseas Territories under the Economic Cooperation Administration. He concerned himself with aid issues in Washington in the General Counsel's Office of the various successor agencies to ECA until he came to the Center for International Studies in 1957 to direct a broad program of research into economic and political change in a number of the new states of the African continent. In the course of this program, carried on partly in Cambridge, Massachusetts, partly in London, and partly in the field, he made repeated visits throughout the area south of the Sahara.

He interrupted his researches on frequent occasions to perform negotiating missions for the United States government.

This book is the result of the combination of academic and operational reflections generated from his experience. We present it in confidence that it will be helpful to all those who would improve their understanding both of the new Africa coming into being and the new problems with which it confronts the United States.

Max F. Millikan

PREFACE

My introduction to things African came in 1950, when as Assistant General Counsel of the European Headquarters of the Marshall Plan in Paris I was asked to go on a special mission to Madagascar. Strangely enough, it was the Korean War on the other side of the globe which precipitated the mission. A little known and somewhat obscure provision of the original Marshall Plan legislation authorized the Economic Cooperation Administration to bring into production new sources of strategic materials and to accept in repayment for loans granted to this end scarce materials for the United States' strategic materials stockpile. Two of the materials much in demand for the stockpile at the outbreak of the Korean War—large flake graphite and phlogophite mica—were to be found on the island of Madagascar, some 150 miles off the shore of southeast Africa. Hence my mission there late in 1950.

Armed with a briefcase full of legal documents and mining reports, a slide rule, a portable typewriter, and authorization to negotiate agreements to bring new mines into production and expand the output of existing ones, I set out on my one-man mission. It carried me in an eight-week period up and down and across most of that large and remote island in the Indian Ocean. I traveled mostly by automobile but not infrequently on foot, by the period-piece railroad, which defied the laws of gravity, by the island airline, equipped with refitted captured German transport planes, and on a motley assortment of river boats and ferries.

I was completely taken with the experience, and ever since I have had both a professional and personal interest in all things African. I wanted to know and understand more about what has in many ways been a lost frontier in world affairs.

In Madagascar I found the Africa of Conrad and Gide but I also encountered the stirrings and sounds of the new which were

ix

to plunge Africa from the backwaters of history into the limelight of world affairs before the decade of the 1950's had run its course. The Africa which led Conrad to write of his voyage up the Congo River in 1889, "We penetrated deeper and deeper into the heart of darkness"—and which led Gide to write, after traveling through the Middle Congo some thirty-five years later, "We are on the other side of hell . . . barbarism is behind"—was still very much in evidence in 1950. But there was also the Africa on the brink of the independence revolution which was to sweep across two thirds or more of the African continent by the early 1960's. The scars and the repressive aftermath of the abortive rebellion of the Malagasy against French colonial rule in 1947 was still fresh in the minds of the colonized as well as the colonizers.

Also, side by side with Conrad's "prehistoric man" who lived in the heart of darkness, and Gide's "native" to whom the logic of "cause and effect" was unknown, there was found in the Madagascar of 1950 a small but growing elite of educated Malagasy who were preparing to put into practice some of the new learning they had acquired from their colonizers. These transitional Malagasy, hovering between traditional and modern society, were soon to lead an independent state.

It seemed to me then that if one could learn more about this vital transitional group of Africans in Madagascar and across the length and breadth of Africa generally, one could gain an inkling of—perhaps even insight into—what was to happen in Africa later in the 1950's and in the 1960's. It also seemed to me that an understanding of their changing societies, and of the political and economic circumstances which were the context out of which the new Africa would emerge, was probably indispensable to knowing more about the transitional Africans as people. Thus in the period 1950–1956, while working in Paris, London, and Washington in various capacities, I supplemented my official trips to British and French African territories with a rich diet of reading and discussion of things African wherever and whenever possible.

In late 1956 I accepted the invitation of Dr. Max F. Millikan, Director of the Center for International Studies at the Massachusetts Institute of Technology, to join the senior staff of the Center to develop and direct an African research program. The present volume grows out of the special structure of that program, which has been an attempt to apply the general research philosophy of the Center to African development. Specifically, this volume attempts to describe, analyze, and interrelate the processes of political and economic change in Africa south of the Sahara, to relate the internal dynamics of the new states of Africa to their international behavior (as well as noting the feedback of their international performance into their internal policies), and finally, to weigh the implications of the actions of the new African states at home and abroad with regard to the foreign policy of the United States and other Western nations. In other words, this volume attempts to examine the African presence in world affairs deriving from the internal dynamics of African economic growth and political change. And it attempts to do this on a multi-disciplinary basis, drawing principally on the disciplines of economics and political science.

It is with pleasure that I acknowledge the contribution of three of my colleagues at the Center for International Studies to the work of the African project and more particularly to my own work. First, I should like to thank Dr. Millikan for his invitation to join the Center staff, for the large degree of confidence he reposed in me as Director of the African project with almost unlimited discretion and freedom of action to carry out the research program, and for his generosity in writing the foreword to this volume.

Second, I should like to express my appreciation to Professor Walt W. Rostow for the innumerable imaginative and stimulating suggestions he advanced, particularly in the early stages of our work with respect to formulating the terms of our research efforts and working out a suitable research design, and for his unfailing friendly interest in the African project throughout the time he was at M.I.T.

Thirdly, I should like to express my everlasting thanks and appreciation to Richard W. Hatch, who from the inception of the project gave generously of his time and wisdom. It is with marked pleasure that I acknowledge my very considerable debt to this friendly, understanding, and talented editor and critic.

In connection with the final manuscript of the book, I am indebted to three more colleagues at M.I.T. Professor Everett E.

Hagen, and Donald L. M. Blackmer, Assistant Director of the Center for International Studies, provided me with detailed page-by-page criticism. In doing so—because we did not always see things the same way—they led me to a useful re-examination of several important points in the book. Mrs. Jean Clark, Assistant Editor of the Center, was most helpful on all the technical aspects of the book, particularly the preparation of the tables, notes, and index.

I should like to express my thanks to two part-time colleagues on the project, Mrs. Ona B. Forrest and Gordon Unsworth. Mrs. Forrest throughout the life of the project, and Gordon Unsworth in its early years, have been valuable associates and particularly helpful to me. I am grateful to the United Nations Secretariat for making them both available to participate in our work at M.I.T.

I should like to say a special word of thanks to Professor Kenneth Robinson, Director of the Institute of Commonwealth Studies at the University of London, for his friendly and stimulating interest in my work and for his generosity in making the facilities of the Institute available to me for a research base whenever I was in London.

In London, too, I should like to thank the dynamic editor of *West Africa*, David Williams, one of the most knowledgeable persons I know on African affairs, for the many stimulating discussions we had on the broad range of African economic and political problems. I could not express my thanks to Mr. Williams, however, without also expressing my appreciation to his charming wife, Penelope, who most graciously put up with our many long discussions, some of which lasted into the small hours of the morning.

I should also like to express my appreciation to His Excellency Hanon Yavor, successively the Israeli Ambassador to Liberia and to Nigeria, whose knowledge of African affairs is outstanding. On many occasions in both Monrovia and Lagos he was willing to sit for long hours and discuss and debate with me the whole range of African politics.

Nearer home, I should like to express my gratitude to Taylor Ostrander, Assistant to the Chairman of American Metal Climax, and his wife, Ruth, for their friendly and sustained interest in my work, for Mr. Ostrander's most valuable help in arranging for my trip to the Northern Rhodesian Copperbelt, and for his many valuable introductions to key African and European personalities throughout the Federation of Rhodesia and Nyasaland.

I should like, too, to express my thanks to Alan Pifer, formerly Executive Associate and now Vice-President of the Carnegie Corporation of New York, who in addition to being an understanding officer of the foundation which generously financed the overseas work of myself and my four colleagues, proved to be a most interested and helpful friend of the project. On any number of occasions he shared his rich knowledge of many parts of Africa with me.

At this point it is also appropriate to express my thanks once again to the Carnegie Corporation of New York for making possible the two years of field work undertaken by the African Project. The Corporation is, of course, not responsible for any of the opinions or judgments contained in this volume.

I should also like to express my debt to the authors and publishers of the growing body of literature, official, semi-official, and private, coming out of Africa on things African, to which I have made frequent reference in my research. I should like specifically to thank the following organizations for their kind permission to quote from volumes they have published or are otherwise responsible for: Editions Présence Africaine for permission to quote from *Toward Full Re-Africanisation* by Sékou Touré; Editions Présence Africaine and the American Society of African Culture for permission to quote from *African Socialism* by Léopold Sédar Senghor; Cambridge University Press for permission to quote from *Zik* by Dr. Nnandi Azikiwe; Frederick A. Praeger for permission to quote from *I Speak of Africa* by Dr. Kwame Nkrumah; and Curtis Brown Ltd., and Harper & Row, Publishers, for permission to quote from *Mister Johnson* by Joyce Cary.

I have put off to the penultimate paragraph the expression of my gratitude and appreciation to the many people in Africa who gave generously and willingly of their time, knowledge, and friendship. It would not be possible for me to list all of them or to say all of the things I should say with respect to each of them. Hence I shall make my expression a symbolic one by expressing thanks to a small group of Africans whom I have come to know best and who are from the African country which I have come to know best, the Federation of Nigeria. My thanks then to Chief S. O. Adebo, formerly Chief Secretary and Head of the Civil Service in the Western Region and now the Nigerian Permanent Representative to the United Nations (with the rank of Ambassador) and Economic Commissioner General of Nigeria in Washington, D.C., charged with maintaining liaison with the International Bank for Reconstruction and Development Consultative Group on Aid to Nigeria; and co-author of the pioneering Phillipson-Adebo report of 1953 on Nigerianisation of the public service, which I have made frequent use of in my research on Africanization; to Chief Isaac Dina, Permanent Secretary of the Treasury in the Western Region and also the successor to Chief Adebo as Head of the Civil Service in the Western Region; to Andrew I. Wilson, Esq., Permanent Secretary to the Ministry of Economic Planning and Community Development for the Western Region; to Dr. Pius N. C. Okigbo, Economic Adviser to the Premier of the Eastern Region and author of the most useful study, *Nigerian National Accounts, 1950–57*, published in 1961; to L. O. V. Anionwu, Esq., formerly Chief Nigerianisation Officer, then Permanent Secretary of the Ministry of Foreign Affairs and Commonwealth Relations, and now Nigerian Ambassador to Italy; and to Ali Akilu, Esq., Secretary to the Premier of the Northern Region. To all of these outstanding civil servants, and through them to all of the many Africans who were so helpful and so hospitable, I express my warm thanks.

Finally, I should like to thank my wife who, if I may borrow a phrase from Van Wyck Brooks, not only edited the substance of my work on this book and on the preceding one [1] but, more importantly, edited me throughout the period of the project, at home and abroad, and to our three children who helped their mother perform this most difficult task. It is with pleasure that I dedicate this volume to them—to Jay, and Gigi, Mitch, and Laura.

Arnold Rivkin

Cambridge, Massachusetts
March 1963

CONTENTS

PART FOUR—*The African Presence in World Affairs*

PART ONE

Introduction: *Concepts and Themes*

It would seem that what is true of Nigerian politics is similarly true of her economics, namely the need to reconcile systems to objectives. It is necessary to set out national economic objectives and then to reconcile foreign policy to them. Economic development is the natural way of adjusting a traditional society to the exacting demands of a modern democratic way of life.*

CHIEF H. O. DAVIES
Lawyer, author, and sometime newspaper publisher in Nigeria

* *Nigeria: Prospects for Democracy*, London, 1961.

Chapter 1

THE MULTI-DIMENSIONAL AFRICAN PRESENCE

The African presence in world affairs is a distillation of the problems of economic growth and the quest of the new African states for political stability. Thus it is not the single presence postulated by President Nkrumah under the rubric of the African personality. It is a multi-dimensional presence arising from the sudden dramatic thrust of twenty-eight new nations on the world scene in a seven-year period.* The new states include members of the British Commonwealth, the Franco-African Community, and the Arab League. They are all members of the United Nations. The new states may be members of the Casablanca bloc, the Monrovia bloc, and, within the latter, the Brazzaville bloc, or on the threshold of one of the African blocs. They may also be members of the Afro-Asian bloc, or the Belgrade "neutralist" bloc, or have a foot in several blocs.† Their spokesmen include an emperor and several kings as well as presidents and premiers. The heads of state and government are mostly French-speaking and English-

* See Appendix I for complete list of independent African States as of March 31, 1963, with dates of accession to independence and other relevant data.

† See Appendix II for membership of independent African States in the various African blocs and other regional and international state systems.

3

speaking. Among the French-speaking are such varied figures as Léopold Sédar Senghor, Houphouët-Boigny, Sékou Touré, Habib Bourguiba, Cyrille Adoula, and Joseph Kasavubu. Among the English-speaking there are such contrasting personalities as Alhaji Sir Abubakar Tafawa Balewa, Kwame Nkrumah, Sir Milton Margai, William V. S. Tubman, Julius Nyerere, and Milton Obote. And so on the world scene the African presence takes on varied forms and speaks with many voices.

The Demise of Colonialism

In its broadest impact on world affairs the African presence signifies the end of anachronistic colonial empires.

In the British and French cases the African surge toward independence—African nationalism—has been met by an appreciation of the dynamics of postwar colonial change—European decolonization. Accommodations have been made and are being made. In sub-Sahara Africa violence has been notably absent in the birth of nearly two dozen states out of the British and French holdings there. Only Algeria most recently and Morocco and Tunisia at an earlier time in North Africa, and the Federation of Rhodesia and Nyasaland now and Kenya somewhat earlier in sub-Sahara Africa, have seriously marred the relatively peaceful transition to statehood of colonies of the two major African empires, the French and the British.

Belgium, the third of the big four European colonial powers in Africa, has had its empire abruptly liquidated. Its major holding, the Congo, came to independence and crisis is mid-1960. Its trust territory, Ruanda-Urandi, became independent just two years later as the Republic of Rwanda and the Kingdom of Burundi. The African presence projected on the world scene by the Congo crisis is one of violence, chaos, tribalism, primitiveness, and bewildering factionalism. Sadly, in the new states Rwanda and Burundi many of the same seeds of crisis have been planted and may germinate at any moment.

The Congo dimension of the African presence has permeated not only the Congolese presence *per se* but also that of the many other African states which have played leading roles in the Congo affair. Thus a Ghanaian battalion of the United Nations forces in the Congo mutinied and had to be recalled and disbanded; repeatedly Ethiopian troops have been accused of pillaging and of quarreling with other United Nations units; Ghanaian, Guinean, and United Arab Republic diplomatic personnel were accused of interfering in the internal affairs of the Congo and intriguing against the Kasavubu government, and were summarily ousted. And one of the most divisive factors in the relationships among African states has been their differing attitudes toward the various Congolese factions.

The most intractable of the Congolese problems, the Katanga secession issue, has revealed much about the African presence in world affairs. It has illustrated the special meaning Africans tend to attach to the term "self-determination." Obviously, for many it does not comprehend "secession" from an independent African state, no matter how determined the would-be secessionists may be to attain independent status or how legitimate their claim for such status. Self-determination in the African sense tends to be operative only against colonial powers.

Only Portugal of the four major colonial powers remains fully engaged, and apparently determined to remain so, in Africa. The African presence as projected by Portuguese Angola is characterized by violence, bitterness, and destructiveness. The posture appears to be one of lashing out on all sides and a determination to prevail or pull the total edifice down, come what may. The Portuguese government seems to be saying, "We shall keep the structure we have created or destroy it in the process of defending it against all comers"; and the Angola rebels seem to be saying, "We shall have what is rightfully ours even if we have to reduce it to ashes to get it." The Portuguese empire in Africa is doomed, and the Africans in Portuguese areas of Africa seemed doomed to an orgy of blood-letting and chaos before and after independence which will make preceding events in the Congo, unbelievably cruel and chaotic as they may now seem to be, appear as proper as a garden party.

The Italian empire in Africa was liquidated by United Nations fiat as a result of Italy's defeat in World War II. The last segment of this poverty-stricken and, as the conquest of Ethiopia demonstrated, hard-won empire, Italian Somaliland, acceded to independence in 1961 and signalled Italy's disappearance as a colonial power.

The Spanish empire in Africa, always small and peripheral, persists under increasing African attack—physical as well as verbal. The African presence here has manifested itself in sporadic and repeated incursions of Moroccan "irregulars" into Spanish Sahara, periodic outbreaks of violence against the Spanish enclave of Ifni, once again at the hands of Moroccan irregulars, and reiterated Moroccan claims, larded with threats of force, to the Spanish-held cities along the northern rim of Morocco. Spain has already evacuated the Spanish zone in Morocco, which, along with the internationally administered city of Tangier, has become an integal part of the Kingdom of Morocco.

Thus the African presence in the world arena has loomed larger and larger as the empires which contained that presence recede into the backwaters of history. The process is a dual one—an African thrust and a European withdrawal—planned or otherwise. Where the European withdrawal has been timely and flexible it not only has accommodated the African thrust, it also has facilitated it. In radical nationalist African circles this midwife role has bred resentment. It has robbed the independence revolution of martyrs and struggle. The "struggle for independence" was rendered a literary term rather than a descriptive one of physical strife at the barricades. Where the European withdrawal has been ill-timed and out of joint with the political and social realities it has left a bitter legacy of death and destruction. A precipitous withdrawal in the Congo after a sterile period without preparation brought on Africa's most chaotic crisis. A delayed withdrawal in Algeria brought on the most costly of all African wars—in human and material terms. Either way, timely or belated, European withdrawal interacting with the African nationalist push has created a duality which is an integral part of the African presence and accounts for the rigorous, unrelenting, compulsive anti-colonialism of Africa, a major attribute of its presence on the world stage.

There is a second significance to events born of the colonial liquidation. Katanga has dramatically demonstrated a special aspect of the egalitarian spirit so often associated with the African presence. Even African socialists and self-avowed Marxists have adopted the line that "historically" African societies have tended to be egalitarian. Thus they deny the applicability of the basic Marxist concept of the class struggle to African societies and are deviationists on this fundamental element of Marxism. Katanga, however, has revealed what others before have suggested, i.e., those who have do not always care to share with the many who do not have. Thus the Ivory Coast, Gabon, Mauritania, and Katanga have not been overjoyed by the proposals and prospects for larger political groupings. The first three by accidents of history—and some Africans would allege by French design—came to independence as separate independent states. Hence all they need do is resist Pan-Africanist pressures to join larger political associations, unions, or groupings. Katanga, once again by accident of history—and some would allege as a result of Belgian ineptitude—came to independence as a part of a larger unit. Hence its lot is a more difficult one. In order to retain unto itself its riches it must secede. In doing so, or in attempting to do so, it has brought down on its head widespread and near-universal African wrath.

Thus the egalitarian spirit as a guiding principle of foreign policy tends to be somewhat selective with respect to the choice of political friends and political groupings for the states disposing of wealth, and somewhat more universal for those aspiring to a share in that wealth.

Perhaps most importantly the Katanga incident reveals a quality in the African presence which has wide significance for world peace. Many African states have been willing, a smaller number prepared, and a still smaller number anxious to employ force on a large scale to achieve their objective of crushing an independent secessionist Katanga, even though this involved significant external intrusion in the internal affairs of the Congo by the United Nations and foreign powers, and even though this meant non-Africans killing Africans.

What the attitude of certain leading African nationalists would be if a secessionist tendency in one or another of the new states happened to coincide with the national interest of their

states, or their Pan-Africanist orientation, or their ideological outlook, remains to be seen. Indications are that for a good many
pragmatism rather than consistency or abstract principle would
prevail; i.e., self-determination would be reinstated, not as secession,
which has already been declared unacceptable, but as "national
liberation." Thus in pursuit of another African nationalist concept—"national liberation" of African countries from neo-colonialist "stooge governments"—subversion is an accepted tactic. In the
struggle for control in the former Republic of Cameroun, since
October 1, 1961 the Federal Republic of Cameroon, Guinea and
Ghana gave covert support to the rebellion, largely centered in
the Bamiléké area of the republic, as well as recognizing the exiled
leader of the rebellion, the late Dr. Félix Moumié. If Moumié
or his movement could have seized control of an area of the country, Guinean and Ghanaian recognition of Moumié as the "legal
government" of the country would have amounted to recognition
of a secessionist government laying claim to being the rightful
government of the entire country. So, in the Congo, recognition by
Guinea, Ghana, and the United Arab Republic of the Gizenga
régime in Stanleyville before the formation of the Adoula government as the "legal government" of the Congo amounted to recognition of a secessionist régime with pretensions to govern a larger
geographic area than it occupied or controlled.

However, when the Somali Republic recently invited the
Somalis living in colonial Kenya "to secede," Jomo Kenyatta,
president of the Kenya Africa National Union, one of the two
leading nationalist groups pressing for early independence for
Kenya, stormed that "colonists were using Somalia to foster a
policy of divide and rule." He then went on to warn against
"another Tshombe in Kenya." [1] "Self-determination" apparently
was not applicable even though what was proposed was withdrawal
from a colonial area; "national liberation" apparently was equally
inapplicable even though, once again, what was proposed was
withdrawal from a colonial area which at the time of the proposal
was in KANU terms run by an "African stooge-colonialist" coalition. Only "secession" was applicable, even though what was
proposed was withdrawal from a colonial area and adhesion to an
independent one, and even though Somalia's claim to incorpora-

tion of the Somalis in the desert wastelands of the Northern Frontier district of Kenya into Greater Somalia was no different from her claim, which has general support among African nationalists, to incorporation of the Somalis in French Somaliland into Greater Somalia.

It would thus seem clear that the African presence is, if anything, pragmatic. Self-determination applies only in anti-colonial situations; it becomes secession in African contexts. And secession, for some African nationalists, could readily become "national liberation" by the "legal government" ousted from its rightful place by an African "stooge government" operating in conjunction with a European "neo-colonialist" power. In this view it would be justifiable to use force and subversion to "liberate" the country held in thrall by the "stooge" government. In the words of Tawia Adamafio, the then Minister of Information of Ghana, "Ghana's Government does not consider all attempts to overthrow governments as crimes—it depends upon the government at which they are aimed." [2] And he might have added, "it depends on who is aiming."

The New Africa and World Peace

Looking outward again, the African presence has been an unprecedented one at the United Nations; there are no precedents for the Congo crisis and the United Nations' role in it, for the marathon Algerian crisis, for the pocket war in Bizerte, the Portuguese debacle in Angola, and the unending relentless African crusade against Western European colonialism, the only kind they have known in recent generations. Any one of these would have left its mark on the United Nations. Altogether, in sequence and simultaneously, as they have been from time to time, they have had a cumulative impact on the United Nations which will fundamentally alter its course. The Soviet troika proposal for reorganization of the Secretariat and the open Soviet campaign against the late Secretary-General, Dag Hammarskjöld, were in large part at least an outgrowth of the Congo crisis. The French disdain for the United Nations has been an outgrowth first of the Algerian, then the Tunisian, and finally the Congo crisis. The British suspicion of the United Nations, born in the Suez crisis and nurtured in that of the Congo, has grown by leaps and bounds with what Lord Home, the British Foreign Minister, has labeled the "irresponsibility" of the United Nations on colonial issues. In the British view this "irresponsibility" reached its climax with the General Assembly's "meddling" in the "internal affairs" of Southern Rhodesia, i.e., the struggle of Africans to oust Europeans from political control of Southern Rhodesia, the "self-governing" territory in the Federation of Rhodesia and Nyasaland. When the recurrent Republic of South Africa apartheid issue and related South-West Africa League of Nations mandate problem are added to the other items which have crowded the African agenda of the United Nations in recent years, it can be truly said the African presence dominated the 1960, 1961 and 1962 agendas of the United Nations and promises to do so again in coming years.

As was to be expected, Africa and its presence also dominated the proceedings of the United Nations Trusteeship Council. In 1961 the trust territories of French Togoland, French Cameroun, Italian Somaliland, and British Tanganyika all became independent states. And the British Cameroons, North and South, became independent and federated respectively with Nigeria and the Republic of Cameroun. The then remaining trust territory in Africa, Belgium's Ruanda-Urundi, was on the agenda several times with respect to tribal violence, a *coup d'état*, an election, and controversy over plans for a termination of the trusteeship. The territory acceded to independence as two states on July 1, 1962, amid suspicions between the new states, one a republic and the other a monarchy, recriminations by the radical nationalist African states and the Soviet Union over the temporary continuation of the presence of Belgian troops in the new states, and dire predictions of crises to come to these poor, overcrowded new states. The status of the mandated territory of South-West Africa rounded out the Trusteeship Council agenda.

There are many other manifestations of the African presence in world affairs which have potential for affecting world peace and the political balance of power in world affairs. Inherited colonial boundaries, denounced by one African nationalist leader after another as artificial and contrived, are one of the richest sources of actual and potential controversy and conflict. The number of situations with low boiling points are many and varied. On the fringe of the Sahara, Morocco lays claim to the entire territory of the Islamic Republic of Mauritania; the United Arab Republic has laid claim to a number of points along its shared border with the Sudan (although at this writing these claims have apparently been resolved or at any rate shelved); Algeria lays claim (which France recognized in the Evian agreement) to all of the Saharan hinterland administered by the French as separate departments, although Tunisia and Morocco both claim areas in the Sahara departments contiguous to their borders; Somalia and Ethiopia have been engaged in a minor and intermittent shooting war concerning border areas and grazing rights; Somalia also has claims on French Somaliland and northern Kenya as part of its dream of a Greater Somalia incorporating all Somali peoples; Zanzibar, under the suzerainty of the Sultan of Zanzibar, holds title to the valuable Mombasa strip on the coast of Kenya which Kenyan politicians, as independence approaches, are increasingly demanding be incorporated in an independent Kenya; the Federal Republic of Cameroon has not withdrawn its claims to the Northern Cameroons, incorporated as a result of a United Nations plebiscite into the Federation of Nigeria; and Ghana has on many occasions intimated that the way to resolve the division of the Ewe tribe between Ghana and Togo is to incorporate Togo into the Republic of Ghana. One could cite a good many other sore spots.

Related to this irredentist aspect of the African presence but a serious consideration in its own right is the incipient arms race in Africa. The new independence, the asserting of the new sovereignty, the flexing of the new muscles of the new national defense forces, the prestige race, the Pan-Africanist competition—all combine with territorial ambitions to create a dangerous backdrop, as well as motivation, for the newest of the world's arms races, that of Africa.

Ghana has set the style and the pace. Navies and jet air forces are the African build-up order of the day. The nearby independent states of *l'expression française* have turned to France for aid in building their military forces, and they have looked to one another too. Thus the Ivory Coast is the center of a military build-up, and her associates in the *Conseil de l'Entente*—Dahomey, Niger, and the Upper Volta—are looking to her for support. Togo, on the other hand, has been looking not only toward France but also toward Nigeria, which appears to feel unable to let Ghana outpace her. Nigeria also appears inclined to speculate uneasily about the mission of a jet air force in a country the size of Ghana. In the main, all the new African states are building up national forces with undefined missions but with equipment of a military-technological level which makes them capable of external ventures far beyond their borders and territorial waters.

Joint military commands too have been broached by Ghana, Guinea, and the United Arab Republic as an aspect and dimension of their Pan-Africanist philosophy. In fact Ghana and the United Arab Republic have taken preliminary steps toward such a grouping of military forces. These self-styled neutralist Pan-Africanist states have been quick to denounce groupings of armed forces of other states elsewhere as aggressive military blocs, e.g., NATO. It seems quite likely that if a grouping of West African states of French expression with a political outlook conflicting with or differing sharply from, say that of Ghana should evolve, it too would be viewed by them as threatening and aggressive. The judgment would seem to depend on who is making the military alliance. As Minister Adamafio said with respect to the acceptability of conspiracies to subvert: "it depends upon the government at which they are aimed."

Thus the African presence has brought to the world scene a basketful of disturbing boundary disputes coupled with a disquieting arms race which could explode world peace in any number of directions. The African presence is a many-pronged and many-sided one. It is a force for peace, at the highest level of generalization and abstraction being opposed to the nuclear armaments race. It is a potential and threatening force for war at the level of affairs within their own control, the level of African interstate relations. The seeds of world war are always present in interstate crises involving violence; they are even present in internal crises involving violence, as the Congo has all too clearly demonstrated.

Economic and Cultural Development

The African presence has still another critical dimension in the determination of the African states to give meaning to their political independence by developing supporting economies. They are determined to "catch up" with the developed states, with other areas of the world, and with one another. Many, intent on raising the standards of living of their people and giving meaning to the "revolution of rising expectations," have made economic development a priority objective in their national plans.

The African concern with economic growth gave birth to the United Nations Economic Commission for Africa, the Mutual Assistance Foundation of the Commission for Technical Cooperation in Africa South of Sahara, and the customs unions in former French West and Equatorial Africa; brought about the accession of African states into membership in the International Bank for Reconstruction and Development, the International Monetary Fund, and the International Development Association; speeded the renovation of the European Economic Community; and inspired many other bodies, agencies, conferences, and meetings concerned with African development. It has also led to major new aid programs for African development in the United States, the United Kingdom, France, Israel, and other free world powers, and to comparable programs in the Sino-Soviet bloc. The entrance of Israel, Yugoslavia, and both Nationalist and Communist China into the economic aid and technical assistance fields in Africa is an important new development on the world stage and a dramatic response to the new African presence there.

Moreover, the relentless African search for growth and stability has carried the African presence into the far corners of the world. The highly mobile spokesmen of African independence, sovereignty, development, unity, and politics travel the world over. They go to the East, to the West. They go to Israel, and to the Arab World. They go the rounds of the underdeveloped world. Only Latin America has been off the beaten path for these relentless travelers, and now that is changing too. As for their own newly discovered continent of Africa, they streak up one side and down another. Every capital of every new state must be the seat of at least one important conference, and some of many.

In the cultural area Senghor's *négritude* and Nkrumah's African personality doctrines have added still another dimension to the African presence. The exchange students and visiting teachers, the scholarship and fellowship students, the multiplicity of special junketing groups with interests ranging from the arts to technology, and coming from one end of the world to the other, have added overtones and shadings to the presence, aside from making it even more ubiquitous on the world scene.

Major African Blocs

What all this adds up to politically is an African presence whose multi-dimensional interests and manifestations have been systematized by the emergence of two major, if still fluid, blocs of African states. Although they are made up of states with special interests which vary and may even conflict on many of the principal elements of the African presence, there is agreement on central themes within each of these two blocs. And even if the two blocs coalesce at some point in response to repeated initiatives of one or another African state, such an association would be an unstable one. It would merely serve to conceal and plaster over the basic differences which would persist. Such an association, should it come about, would merely shift the conflicts and tensions from an *inter*-bloc locus to an *intra*-bloc locus. And the shift in locus, should it occur, would probably be accompanied by a shift in terminology, so that blocs become either, on the one hand, regional groupings and organizations, or, on the other, wings and *tendances* within a continental-wide organization of African states. Either way, in our view, the differences between *existing* blocs would continue irrespective of the new terminology, and our analysis of the differences, if valid with reference to the existing blocs, would continue to be valid for the restyled regional groupings, and *ad hoc* internal wings or factions of a new association of African states.

The smaller and older (and less stable) is the Casablanca bloc, consisting of the Republics of Ghana, Guinea, and Mali (themselves grouped in the Union of African States), and the Kingdom of Morocco and the United Arab Republic (themselves linked in the Arab League).* The younger and by far the larger is the more inclusive Monrovia bloc, originally composed of twenty African states of varying political hues, ranging among the English-speakers from Nigeria to Ethiopia, and among the French-speakers from Senegal to Gabon. In late 1962 the bulk of the Monrovia bloc initialed a new charter at Lagos and organized themselves into the Inter-African and Malagasy States Organisation. The Casablanca bloc would categorize itself as militant nationalist, radical Pan-Africanist, positive neutralist, anti-colonialist, African-Arab socialist (except Morocco), and activist. The Monrovia bloc would, by contrast, categorize itself as a grouping of independent states for limited purposes and with shared interests in protecting their political independence, in evolving economic and cultural cooperation, and in peaceful change—as opposed to all blocs, including neutralist blocs, and therefore non-bloc—and as a body of states primarily concerned with their internal political and economic development, and with independent foreign policies reflecting these basic national interests.

In practice these basic characterizations lead to widely different policies and performances by the two blocs. A brief look at a few major areas of African policy will suffice to demonstrate the gulf in outlook between the two competing blocs. The Casablanca

* The Republic of Algeria, which is also a member of the Casablanca bloc, only became independent in July 1962—after all of the research and most of the writing of this book, which deals primarily with the problems and roles of the independent African States, were completed. Hence, except where Algeria is a direct and principal participant in a situation, it is omitted from the discussion.

powers look outward toward political unions as the *sine qua non* of all African progress. They would apply their internal doctrine of the "primacy of the Political Kingdom" to all of Africa. Thus in their view the only way any radical advance could be made in the economic sphere would be through the early achievement of an Africa-wide political union. Political union is viewed as a pre-condition to African growth and also, because of the interrelation-ship of growth and stability, to political stability. The outlook of the Monrovia powers would differ by 180 degrees. They look in-ward to find growth and stability in their own internal develop-ment. They believe in a multiplicity of economic, social, and political contacts among African states which, if they are sound, may in time eventuate in close political associations and even unions.

The quotations which follow from two leading African na-tionalist leaders, who used to hold one another in considerable esteem and who both profess to be Pan-Africanist in outlook, pro-vide a dramatic confrontation of these two sharply different views of African objectives.

First, President Nkrumah, the self-avowed Pan-Africanist leader of Africa, and beyond question one of the leading, and some say *the* leading, spokesman of the Casablanca bloc, categorically declared in a special introduction to his recent book:

Never before have a people had within their grasp so great an opportunity for developing a continent endowed with so much wealth. Individually, the independent states of Africa, some of them poten-tially rich, others poor, can do little for their people. Together, by mutual help, they can achieve much. But the economic development of the continent must be planned and pursued as a whole. A loose confederation designed only for economic cooperation would not pro-vide the necessary unity of purpose. Only a strong political union can bring about full and effective development of our material resources for the benefit of our people.[3]

Second, Dr. Azikiwe, Governor-General of the Federation of Nigeria, former premier of the Eastern Region of Nigeria, and one of the earliest and best known of the African nationalist leaders, equally categorically declared in a speech in mid-1959, which he has recently published in a collection of speeches as representative of his point of view:

I believe that economic and social integration will enable Nigeria and its neighbours to bring to pass the United States of Africa, which is the dream of Africa nationalists. It would be capital folly to assume that hard-bargaining politicians who passed through the ordeal of victimization and the crucible of persecution to win their political independence will easily surrender their newly-won political power in the interest of a political leviathan which is populated by people who are alien to one another in their social and economic relations. It has not been possible in Europe or America, and unless Africa can show herself different from other continents, the verdict of history on this score will remain unchallenged and unaltered.

Lest there should be any mistaken notion of my stand on the alignment of interests of African States, may I reiterate that I firmly believe in the attainment of an association or union of African States either on a regional or continental basis in the future. I would regard such a future as not within the life-time of the heroes and heroines who have spearheaded the struggle for freedom in Africa, these four decades. But I honestly believe that social and economic integration would so mix the masses of the various African territories into an amalgam of understanding that the objective might be realizable earlier than we expected.

In other words, the prerequisites of political integration in Africa are the economic and social integration of African peoples. Otherwise, we shall be precipitating a crisis which will find African leaders jockeying among themselves for leadership of peoples who are not only alien to each other but are unprepared for such a social revolution. This would be disastrous to the ideals of Pan-Africanism which all of us, as sincere nationalists, have been propagating all these years.[4]

An offshoot of the conflicting views of the two blocs on political unions is to be seen in their differing attitudes toward subversion of African government by other African governments. Apparently the rules of the game used by the Casablanca powers allow for, and in fact call for, the "national liberation" of "stooge" governments by the Casablanca powers. We have already quoted Minister Adamafio of Ghana to this effect, cited the Guinean intrusion in the Republic of Cameroun, and alluded to the expulsion of the Ghana, Guinea, and United Arab Republic diplomatic missions from Leopoldville by the Kasavubu government on the ground of interference by these diplomatic missions in the internal political affairs of the country in the interests of an opposition faction intent on taking over power. During the course of 1961 two other cases of subversion were alleged by independent African states against neighboring states, with at least *prima facie* evidence adduced of their complicity. Sierra Leone arrested and expelled two Ghanaians on charges of attempting to subvert the government, and Liberia declared *persona non grata* and demanded the recall of a Ghanaian Embassy official in Monrovia on the same ground.

The Monrovia powers have made clear that they abhor the resort to subversion, coercion, or outright force by one African state against another. In fact, a hallmark of the Monrovia bloc, imprinted on the original Monrovia Conference resolutions, is the unequivocal position that all these practices are strictly off-limits. Existing borders are only to be changed peacefully, by consent of the states involved. Senegal, for example, which contemplates a possible union with the British enclave of Gambia, has made it clear through President Senghor that union will come about only if Gambia freely decides it wants to be united with Senegal.

Finally, the tendency of the Casablanca powers to identify their own "revolutionary" movement with world-wide revolutionary forces and their tendency to equate anti-colonialism exclusively with the West lead them to a brand of neutralism which increasingly brings them out on the Communist-bloc side on major cold-war issues and to a posture of rapport with the Communist bloc. The tendency of the Monrovia powers, consistent with their emphasis on national independence and internal development, is to adopt the position in foreign affairs of deciding issues on their merit and in terms of their respective national interests, which frequently coincide with or are compatible with those of the West.

All of these and many other differences between the two major African blocs, which would be swept under the rug but by no means resolved if the two blocs should effect a formal merger, are considered in detail at appropriate places later on in the book, as are also the differences, already briefly suggested, between powers of the two groups and among members of the respective groups.

Basic Interrelationships

There are therefore very different embodiments of the African presence on the world scene when one adds specific national interests to the more general manifestations we have discussed in this chapter. The concern of this book is to examine and analyze the principal manifestations of the African presence in world affairs in light of their implications for world peace, the political balance of power, and the decade of development the United States has called for in the 1960's. To do this we believe it indispensable to have a clear view of the underpinnings of the external posture of African states in the world arena. We believe definition, examination, and analysis of the internal African economic and political structures, systems, and problems is the starting point for an understanding of the external presence. We think this for two reasons.

First, the problems of state-building, nation-building, economy-building, and technological revolution—the four major transformations all the new African states are undergoing or are confronted with—interact on one another; and, perhaps more important for our purposes, the totality of these problems, and the ways they are resolved, interact on and contribute to shaping the total external posture of the new states. For example, the one-party political systems of Ghana, Guinea, and Mali interact with their "African socialist" economic systems to produce left-authoritarian states which seem to find in pro-Communist bloc neutralism a congenial foreign policy posture. Conversely, the internal politico-economic situation in Ghana, and to a lesser extent in Guinea and Mali, has been the source of considerable criticism, concern, and even hostility in the West and has rendered the relationships of Western states with them difficult, and in the case of Ghana even tense.

Second, in Africa many of the internal problems tend to merge effortlessly into external policy and the international arena. When a state such as Guinea decides as a matter of domestic doctrine that its internal political stability can be achieved only as part of a larger Pan-African movement which would generate such strength that, once and for all, neo-colonialist designs on her security—internal as well as territorial—would be rendered impossible, then internal political problems are inextricably interwoven in the fabric of foreign policy. Thus political opposition in Guinea on almost any domestic issue tends to be viewed not only in terms of the government's strength at home but also in terms of its role in the Pan-Africanist movement. All purges prominently feature charges of conspiracy of disaffected Guineans with foreign agents and powers for the purpose of undermining state security. True to form, a serious conspiracy uncovered in November-December 1961 led to charges of subversion by a foreign power, in this case an "Eastern European power," later identified as the Soviet Union. The Soviet Ambassador to Guinea was recalled at Guinea's request. Earlier charges usually were against conspiracies involving subversion by "Western imperialist states."

Thus the principal problems confronting the new African states are for convenience divided in this book into two categories —problems of economic growth and problems of political stability. They are viewed as a development nexus in the next chapter, and are examined both as such and as separate but interrelated problems in subsequent chapters.

Chapter 2

THE AFRICAN DEVELOPMENT NEXUS: GROWTH AND STABILITY

The African nationalist leaders, having achieved their objective of independence from colonial rule, have uniformly set about building the nationalism for which they led their countries to independence. The way they go about their task will determine the course of African development for years to come.

At the outset, as an inevitable concomitant of independence, the new leaders of independent Africa have made political stability the foundation stone of their nation-building. For some this has meant the consolidation of personal power; for others it has meant the growing control of the state machinery by a single-party political apparatus; for others it has meant the creation of a durable political structure and democratic political processes. For whatever reason, all of them have been concerned to build national cohesion by submerging the divisive qualities of regional, tribal, and religious differences in new concepts of nationality and African personality, to maintain law and order, and to satisfy increasingly the aspirations of their peoples for improved standards of living.

Having perceived the obvious link between political stability and the satisfaction of the felt wants of their people, the African

21

leaders have for this reason alone made economic growth, at least in theory, the number one priority after independence. Many of them have also recognized the unifying role which economic growth could play in breaking down separatist tendencies, dissipating particularism, and minimizing the differences characteristic of the heterogeneous tribal structure of Africa by pulling more and more people into the market economy, where the premium is on individual performance rather than on tribal affiliation or clan status. Finally, many of them have recognized the role which improved living standards could play in creating among increasing segments of the population a vested interest in the maintenance of law and order.

Priority of Economic Development

For the African leaders who have perceived the multi-faceted potential of economic growth, such growth has been the number one priority of their governments in fact as well as precept. These men have tended to look inward to find stability in internal growth.

The Minister of Commerce and Industry of Nigeria, the country in Africa which best exemplifies this approach to growth and stability, tied these two objectives of national policy together in an unmistakable way during a major policy declaration on behalf of his government soon after independence. He stated in a formal speech delivered in Lagos to a joint conference of Federal and Regional Ministers and a special delegation of the Federation of British Industries then visiting Nigeria:

We live in challenging times, and events in the continent of Africa over the next decade will undoubtedly influence the future of mankind. We are not unaware of the heavy responsibility which we bear to ensure the maintenance of stability and good government in Nigeria and we intend to continue the path of moderation which we have so far followed. Nevertheless, we are faced with many urgent problems, not the least of which is the need to raise appreciably over the next few years, the living standards of our people. If we cannot achieve this then we have failed in our responsibilities, and this is the major challenge which faces us.

We offer you a warm and sincere welcome and we will continue to ensure conditions of stability in which real industrial growth can proceed. We also offer you a market of a size unique in Africa and a friendly, hard-working people. These things we can offer; and it is our sincere hope that we shall not find that we have offered them in vain. For, Gentlemen, to ensure stability we must ensure that we have a contented and happy people, and for this to be so, they must be assured of a rising standard of living.[1]

For other leaders, for a variety of reasons thought to be overriding, there has been something of a discrepancy between theory and practice. They have tended to look outward to find stability in larger groupings of states and in notions of Pan-Africanism and in doing so have tended to downgrade the priority accorded in practice to economic development. They have tended to focus their energy, their limited pools of trained manpower, and even their accumulated savings, where they exist, on the achievement of Pan-Africanist goals.

The President of Ghana is the leading advocate of Pan-Africanism, seeing in it the solution to all of Africa's manifold problems—political and economic. In larger unions of African states Dr. Nkrumah finds the one true route to growth and stability for the independent states of Africa. In a major address to the Conference on Positive Action and Security in Africa held in April 1960 at Accra, Dr. Nkrumah spelled out in detail his philosophy of growth and stability. After condemning as "new imperialism"[2] the inclusion of African states "in common market and trade preferences areas set up by industrial Europe," he said:

But Africa must be developed industrially, for her own sake and ultimately for the sake of a healthy world economy. This can only happen if the artificial boundaries that divide her are broken down so as to provide for viable economic units, and ultimately a single African unit. . . . There can be no peace or security in Africa without freedom and political unity. . . . Our salvation and strength and our only way out of these ravages ["international wars, rebellions, and revolutions"] in Africa, lies in political union. . . . The overriding importance of African unity demands the sacrifice of all personal, tribal and regional objectives and considerations. . . . The only answer to the several difficulties facing our continent is actual union of our various states and territories. If we cannot make an effort in this direction, we might as well begin to throw up our hands in despair and forget about Africa.[2]

In his book *I Speak of Freedom*, Dr. Nkrumah linked Ghanaian development with Pan-Africanism this way:

Finally, I put the development of Ghana in its African context, and spoke of Pan-Africanism and the emergence of an African personality in international affairs:
As I have often emphasized, the freedom and independence of Ghana is meaningless unless it is linked up with the total liberation of Africa . . . until we ourselves purge from our own minds . . . tribal chauvinism and prejudice of one against the other, we shall not be able to cultivate the wider spirit of brotherhood which our objective of Pan-Africanism calls for.[3]

And to hammer home his notion of achieving development and security in African political union Nkrumah categorically declared:

There is strength in the political unity of our continent and that is why the Convention People's Party, as the vanguard for African liberation, is always against any policy for the balkanisation of Africa into small, weak and unstable states. We believe that considerations of mutual security and prosperity of our people demand that all the independent states in Africa should work together to create a Union of African States.[4]

The excerpts quoted from the Nigerian minister and the Ghanaian president are important not only to illustrate the differing views of their countries toward the achievement of growth and stability, the development nexus of Africa, but also to characterize the fundamental African-wide dialogue between the Monrovia and the Casablanca powers, of which their countries, respectively, are the recognized leaders. The former stress internal development of their countries as their principal national objective. Then, in good time, economic cooperation and political collaboration among independent African states could bear fruit and possibly lead to closer associations among, and even integration of, African states.

The latter emphasize African-wide political unity as their principal national objective. Then economic development and political cohesion would follow as the night the day for the independent African states banded together in African political union. The neo-colonialist would be barred from the continent for all time, and in the political kingdom of African nationalism, undisturbed by foreign forces, all would be possible.

Thus the differing conceptions have a direct bearing on the emphasis accorded economic growth as a national objective and on the pace and pattern such growth is likely to assume; but there is no dispute over the desirability of achieving political stability as a precondition to economic growth. In fact, many with an eye to foreign investment would make stability an indispensable pre-requisite of growth. These states stress their political stability in appeals to prospective overseas investors. One of the more aggressive African states on this score has been the revivified Republic of Liberia. Typical of its campaign to attract foreign investors are the following official statements:

American businessmen who may be interested in opportunities for investment in Liberia will receive encouragement from us. We have a stable Government and a free economy that is growing rapidly.[5]

In Liberia the American investor enjoys the cooperation of a government which President Kennedy has described as a "symbol of stability." [6]

In states with tendencies similar to Nigeria's, that is, where economic development assumes a priority position—at times *the* priority position—in the scheme of things, political stability is viewed not only as a precondition but also as a consequence of economic growth. The circular interaction of stability and growth is central to the politico-economic philosophy of internal development, with simultaneous concentration on the interrelated tasks of state-building, nation-building, economy-building, and techno-logical transformation of subsistence societies to modern ones.

In states leaning Ghana's way, however, economic development is not an end in itself; it is a tool and a resource to further Pan-Africanist associations, which in turn will ensure over the long run "real" development and security for all African states.

The wealth of Ghana has, despite official denials, been lavished on Pan-Africanist politics the continent over. At the overt level, loans of $28 million and about $14 million were made to Guinea and Mali, respectively, as part of the package that was involved in founding the Union of African States—Ghana, Guinea, and Mali. At the covert level practically every African nationalist group and every disaffected African exile and émigré is able to find a place in one or another of Ghana's Pan-Africanist secretariats, staffs, or societies. The image of a prosperous and dynamic Ghana also is expected to serve as an inspiration to others and an example of what could be achieved by union with Ghana.

Thus internal unity, imposed quickly and at whatever cost, was felt necessary by Nkrumah if he was to be free to focus on external affairs and to project onto the African scene a monolithic Ghanaian personality as the model for the total continent. The African development nexus in Ghana points outward. The stability and growth objectives interact, partly by design and partly, here as elsewhere, inevitably, to produce a Pan-Africanist posture—desired certainly, and to an extent destined by the left-authoritarian course being pursued within the borders of Ghana.

Economic Growth Models

Every new African state at independence is confronted with a vital decision—perhaps the most vital to be made by the new leaders with respect to their fledgling economies, and of major importance to their evolving political structures. What type of economic growth model should the new state seek to follow? The spectrum of choices available is indeed a broad one, ranging, at least in theory, from a totally free economy on the one hand to a totally controlled one on the other. In practice, of course, there are few economies which could be placed at either end of the spectrum. Most economies in practice tend to be some combination of public and private sectors, of voluntary performance and public regulation, of incentives and coercion, of rewards and penalties—in short, of carrots and sticks.

The choice is not, as has been suggested, between capitalism and socialism. The choice is rather between a type of economy which seeks to decentralize economic decision-making and encourage individual economic initiatives and a type of economy which seeks to centralize in government hands economic decision-making and discourage individual economic initiatives. There are many degrees and variants of each type of economy, and many of the different types are to be found in different parts of Africa.

Economies which emphasize individual economic decision-making tend to evolve in the context of democratic political systems characterized by widespread political decision-making and respect for individual rights, whereas economies which emphasize government control of economic decision-making tend to evolve in the context of authoritarian political systems characterized by concentrated political decision-making by a controlling, monolithic one-party apparatus and primacy of the state over the individual in all spheres of activity.

The political decision underlying the choice of an economic growth model is thus part of a pattern. A democratic political pattern usually calls for an open economic structure that is consistent with and reinforcing of the free exercise of political rights by individuals; an authoritarian pattern usually precludes dissenting elements anywhere in the social structure and therefore imposes authoritarian control to ensure "correct" performance in so vital an area as the national economy. In states which fall somewhere between the democratic and the authoritarian extremes of the political spectrum, the economies more often than not will reflect this intermediate position, with all its internal inconsistencies.

The equation may be reversed and still hold true. An open, private-sector economy appears to require a total environment in which individuals are free to make their own decisions—that which tends to accompany a democratic political system; a closed, state-owned or state-controlled economy requires an authority to control performance which only an authoritarian political system can provide. At any rate, this appears to be the situation in Africa. Nigeria's is the open, private-sector economy growing in an atmosphere of democratic tolerance. Ghana and, perhaps for this purpose even more clearly, Guinea have state-run, public-sector economies operating in a milieu of authoritarian and at times totalitarian controls. Mid-way on the right, the Ivory Coast has a mixed economy with tendencies toward a quasi-open, private-sector economy, operating in a one-party state with a non-doctrinaire and somewhat eclectic authoritarian pattern; and mid-way on the left, Tunisia has a mixed economy with tendencies toward an expanding but by no means inclusive public-sector economy, operating in a one-party state with a mildly doctrinaire and effective but not overbearing authoritarian system.

One way or another the political and economic systems—and, as we attempt to explore in Parts Two and Three of this book, the problems of growth and stability themselves are conjoined—interact on one another and together influence the external role of the new states. The African presence reflects and feeds back into the African development nexus of growth and stability. Moreover, confronting the new African states in their efforts to modernize there are in the colonial legacy four critical problems, each of which has a bearing on the dimensions of growth and stability. These are the problems of modernization of traditional agriculture, Africanization of the public services and the private sector of the economies, the push for education, and the role of welfare concepts in nascent states with underdeveloped economies. The resolution of any or all of these problems would not only have a direct and immediate effect on growth and stability but also contribute to the cumulative effect of economic growth in enhancing political stability.

Making Political Decisions

In the search for stability the new states are also confronted with major problem areas which share the same dual dimensions as the four critical growth problems. The building of state structures and political systems, the development of national policies toward nationalism, Pan-Africanism, and Eurafricanism, and defining the role of neutralism and the United Nations in their quest for security and stability—all are fundamental political questions confronting, and at times confounding, the new states. They set the political framework within which the economy must be constructed, and they impose burdens and limitations on the use of resources. We have already mentioned the direct interplay between economic growth models and political systems. There are also direct consequences for the emerging economies from the attitudes and policies of the new states toward investment policy, trade, aid, and a multiplicity of other factors. Should development take place within the confines of Gabon, or the Ivory Coast, or Ghana, or Nigeria, or be made contingent upon and interrelated with development in the wider area of West Africa? Or even more widely, in the area of tropical Africa? Should development emphasize a transportation grid within country A or B, or should it stress regional roads and rail links between country A and B? Even more pressing, should armed forces be established by the new states with implied missions going far beyond internal needs and local defense?

Almost imperceptibly domestic political decisions on the nature of the state, the way to ensure the political stability and territorial integrity of the country, and the form in which to seek to achieve economic growth spill over into official attitudes toward external events. If the assessment is that stability and security are to be found in internal development, the nation's policies regarding Pan-Africanism, political union, "national liberation," neutralism, and so on, are likely to lead to the outlook in foreign affairs characteristic of the Monrovia powers. And similarly, the assessment that stability and security as well as growth are to be found in larger groupings of African states and as part of a worldwide social revolution is likely to lead to the Casablanca powers' outlook in world affairs. More specifically, a policy favoring, for example, economic connections with Western Europe as a way to facilitate economic growth through an augmentation of foreign resource earnings leads to certain attitudes toward the Common Market, toward private overseas investment and trade, toward foreign aid, etc. A different policy, looking toward the severance or dilution of economic relations with West Europeans as a way to achieve African unity, leads to other attitudes toward the Common Market, trade and aid relations with the Communist bloc, neutralist posture, etc.

Scope of the Discussion

It is in this context that the complex of internal economic and political problems awaiting decision are focused on in Parts II and III of this book. Throughout the discussion in the two Parts are instances which may specifically illustrate where and how the problems under discussion may impinge on or interact with one another. However, the individual chapters are primarily intended to suggest, by the nature of the analysis and the over-all treatment of the respective problems they deal with, the general areas and scope of likely interplay of the development problems considered. For example, Chapter 8, in analyzing the problem of political structures, deals with the question of local government. The connection of local governmental institutions and powers to the nature of the political structure and the type of political system being established is direct and, once pointed out, relatively easy to perceive. Perhaps somewhat less direct and somewhat more obscure is the relationship of local government to economic development. Nevertheless, the relationship—and thus potential interaction—of the two exists. The precise nature of the interaction —the nexus—would undoubtedly vary with the multiplicity of specific factors to be found in particular contexts. It is likely to be more apparent in some contexts than in others. States with strong local government units are likely to be not only less centralized politically but also less centralized economically. And there is undoubtedly a causal relationship involved in the correlation.

The possible dimensions of the relationship, however, between local government and economic development, and the potential patterns of their interaction, are probably innumerable. They are the subject of a recent special study by a prominent British economist, who at the outset asks: "What is the relation between local government and economic development?" and then observes that "it is entirely proper that the development of local government in these [underdeveloped] countries should now be regarded as in part an economic problem: it is because it is in part an economic problem that the present writer (an economist) has been drawn to its study." [7]

The explicit identification of the link by the author, although long inferred, between local government and economic development also makes explicit the fact that the nexus is a field of study by itself. Similarly any number of other links whose existence could be inferred, or which are suggested by the eight chapters of Parts Two and Three of this book, are likely to constitute fields of study by themselves. In addition, not all the links will be present at every stage in the development process or necessarily in every state to which we allude. Hence for the most part we have been content to avoid specific reference to linkages. We believe that to have done so would have made the book unmanageable and also would have diverted attention from the principal objective of these chapters: to identify and analyze the principal problems of African growth and stability and to establish that they constitute a vital nexus in African development. Thus the innumerable points of contact and interplay of the forces of growth and stability are at times made explicit in the book to illustrate or make a point, but more often they are merely suggested to the reader by the material presented and analyzed.

The development nexus in each African state is a fusion of these problems and the attempted national solutions. Sometimes the specific problems are deliberately interrelated; often we would speculate they are not. The interplay of the problems and the proposed solutions would in part result from conscious design, but it also would in part flow from the very nature of the problems being dealt with and the methods being used to resolve them.

The following words of a prominent British economist, in an introduction to a recent collection of papers on federalism and economic growth, nicely sum up the nature of the African development nexus:

As an illustration of these various socio-anthropological forces of separatism and cohesion, the case of Nigeria was discussed in some detail, and proved to have considerably more than local interest. . . .

The important factors in preserving the unity of Nigeria were thus felt to be—largely although not wholly—those which would be strengthened by the process of economic development, although they were not in themselves specifically economic. It is characteristic of a backward (underdeveloped) country that economic intercommunications, or, as economists put it, "intersectoral flows," are poor and weak. So long as this condition persist, extra-economic cohesive forces are likely also to remain relatively weak, but almost as a by-product of economic development they are likely to grow in strength. . . .[8]

PART TWO

Problems of Growth

*The road itself seems to speak to him [Mister Rudbeck, British District Officer, Northern Nigeria]. "I'm smashing up the old Fada—I shall change everything and everybody in it. I am abolishing the old ways, the old ideas, the old law; I am bringing wealth and opportunity for good as well as vice, new powers to men and therefore new conflicts. I am the revolution. I am giving you plenty of trouble already, you governors, and I am going to give you plenty more. I destroy and I make new. What are you going to do about it? I am your idea. You made me, so I suppose you know." ***

JOYCE CARY
*Novelist, and one time
British Colonial Officer in Nigeria*

* *Mister Johnson*, London, 1939.

Chapter 3

CHOICE OF A GROWTH MODEL

The fundamental economic issue confronting the new African states is one of choice. What shall be their model of growth, their road to development?

The deceptively simple Communist formulation—the choice between "the capitalist road or noncapitalist" [1]—is of course a fiction. The possible growth models are legion. The possible choices available theoretically constitute a continuum ranging from pure capitalism at one extreme to pure communism at the other; but in the real world of economic development the pure model does not exist. The real choice must be made from the wide range of mixed economies in which the relative size and importance of the private and public sectors, the degree of individual freedom to make economic decisions, and the extent of state direction of economic activities all vary.

This fact is clearly reflected in the beginnings already made by the new African states. Their emerging economies reflect a wide diversity and incorporate, along with many aspects of their colonial heritage, a selection of socialist, communist, and private enterprise economic theory. The search is for an African way, a synthesis suitable to African "realities." A prominent African economist-statesman, Mamadou Dia, of Senegal, sees the choice this way:

Between Indian prudence and the ardor of democracies claiming to draw their inspiration from Marxist-Leninist doctrine, we think there is place for a solution which is a synthesis adapting socialism to African realities.[2]

Other African leaders looking for an African way would perceive a broader spectrum of choices and envisage other possible syntheses. But none the less, all seem to be seeking some blend, some amalgam of theory, doctrine, and reality combined to satisfy their development needs and aspirations.

The new states also have borrowed economic techniques, institutions, and mechanisms from many corners of the world. At times these have been blended in interesting new ways. For example, in agriculture, advanced technology, much of it Western in origin and spirit, is being combined with Israeli agricultural organization, *kibbutzim* and *moshavim*, and authoritarian methods modeled on the Chinese and Russian communist practices in an attempt to produce a modern agricultural sector.

Importance of the Public Sector

The point of departure for the choice of the nascent African states is common to all of them. From the outset it is predetermined that all of the economies of the new African states will have large public sectors. In the first instance this condition derives from the colonial structure. The indigenous entrepreneur and indigenous capital accumulation were the exception rather than the rule during the colonial era. Enterprises were either owned by private foreign interests or by the government of the colonial territory. The governments of the new states inherited the property held by the colonial government—physical property such as railroads, monetary reserves such as the accumulation from the sale of cocoa in the Gold Coast, or, in rare instances, portfolios such as that of the Belgian Congo, holding shares, options, voting rights, etc., in a complex of private and quasi-public corporations.

Aside from the direct legacy in the public sector, the colonial economic structure left limited raw material with which to build the private sector. In the absence of indigenous private capital and entrepreneurs the temptation for the new states has been to fill the gap with public capital and state ownership and management.

The propensity for public ownership and management arising from existing indigenous shortages has been accentuated in those states with left-authoritarian political systems (described in Chapter 8) which maintain that their independence will not be complete or "real" until they have reinforced their political independence by the total decolonization of their economies. So important has this objective of economic decolonization become to the left authoritarian states that Ghana, Guinea, and Mali have gone to the extent of writing a specific provision into their charter of the Union of African States (the so-called Ghana-Guinea, Mali Union) relating to the achievement of the objective. The Charter provides that:

Article 4.—The Union's activities shall be exercised mainly in the following fields:

(d) Economy—Defining a common set of directives relating to Economic Planning, aiming at the complete decolonisation of the set-ups inherited from the colonial system, and organising the development of the wealth of their countries in the interest of their peoples.[3]

To President Touré decolonization has meant severely limiting and circumscribing the sphere of the private foreign investor. For practical purposes the indigenous private sector was nonexistent in Guinea, providing little to build on and, by the same token, offering little resistance to government intervention. Since independence the access and activity of private foreign investors have been limited by the preemption of certain fields exclusively for the government, by nationalization of others, and by strict regulation of the private sector generally. By and large Guinea has encouraged the foreign investor only in major mineral resource exploitation and in processing projects requiring significant amounts of capital, foreign exchange, and technological knowledge. To

President Nkrumah economic decolonization has meant earmarking some fields of economic activity exclusively for government, some for cooperative societies (which in Ghana has come virtually to mean government), some for mixed government-private investment (primarily foreign investment), and some for private investment, primarily indigenous private investment. The foreign investor, welcomed for some purposes, is to be barred from others which are deemed to be rightfully the province of Ghanaians. Thus in both Ghana and Guinea, interestingly enough, the basic natural resource of the countries, mineral wealth, which in other socialist-oriented areas as a matter of doctrine has been reserved for the government, has been held out for private foreign investment. It is also interesting to note that in Nigeria, Chief Awolowo, leader of the opposition at the federal level and head of the Action Group, one of Nigeria's principal parties, has called, to little avail, for nationalization of "the natural resources of the nation" now in the hands of outsiders and has made tin-mining the number one target for his campaign.

To President Nasser of the United Arab Republic decolonization has meant, in the end, nationalization of all investment of any scale, foreign and internal, and a totally state-directed economy. In contrast to the situation in Guinea, and to a considerable extent in Ghana, there were indigenous private investments of some scale in the United Arab Republic, particularly in agriculture. Moreover, unlike Guinea and Ghana, where land tends to be tribally held, land reform has meaning in the United Arab Republic, where a small class of large land-owners existed, with a large landless class working the land. (But this is a Middle Eastern pattern rather than an African one.)

These same states have further accentuated the growth of the public sectors of their economies by their adherence to an economic philosophy termed "African socialism" south of the Sahara and "Arab socialism" in the United Arab Republic. In many ways building socialism in these states is the counterpart of decolonization, for the indigenous institutions substituted for the dismantled colonial ones are part and parcel of the same process; e.g., the state trading organizations established in Guinea result both from a policy of ejecting French interests (decolonization) and from Guinean economic doctrine (African socialism). Sékou Touré formulated the dual process this way:

Independence is the means taken by the Party [*Parti Démocratique de Guinée*] to destroy the structures of the colonial system which hampered the improvement of the living conditions of the people of Guinea. But one cannot destroy a system without replacing it by another [i.e., African socialism].[4]

In other ways, however, the term "African socialism" implies more than providing substitute structures for colonial economic structures. It covers policy on forced saving, compulsory labor, limitations on earnings, role of trade unions, allocation of resources (e.g., heavy industry versus consumer industry), patents and copyrights, and all the other problems of priorities and relationships comprehended by an over-all economic theory.

In all the new states, ideology aside, there is a compulsion to achieve growth in a hurry. There is a sense of urgency about recognizable achievement. This is in part compounded from a desire of the underdeveloped states to catch up, to close the gap with the developed states, the former colonial power, and the West generally, and in part from the mounting internal pressures for better standards of living, which have been held out frequently as a consequence if not a concomitant of political independence. And because these two drives can be incompatible, and are likely to be if the rate of growth is too small or the pace too slow, many of the African leaders have resorted on the one hand to more and more exhortation and coercion to induce an accelerated rate of growth, and on the other to increasing repression and distraction to avoid or silence discontent with the failure to achieve the necessary rate of growth.

Catching up means many things. It means modernization, building a state and a society which dispose of the symbols or indices of progress—a modern capital city, a national university in an appropriate setting, state-owned commercial airline and shipping companies, armed forces including navies and air forces, social overhead infrastructure, and all of the physical paraphernalia of developed economies. It means industrialization, preferably including some heavy industry, with aluminum- and steel-making ranking high. It means agricultural development, including expanding food production. It means an expanding level of social welfare services emulating those of the states with advanced economies. It means a growing national product.

An improved standard of living means many things too. In most African states it means higher wages and more fringe benefits. The colonial standards with respect to salaries and benefits for Europeans, notwithstanding their completely inapplicable rationale for independent states, have all too often become the goal. (In the doctrinaire left-authoritarian and puritanical state of Guinea this trend has been officially proscribed. Elsewhere, as in Senegal, it has been recognized by African leaders as a serious development problem involving the growing role of trade unions in their countries.) [5] Universal free primary education and wider educational opportunities generally have also become widely accepted goals. Welfare service and amenities have become lesser goals in differing degrees in various places. Ownership of bicycles, motor scooters, and automobiles has become an important index for measuring living standards, as has better housing, which means a growing per capita income.

Thus a lack of local capital and entrepreneurs, combined with an urgent drive to compress into the span of one generation the generations of development which have led in advanced economies to high levels of production, creates conditions compatible with, and many would say determinant of, a large and dynamic public sector. This would be particularly so for the ideologically oriented left-authoritarian states espousing African socialism. For them the conditions created would be said to make a large public sector historically inevitable.

Role of the Private Sector

What remains open for examination, once it is recognized that all of the new African states are destined to have an active and important public sector, is the role of government with respect to individual economic activity, e.g., fixing of wage levels, forced saving, compulsory labor, availability of consumer goods, trade union activity, and so on, and the economic role left to the private sector, indigenous and foreign, e.g., small business, transportation, consumer-goods manufacturing, export trade, and mineral extraction.

It seems clear that authoritarian economic development models exercise considerable attraction for many of the leaders of the new African states. The left-authoritarian states, as we have already suggested in connection with Pan-African doctrine, more or less subscribe to President Nkrumah's doctrine that the "political kingdom" comes first: that once political power is obtained all else follows—or, at any rate, becomes possible.

Nkrumah first consolidated his political power, including the institution of a new constitution providing for a strong presidential system and the systematic elimination of all meaningful political opposition, and then unveiled his Marxist socialism rechristened "African socialism." This is essentially an authoritarian model, with the state using its powers to expand the public sector, circumscribe and control the private sector, and increasingly to restrict individual initiative. Compulsory savings through the required purchase of National Development Bonds and other techniques, national labor service in the Workers' Brigade, government control of trade unions, government fixing of wages, government control of the national farmer's association, cooperative movement, youth movement, women's association, and so forth—all combine to leave the individual little leeway for economic decisions. The government's increasing encroachment on what has been thought of elsewhere as the private sector has been obvious for all to see, and has been characterized by government investment in every conceivable type of industrial and business enterprise and government participation and control of business activity.

In President Touré's view the political structure and system, once determined, set the framework for the economic structure and system. "Such is for each country the nature of its political system, such is or will necessarily be that of its economic organization. In fact, political economics has no other object than to regulate the problems of the economic order according to the given political conditions." [6] Growing more specific, Touré's belief is that: "Our political regime condemns individualism and theft, oppression and exploitation. So our economy must, thanks to our planning in the introduction of many technical means, in the co-operation and the equitable repartition of wealth . . . further to the utmost a general progress, a perfect balance of the nation." [7] Touré having chosen for Guinea "a dictatorship of the people," "a popular dictatorship"—what Talmon has aptly designated a totalitarian democracy—it follows that the economy being constructed in Guinea will be an authoritarian one.

Thus the public sector predominates and grows in Guinea, and the individual area of decision-making in economic affairs has all but disappeared, except for tactical concessions such as the re-introduction of a degree of private trading following public admission by President Touré late in 1961 of the failure of the state trading monopoly, or for black marketing and corruption. "Everywhere," in the words of Touré, "the Party has preeminence, . . . everywhere, it must think, act, guide, and control the action of the labouring masses." [8]

The military dictatorship in the United Arab Republic, once having consolidated its monopoly of political power in the country in a one-party "national front," also evolved an authoritarian development model, denominated "Arab socialism." Its chief ingredients have been nationalization and all-pervasive government control of the economy. The imposition of Arab socialism, however, precipitated the dissolution of the original United Arab Republic; Syria abruptly withdrew late in 1961, and the federal link between the Republic and Yemen broke over the same issue a few months later. [9]

It is pertinent to note that states with left-authoritarian development models, such as Guinea, Ghana, and the United Arab Republic, tend to relate their internal economic development to external policy objectives. Thus, as we have already seen, Dr. Nkrumah has emphasized that a central purpose behind the need for Ghanaian economic development is to further "African unity." In his words:

For we know that it is only if we [Ghana] become economically strong and politically stable that we can carry through with sufficient determination our policy for the freedom and unity of the African continent.[10]

Ghanaian resources have been used directly to induce African political union through loans to Ghana's associates in the Union of African States—Guinea and Mali; they have also been an important factor in financing many of the anti-colonial independence movements and the political movements of disaffected African émigrés from independent states. There have been allegations at various times by Congolese politicians and others of Ghanaian financial support to particular factions in the Congo and elsewhere. All of these expenditures could be and probably are rationalized as furthering African unity.

Dr. Nkrumah has also emphasized that successful Ghanaian economic development would serve as a model, an example, an inspiration for other African states—this too in the name of African unity. In Dr. Nkrumah's words:

> Let us demonstrate to the world that our conception of the African personality means not only optimism, cheerfulness, and an easy, confident outlook in tackling the problems of life, but also a disdain for vanities, and a sense of social obligation which will make our society an object of admiration and of example.[11]

President Touré also appears to view Guinean economic development as part of a larger process of Pan-African decolonization and development. In his book *Toward Full Re-Africanisation,* Sékou Touré declares:

> We are conscious that, as long as the whole of Africa is not liberated, Guinea will not feel safe. . . . Guinea registers the pain of the colonized people of Africa. . .
>
> It is therefore to drive all pain out . . . that we must examine the condition of the instruments which will serve to carry out this fight victoriously; the P.D.G.–R.D.A. [*Parti Démocratique de Guinée*], the State and its institutions, the People and its political, social, economic and cultural practices! [12]

In the meantime, while awaiting the larger events, Guinean economic development assumes the character more or less of a hold-

ing action. The focus of Guinea—in economic growth and political
stability—has been Pan-African.

Similarly Colonel Nasser seems to view Egyptian economic
development as a prestige symbol in Middle Eastern affairs and
to a lesser extent in African politics. He has also made use of a
key doctrine of Egyptian development policy, nationalization, as
an instrument of foreign policy. He struck out against the West
generally when he nationalized the Suez Canal, and again when
he nationalized French and Belgian investments as a retaliatory
action against those countries for policies they pursued in third
countries which he disapproved of, i.e., in the Sahara and the
Congo respectively. Nasser, like Touré, has focused on external
affairs, looking for domestic growth and stability in concepts of
larger political units (with their combined economic resources)
like the United Arab Republic, Pan-Arabism, and a very special
version of Pan-Africanism. So far the oil riches of the sheikdoms
of the Arabian peninsula and Saudi Arabia have escaped Nasser's
embrace. Only the poor neighbors of Syria and Yemen responded
to his vision of a United Arab Republic, and even they have found
it desirable to break away from the embrace.

At the opposite pole from the African and Arab socialism
of Guinea, Ghana, and the United Arab Republic in the African
context is Nigeria. The Federation of Nigeria is one of the few
African states with a democratic political framework. It is also
one of the few with a significantly large and dynamic private sector, a free trade union movement, a free press, and a growing body
of private entrepreneurs. There are serious institutional deficiencies
and limitations on the growth of the private sector in Nigeria—
e.g., lack of an agricultural credit system, inadequate agricultural
extension services, and insufficient channels for funneling substantial investment into the private industrial sector—but the
Nigerian government is attempting to meet these and other growth
problems with significant participation of private enterprise and
with limited government intervention and control. Thus Nigeria,
although it will have its large public sector, intends to put it in
a context of an expanding economy with a growing private sector.
It is probably the only African country seriously engaged in such
an attempt.

In its concentration on internal economic development within the framework of democratic institutions Nigeria has tended to resist the diversions of external adventures, seeking to emphasize economic cooperation rather than political affiliation in its relationships with other African states. Nigeria has been wary of the conference circuit which has afflicted African politics and absorbed the energies, to say little of the resources, of many of the new African states. Thus the contrast between Ghana, Guinea, and the United Arab Republic on the one hand and Nigeria on the other relates not only to the structure of their economies but also to the role they envisage for their economies in external relationships.

Between Guinea, Ghana, and the United Arab Republic on the one hand and Nigeria on the other the gradations and variations of economies are many in the new African states. Senegal is developing its own brand of "middle-of-the-road" African socialism that emphasizes traditional African communal practices in rural agricultural areas and at the same time seeks to preserve its Eurafrican economic ties with France. In the words of the President of Senegal, "We stand for a middle course, a *democratic socialism*, which goes so far as to integrate spiritual values, a socialism which ties in with the old ethical current of the French socialists [from Saint Simon to Léon Blum]. . . ." [13] Tunisia is engaged in pragmatically evolving a mixed economy responsive to its problems of capital shortages and a persistently large body of unemployed workers. Many public enterprises of a labor-intensive nature have characterized Tunisia's development efforts. Liberia's economy has a private sector with a small but growing number of large foreign private investors, particularly in rubber and iron ore, and a relatively tight circle of large Liberian investors. The Liberian economy, like the government and society, has been the exclusive preserve of the True Whig Party, the single party in the country. The Ivory Coast has a sizable private sector by African standards, with a considerable overseas French investment. The economy has been characterized by President Houphouët-Boigny as a "liberal economy," concerned with "stability and freedom for private enterprise," [14] and without many of the economic controls now found in Guinea, Ghana, and the United Arab Republic. The economy is evolving against the background of a right-authoritarian political system. And one could go on with other examples.

Meaning of the Choice

The important point is that most African economies, despite existing propensities and structural factors, can evolve in many different directions. Even those which have made relatively conscious and distinct choices—Guinea, Ghana, the United Arab Republic, and Nigeria—have a long way to go before the die is irretrievably cast and the final form of their structures and systems becomes determined. There remains the question of whether they can realize the goals they have chosen or whether in practice they will have to modify them. Other states have revealed a trend in their policies, and still others are drifting, or seeking a way, a route, a model for growth which will meet their needs and aspirations. There can be little doubt that the new states will be influenced in their choice of models by the scope, intensity, and nature of the problems of growth in their respective economies, and that in turn the priority attached and type of solution selected for the problems of growth will reflect the choices made. There can be little doubt too that the new states will be influenced in their choice of growth models by their choice of political structures and systems, which in turn will be affected by their choice of economic growth models.

What model or models, then, have the most to offer the new states? What models are most likely to resolve the fundamental problems of African growth—modernization of agriculture, Africanization of the public and private sectors, meeting the push for education, and striking a balance in the allocation of resources so that the productive sectors can be enlarged and, at the same time, accommodate or contain the drive toward the adoption of welfare state concepts?

What model or models are likely to contribute most to the achievement of political stability? What model or models are compatible with the various state structures and political systems African states are already evolving? With authoritarianism? With democratic systems?

These are the vital questions involved in the choice of a growth model—i.e., concentration on internal growth and stability or on finding growth and stability in Pan-African configurations. The choice in every case will affect the pattern and rate of growth, the type and nature of internal stability achieved, and the relationship of African states toward one another. The choice will also influence the relationships of African states to the outside world. The adoption of a left-authoritarian political model and a matching economic one will tend to project one kind of external posture, a certain type of positive neutralist position. The adoption of a democratic political model and a mixed economy with a large private sector will tend to project another kind of external posture, a type of non-doctrinaire national interest position—what President J. K. Nyerere of Tanganyika has described as an "independent" foreign policy deciding individual issues on their merits in terms of the country's national interest rather than on ideological grounds or bloc affiliation.

The choices that African states are now in the process of making are therefore of critical importance to the realization of the nations' objectives of growth and stability and to their interaction within the development nexus of which they are part. The choices are also important to the posture and role the African states adopt and evolve vis-à-vis one another, the Afro-Asian world, the United States and the free world generally, and the Communist bloc.

Whether the chicken or the egg comes first, whether the political form predetermines the economic system or *vice versa*, although fascinating to theorize about, is not of central importance to the view taken in this volume. The view taken here is that the search for economic growth and the quest for political stability interact in an unbreakable nexus, and that this interaction is a crucial—perhaps decisive—factor in shaping the face and posture the new states of Africa present to the world. The chapters which follow on economic growth problems and on problems of achieving political stability approach these problems from this vantage point.

Chapter 4

THE MODERNIZATION OF AGRICULTURE

Economic Importance

The crucial economic role of African agriculture gives it first place on any list of African development problems.

The Economic Survey of Nigeria for 1959 stated:

Agriculture is by far the most important sector of Nigeria's economy. It occupies the majority of the male working population and provides at least 50 per cent of the national product and 85 per cent of the country's exports.[1]

The Commission of the European Economic Community, in a report published late in 1958, described the situation in French Africa (including Guinea) as follows:

The structure of production of the Overseas Countries is that of underdeveloped countries; its salient features are therefore: The overwhelming importance of agriculture production; The relatively limited variety of products; The relatively great importance of the non-monetary sector.[2]

The same report (on p. 537) says of the Belgian Congo, now the independent Republic of the Congo, that: "A first breakdown

48

of the gross national product between the different sectors of activity in 1950 and 1956 gives an idea of relative importance of the chief sectors of production. Agriculture (incl. the processing of agricultural produce) comes first, closely followed by mining." Thus even in the mineral-rich former Belgian Congo agriculture is of prime importance.

An examination of the contribution of agriculture to export earnings—the key to financing the development of underdeveloped economies—indicates that for the largest part of Africa it is the principal contributor, and for all of Africa it is a major contributor. In many economies a single cash crop accounts for between 50 to 90 per cent of all export earnings.

Among the multi-commodity export economies during the period 1950–1957, the principal agricultural exports averaged 87 per cent (including 4.4 per cent for tropical woods) of the export earnings of French West Africa, 83.3 per cent (including 5.3 per cent for timber) of the export earnings of Nigeria, 82.3 per cent (including 2.5 per cent for rough woods) of the export earnings of Mozambique, 82.4 per cent of the export earnings of British East Africa, and 26.1 per cent of the export earnings of the Belgian Congo. The addition of miscellaneous agricultural exports, individually relatively minor in volume and value as a percentage of total agricultural exports, would in most instances raise the foregoing percentages 5 to 10 per cent.

In the predominantly monoculture economies during the same period one crop averaged well over one half of the export earnings. Coffee accounted for 57.6 per cent of the export earnings of Ethiopia, groundnuts for 92.1 per cent of the export earnings of the Gambia, cocoa for 65.4 per cent of the export earnings of Ghana, cotton and cotton seed for 71 per cent of the export earnings of the Sudan, and rubber for over 76.3 per cent of the export earnings of Liberia.[3]

The mounting controversy surrounding the operation of the European Economic Community in Eurafrican trade, which centers on the trade advantages for agricultural commodities of the African countries associated with the EEC, underlines the crucial importance attached to agriculture in the economies of all African countries, especially with respect to export earnings. It is particularly significant that the principal advantages which are at the heart of the controversy all relate to primary agricultural exports of tropical African countries—*inter alia*, cocoa, coffee, and vegetable oils—and also to tropical hardwoods.

Ghana and Nigeria, which are not associated with the EEC, have been particularly outspoken·in their complaints against the duty-free entry into the six EEC countries of cocoa from the ECC-associated countries of former French West Africa. Uganda has protested against the common external coffee tariff which would operate primarily to the disadvantage of non-associated African producers of robusta coffee, among which Uganda and Angola rank highest. Once again, former French West African territories are likely to be the principal beneficiaries of the common external tariff of the European Six of the EEC. Nigeria has also been concerned about the common external tariff on vegetable oils and tropical hardwoods.

All non-associated African countries have expressed concern over other provisions in the Treaty of Rome (March 25, 1957) which may be invoked to their detriment and in favor of the associated countries—primarily in former French West and Equatorial Africa and the former Belgian Congo. Again it is significant that all of these provisions relate to agriculture. They permit the imposition of discriminatory duties on other agricultural products, the imposition of quotas on imports into the EEC area of agricultural products from non-associated areas, and the extension of an agricultural policy to be formulated for the European Six to the overseas associated countries, which would permit, *inter alia*, the negotiating of long-term purchase contracts for agricultural commodities at advantageous prices with associated African country producers or marketing agencies.

The fear of the African states not associated with the EEC is that, with respect to the four or five major agricultural commodities already favored under the Treaty of Rome and others which may be so favored, with little or no warning, the African states associated with the EEC will be encouraged to expand their production behind the shelter of the common external tariff and other discriminatory devices. This could result, particularly in the case of cocoa and coffee marketings to West Germany, in a diversion of trade from Ghanaian, Nigerian, and Ugandan sources to the producers of the independent African states of former French Africa. The non-associated African states are also concerned lest the advantage of the associated African states in trade of vegetable oil, and possibly other semi-processed agricultural products, will encourage the associated African areas to expand their agricultural processing industries, crowding out of the export market such industries in the non-associated countries. Both of these developments could significantly decrease the important export earnings of non-associated African states, and thus their resources for development financing.

Along with the established and, hopefully, expanding export market for African agriculture, the importance of which is highlighted by the Common Market controversy, must be considered the increasing importance of internal agricultural markets in all the developing African economies. The pressing requirements for improved labor performance of both skilled and unskilled workers, which means raising the low African dietary standards; the growth of urban centers; the expanding effort to stabilize labor forces, which means curtailing part-time agricultural production so that the producer must purchase his foodstuffs—these are some of the developments which emphasize the basic role of internal agricultural markets, especially for locally produced foodstuffs.

The all-pervasive importance of agriculture in African development was summed up by the then Prime Minister Nkrumah when, speaking for Ghana, he said, ". . . we want to ensure continued expansion and diversification of agriculture, on which, in the final analysis, all our plans depend." [4] He could have been speaking for all of Africa. In fact, in another address late in 1959 he purported to do just that when he declared that he expected the new regional office of the Food and Agricultural Organization in Accra to develop into "a rigorous African agency for disseminating improved agricultural practices so indispensable to the raising of the nutrition and general standard of living of the people of Africa." [5]

Magnitude of the Problem

The problem of modernizing agriculture is twofold: to increase production and to bring the product into the money economy at one and the same time. The prototype of agricultural tradi-
tionalism is subsistence agriculture, which operates both with
minimum efficiency and almost wholly outside the money economy. Hence the magnitude of the African agricultural problem
can be most briefly stated in terms of the extent to which subsistence agriculture is still the prevailing practice. A United Nations survey, in describing the structural aspects of agriculture in
Africa, defines two categories: "traditional agriculture, chiefly organized with the resources and for the subsistence of rural communities" and "modern agriculture, carried on as a commercial
undertaking entirely within the money economy." [6] It goes on to
comment that:

While the technological structure of traditional agriculture may vary
from area to area . . . it is essentially primitive . . . South of the
Sahara where extensive belts infested by tsetse fly forbid the use of
animals in agriculture, [and] production is based chiefly on manual
labour, frequently complemented by the hoe, the traditional farm
implement . . .[7]

To what extent, then, do primitive methods and production
without market incentives characterize African agriculture? What
proportion of land and how many people are involved?

In terms of land area, the United Nations estimated in 1954,
on the basis of a sampling survey conducted in nine "countries"
in Africa with approximately two-thirds of the population of the
continent, that between two-thirds and three-fourths of the land
cultivated by Africans in these countries was devoted to subsistence production.[8] The "countries" of the survey included seven
in which agriculture is the principal source of export earnings—
Ghana, Nigeria, French West Africa, French Equatorial Africa,
Kenya, Uganda, and Tanganyika—and two in which agriculture
is a major export earner—the Belgian Congo and Southern Rho-

desia. Yet between two-thirds and three-fourths of the land worked by the major part of the African populations in these countries was not contributing to the market economy, including of course the vital export sector.

We lack statistics on population employed in subsistence agriculture, but the United Nations *Economic Survey* notes:

Although production in traditional agriculture is primarily for subsistence, the need for money income makes it necessary for farmers to achieve a marketable surplus. It is not, however, possible to assess the distribution of African manpower between production for sale and subsistence production, since frequently output of the same product is in part commercialized and in part consumed directly, as is the case with food crops generally. Even when certain crops are grown entirely for export, they are often produced in conjunction with subsistence farming within the framework of traditional agriculture.[9]

In its comprehensive *African Labour Survey* the International Labour Office found that it had to forgo making estimates because "owing to the lack of over-all figures it is impossible to make any estimate of the distribution of non-wage earning manpower employed in agriculture between cash cropping and subsistence agriculture." [10] Nevertheless, recent estimates in a study of the associated countries of the European Economic Community put the number of Africans engaged in all agriculture as high as 95 per cent of the population in the former French African associated countries and 85 per cent in the former Belgian Congo.[11] Presumably in areas of Africa not associated with the Common Market—primarily English and Portuguese-speaking areas—approximately the same figures would apply. Thus, despite the difficulties of classification and the shortcomings of the statistics available, it can be safely concluded that well over a majority of the African population is generally engaged in non-market agriculture. And in any event, the overwhelming majority—cash or non-cash producers—is involved in traditional agriculture. The fact that a relatively small number of European producers dominate export agriculture in the former Belgian Congo, the Federation of Rhodesia and Nyasaland (especially Southern Rhodesia), Kenya, Portuguese Africa, and the former French Cameroun emphasizes the underdeveloped state of traditional agriculture in these countries, since here, as elsewhere in Africa, most of the land is worked by Africans, who constitute the bulk of the population.

The underdeveloped state of African agriculture highlights the importance of the largely unexplored potential of this huge sector of African life and reveals the magnitude of the problem of modernization. The words of a study of the structure of the economy of the then Belgian Congo still can be read to apply to just about all of sub-Sahara Africa:

There has been a general expansion in which the production entering the market economy has assumed a larger and larger role. However, the production which remains in the African subsistence economy corresponds to about 80 per cent of total African production.

The magnitude of the problem which remains to be resolved in order to transform African subsistence societies into a market economy is indicated by this percentage.

This percentage is also the measure of the problem of growth confronting all of the new African states on their accession to independence.[12]

The Colonial Background

The foregoing facts in themselves are sufficient to indicate in broad outline the nature of the problem of modernizing African agriculture. The picture is far from complete, however, until those facts are set against the background of the colonial experience and the problem is thus given some historical perspective.

In the first place, little was done by the colonial powers to tackle in any fundamental way the problem of modernizing African agriculture. And what was done was limited in its effectiveness.

The history of the allocation of resources, the most concrete expression of purpose, is most revealing. Going up the scale, the Federation of Rhodesia and Nyasaland allocated to the productive sector, agriculture and industry, 1.7 per cent of total planned expenditures for the period 1957–1961; the Belgian government, 6.4 per cent, in its ten-year plan in the Congo, 1949–1959; and the last pre-independence plan in Ghana allocated 11.3 per cent. The contrast with recent history is too sharp to be ignored. In Ghana's first totally post-independence plan, authorized expenditure for the productive sector was increased to 20 per cent. In agricultural dependent Nigeria the amount of planned expenditures allocated to agriculture and industry, 15.1 per cent in the 1955–1962 plans, which terminated one year after the achievement of Nigerian independence, has been at least doubled in the first post-independence development plan.[13] The Sudan, perhaps setting a record in its first development plan after independence, 1956–1961, allocated 88.1 per cent of its planned expenditures to agriculture and industry. Even though this allocation was drastically reduced to about 62 per cent in a 1957–1958 revision of the plan, this amount is still very high. It is also significant that the allocation to agriculture and industry in post-emergency Kenya following the suppression of the Mau Mau uprising reached 41 per cent of total planned expenditures for 1957–1960. In neighboring Uganda, which had also been disturbed by internal dissension, centering around the then separatist tendencies of the Kingdom of Buganda, the allocation to agriculture and industry was increased from 23.2 per cent for the period of 1946–1955 to 32.8 percent for the period of 1955–1960.

Only in French Africa did a colonial government make substantial allocation of planned expenditures—just over 25 per cent —to agriculture and industry over a long period of time (1946–1957). This level of allocation is being maintained by the newly independent African states of *l'expression française*. However, in Guinea's first post-independence plan (1960–1963), the planned allocation to "production" has been put at slightly more than 47 per cent. In Portuguese Africa the average allocation of planned expenditure for agriculture and industry was 26.5 per cent for the period 1953–1958 and has been increased to 36.5 per cent for the period 1959–1964; but here there has been a substantial program of new European immigrant settlements which has absorbed a very significant part of these allocations.[14]

The Belgian government recognized the need to expand African participation in the productive sectors of the Congolese economy in 1959, almost as a postscript to the Belgian effort to develop the Congo. The following declaration of purpose was not made at the outset of the Congolese ten-year development plan but at its end:

The objective of the collection of measures being prepared is to disengage more and more of the Congolese population from the subsistence economy in order to integrate them into the market economy. This is the ambition of the Government.[15]

Although there is room for disagreement about priorities in the allocation of resources in development plans, it would seem clear that to the European colonial powers modernization of African agriculture—even in the areas concentrating on cash crops—ranked low, and in some areas impossibly low. In those areas where it ranked lowest, the Federation of Rhodesia and Nyasaland and the Belgian Congo, it is perhaps significant that almost all cash-crop production for export has been concentrated in European hands. Tobacco, the chief agricultural export crop of the Rhodesias, has for a long time been practically a European monopoly; palm oil and kernels, coffee, cocoa, tea, and rubber have been a virtual European monopoly in the Congo. Only African production of cotton and groundnuts has achieved significance in Congo agricultural exports. Obviously the failure to provide public resources of scale for agricultural development affected the capital-shy African cultivators much more adversely than the European producers who had adequate private resources or access to them on reasonable commercial terms. Legal, official, and operational measures and restrictions combined with capital shortages to reinforce the dominant position of the European producer. African agriculture was channeled into "self-sufficiency in domestic food supplies" or into special cash crops, e.g., cotton in the Congo, through requirements of compulsory cultivation, through guaranteed prices and markets, and through the types of credit, technical assistance, and advice made available to the African cultivator.

Besides the failure to attach importance to the modernization of African agriculture, there was a combination of fears about doing so—fear of disrupting the traditional subsistence way of life any more than necessary to provide labor for the market sector, fear of food shortages if Africans turned to cash crops on a significant scale, fear of overproduction and surpluses, with attendant dissatisfaction on the part of African producers, fear of too closely integrating African production into the problems of the world commodity markets, and fear of labor shortages for industry, commerce, and European-operated plantations if too many Africans turned to market production. The observations of the East Africa Royal Commission bear eloquent testimony to the pervasiveness of this state of fear:

One of the most untoward consequences of a subsistence economy is the recurring danger of a failure of the basic food supply . . . the inability of the subsistence economy to produce regular marketable surpluses by specializing production without risking a food shortage at critical periods of the year, have led the indigenous populations to seek security by clinging to their customary methods of production. . . . It is not surprising, therefore, that these governments [of East Africa] should endeavour to prevent the occurrence of food shortages. But in the policies which they have adopted they have been unduly influenced by the fears and practices of the indigenous populations, and by encouraging district, regional and even territorial self-sufficiency they have perpetuated the cause of evil which their measures were intended to combat, namely the system of self-sufficiency itself. . . . Instead of encouraging specialization and the free sale of surplus production of food and other agricultural products in suitable areas . . . government policy has frequently looked upon the normal functioning of the market with suspicion. . . . it [government policy] has discouraged African producers from specializing in their production or has discouraged the marketing of food surpluses . . . lest a shortage should occur at some later date. . . . self-sufficiency . . . perpetuates the vicious cycle in which all subsistence economy moves. . . .[16]

In various forms and different degrees some, and frequently most, of these fears colored the thinking and determined the policies of the colonial powers in large areas of Africa. In some areas the measures taken in response to these fears relegated African agriculture to subsistence production; in other areas there was an attempt to achieve balance by confining the impact of the switch to cash-cropping by retaining it within the framework of traditional agriculture. On balance, as the East Africa Royal Commission concluded, no matter how praiseworthy any individual rationale for restricting the modernization of African agriculture might have been, it could only result in retarding both the development of the East African economies and the modernization of the African societies in the area.[17]

A first conclusion from the colonial experience is, then, that for the most part the colonial powers, during the longest part of their tenure in Africa, did not attempt to modernize traditional African agricultural methods. A second conclusion is that, in those instances after World War II where the European colonial powers had some will to improve and transform African agriculture, they generally lacked the ability to do so. The following cases—several of which also clearly illustrate the interplay of political factors on economic development—suggest a lack not only of technical and scientific ability but also of political ability to induce modernization of agriculture.

The impressive list of failures in the area of large-scale agricultural schemes suggests a glaring lack of technical knowledge or experimentation on how to transform the primitive African agricultural system under conditions of African cultivation. Perhaps the classic example in the post-World War II period is the East African groundnut scheme.[18] "Highly mechanized agricultural methods" were applied to a large area in Tanganyika without adequate knowledge of the conditions to be dealt with or the suitability of massive application of temperate-zone mechanized farming techniques and equipment to tropical Africa. The result was a dismal failure and the project was abandoned. In a post-mortem assessment Professor S. H. Frankel, who served on the Working Party which recommended the abandonment of the project, concluded: "Nobody yet knows the scale or system of farming which can economically replace the primitive native effort in these regions." [19]

In addition to limitations of knowledge, the colonial powers generally lacked the authority over or failed to command the respect and confidence of the African populations in sufficient measure to enable them to introduce systematically new organization and techniques of cultivation. At times the colonial powers met passive resistance, at other times active and violent resistance. Persuasion was not effective, perhaps inadequately attempted.

Various degrees of coercion and compulsion generally had only limited success or failed outright.

The United Kingdom tried perhaps more widely and with less recourse to naked force and compulsion than any of the other colonial powers to improve African agriculture. The British experience in three different territories illustrates the limited possibilities of change in a basic area of economic life through use of the powers and sanctions of colonial control. In the Gold Coast, when swollen-shoot was killing an estimated 18,000,000 cocoa trees a year out of a national total of 500,000,000, seemingly the only effective way of bringing the disease under control was to cut and destroy diseased trees. Attempting to compel cutting, the British met strong opposition from the farmers which was at least in part engendered by the political campaign being waged by Kwame Nkrumah and his party against the colonial government. Interesting enough, shortly after he came into office as "Leader of Government Business" Dr. Nkrumah introduced a slightly modified version of the colonial government's cocoa tree cutting plan. "Nkrumah advised Gold Coast farmers not to use cutting-out methods to eradicate the swollen-shoot disease. Later, [after assuming office] he told them 'cutting out' was the only method which would save the cocoa industry from extinction." [20] In Kenya the record of Kikuyu resistance to new agricultural methods which the colonial administration sought to introduce, and the transformation of this resistance into active and bitter political opposition by nationalist leaders, is clear. The opposition and discontent engendered by the colonial effort and the nationalist reaction has been called the major factor leading to, if not the cause of, the Mau Mau outbreak which bedeviled Kenya from 1952 to 1957.

Lastly, the British attempt to develop Nyasaland's traditional agriculture became an important factor in creating the background against which the riots and disorders of early 1959 took place. The report of the Nyasaland Commission of Inquiry, after describing the rules, of ten years' standing, made to prevent soil erosion and the spread of disease, concluded, "The enforcement of these rules led to disputes and a great deal of bitter feeling during the period we have under review [July 1958—March 1959]. . . . We have no doubt that in many districts Congress [the Nyasaland African

Congress] leaders made as much capital as they could out of any government action which was unpopular; and in this respect the agriculture rules were a very happy hunting ground. One shrewd observer, a member of Congress but not belonging to the leadership, agreed there was a policy of 'nagging' the Government. . . ." [21]

The Devlin Commission, as the Nyasaland Commission has come to be known, also observed that "breaches of these [agriculture] rules lead to fines and in extreme cases to imprisonment. They are very unpopular. Their object is little understood because it lies in the long term and the African does not look very far ahead." [22]

In summary, during the European colonial era in Africa only the surface of the agricultural problem was scratched, and that only in the postwar development period. A recent study devoted entirely to the actual and potential agricultural development of Africa south of the Sahara sums up the performance of the colonial powers thus:

Again the background of the nature, ecological relationships, challenges, and potentialities of trans-Saharan Africa in the sphere of agricultural development it must be confessed that all—overseas races and Africans alike—have failed in retaining and improving what is good and in introducing only the better and the best. A review of sins of commission and omission serves as a reminder of what is owed Africa in the years ahead. Paradoxically the outstanding sin of commission is that of failure to make a more timely beginning in thinking, planning, and acting for Africa. In acts of omission all have failed even more seriously and over a wider range. . . . A cardinal omission is a clear enunciation of policy for the development of agriculture and related interests. . . ." [23]

The author's inclusion of Africans in his indictment is for the most part gratuitous. The African rested in a subsistence state, and there in large part he still rests. It was the European colonists who first disturbed the traditional economies and then sought (after 1945) to modernize them. Certainly since 1885 the prerogative has been that of the European colonial powers. Only now, with the transfer of sovereignty to African governments, is the responsibility and the prerogative shifting to African hands.

Some Specifics

It is clearly impossible here to break down the present problem of modernizing African agriculture into all of its components. However, the broad aspects of the problem which embrace most of them should be noted in the ensuing discussion.

With regard to the development of agricultural markets, that is, bringing agriculture into the money economy, the pressing fact is that, although the importance of the export market for African agriculture is already recognized, the development of internal agricultural markets has generally been neglected. The benefits of capital inflow from the export trade are highly visible. The humbler but no less important functions of internal trade often are not.

We have already noted current pressures for the development of internal agricultural markets. In addition, there are likely to be new pressures for expanding the production and variety of foodstuffs for local sale. It is reasonable to expect that, with the growth of cash-cropping for the export market, cultivators engaged in production for the export sector will come to rely for their personal needs more and more on foodstuffs produced by farmers specializing in such agricultural production, and less and less on food of their own cultivation.

If secondary industry is to have any chance to evolve on an economic basis, then the African market for its output must be widened and deepened. One way of achieving this is to expand the earnings of the African farmer so that he has the additional purchasing power which will enable him to increase his consumption of manufactured goods. Cash-cropping for export is only one way of increasing the farmer's income. Production or cash-cropping for internal markets is certainly another way, and, in a sense, an easier and quicker way from the individual farmer's point of view. Production for the local market can be accomplished without the necessity of going through middlemen and marketing boards and conforming to export standards.

The development of markets implies diversification. The

growth of secondary industry will create a demand for such agricultural commodities as cotton, tobacco, and grain for manufacturing purposes. Among the first industrial installations to be found in almost any African country embarking on the journey to economic growth are textile mills, cigarette factories, and breweries. Hence in a growing economy increasing differentiation in production functions, including agricultural production, is likely to prove most economical and over time to result in cultivators concentrating on production of specific commodities for the export market or for the internal market (foodstuffs or commodities for secondary industry).

Diversification, in turn, has implications for other farming activities than crop growing. It is likely that, as a concomitant of the growth of balanced agriculture and as part of the process of differentiation, animal husbandry for the internal economy will grow. The Republic of Chad and the Malagasy Republic have already expanded considerably their livestock production. There is a growing interest in fisheries as a source of food for the internal market. In addition to ocean, river, and lake fishing, fish farms patterned on those found in the Far East have come in for considerable attention in tropical Africa in recent years.

Our emphasis on internal markets does not mean that there is a clean division of the African agricultural market problem. The need to improve and diversify agriculture for supplying the internal market would appear to be a natural extension of diversifying and modernizing the export segment of the agricultural sector. And in some instances modernization of traditional African agriculture must be multi-purposed, affecting both the export and internal segments of the agricultural sector. For example, the increased emphasis on improving and expanding livestock and fisheries production for foodstuffs for the internal market has led to an increase in the production of canned beef, treated hides, skins, and wool, and dairy products, as well as of canned fish for the export trade.

Nor can we assume smooth sailing for the export sector because of its development lead. For instance, the French have encouraged production for export, but largely for the French market, where French African production has received preferential treatment, including the payment of a *surprix* on several key commodities.[24] Hence, in spite of the expenditure of substantial French public funds on the development of African agriculture, the newly independent states of *l'expression française* still face the problem of having to spend more to make their production competitive on the world market. The EEC trade discrimination in favor of the former French African territories, already discussed, continues to provide a shield for the high cost and backward agricultural production of these new states. The danger is that the incentive to discover and develop new and more efficient systems and techniques of production will be dulled by the artificial preferences enjoyed by these states in the EEC. In the Convention of Association between the Common Market Six and the Eighteen African Associated States, replacing the original association arrangement which expired at the end of 1962, this problem gets some recognition. In return for a scheduled reduction in French *surprix* payments and a reduction in tariff preference, a special fund of $230 million has been created to make compensatory payments to the Associated States and to help them diversify and improve the productivity of their agriculture.

Second, moving inward from the economic institution, the market, to what supports it, the farm, there is the whole range of development tasks which comes under the broad heading of production. Central to modernizing agriculture in all underdeveloped economies is the need for improved techniques and systems of cultivation to increase the yield per acre in the first instance, and then to increase the yield per man.

In sub-Sahara Africa, unlike much of South Asia and the Far East, the latter problem exists. For the most part sub-Sahara Africa is not now densely populated, a condition which for the present precludes large surpluses of agricultural labor and provides a motive for increasing yields per man. Moreover, the development of trade, mining and industry, and the increasing availability of primary education, and to a lesser extent post-primary education, have already had the effect of drawing African labor out of agriculture, making it even more important that those who remain on the land increase their productivity if over-all output is to increase *pari passu* with the growing demands of the market.

The production task involves much more than development

efforts aimed at the individual agricultural worker. The African states must embark on extensive programs of village improvement, community development, and rural modernization, not only to increase the efficiency of agricultural workers and their general level of production but also as a means of retaining agricultural labor on the land or stopping the flow of population to urban centers, the relative emphasis shifting with the population situation in the country in question. Ghana and Guinea, and more recently Nigeria, have initiated such programs, a wholesome sign but only a start on what must be a common African movement.

Third, and signifying the very heart of agricultural modernization, are all the critical development factors which are subsumed under the heading of agricultural research and education. It is hardly necessary to spell out either their significance as the very foundation of any program to improve agricultural production or the present state of their indigenous development in Africa.

As to the road ahead, we would note two fairly typical conditions likely to affect the scope of agricultural research and its application. One is the extensive lore, the empirical knowledge, possessed by the African cultivator of the plants and ecology of his area and his distrust of foreign innovations which disregard this store of knowledge and experience.[25] The other, common to many new states in Africa and elsewhere, is that national leaders all too often tend to starve research activities for funds because of the failure to understand the relationship of research to the economic growth so many of them ardently desire. The results of research are sometimes long deferred, and the economic payoff may be even further removed from the ken of the new leaders in a hurry for tangible results.

The part education must play in the modernization of African agriculture is too clearly implied by the great gap between the empirical knowledge behind the prevailing traditional agriculture and the modern agricultural science to be enlarged upon here. The task of closing that gap has been dramatically summed up as follows:

The subject matter [customary African agriculture] is so complex that no modern combination of agricultural research stations and agricultural schools has so far come near devising any better system of agriculture, let alone a better method of education towards such a system.[26]

Such is the challenge facing the new states.

A Perspective

The failure of colonial governments to modernize traditional African agriculture and transform the subsistence agriculture sector into a market sector was bound to mean that economic development, no matter how successful, would be confined in scope for the most part to a thin layer of European investment largely concentrated in primary production for the export market, a growing but, on a continent-wide basis, still limited output of African cash-croppers, and attendant trade and commerce shared between large European interests and an increasing body of African traders.

The consequences set the dimensions of the present agricultural problem. The overwhelming bulk of the African population has remained outside of the modern economy. The potential of the traditional sector for capital accumulation to finance urban and industrial development has been far from fully exploited. The susceptibility of export economies, particularly monoculture economies, to the vagaries of the world market and the elements has not been significantly provided against by diversification. The creation of adequate purchasing power to sustain secondary and tertiary industry has not been widely generated. Cash-cropping, although introduced and encouraged, has not generally been brought to a sufficiently high level of productivity and production of cash-crop foodstuffs for the internal market has not been adequately encouraged. The gap between the export economy and the traditional African subsistence economy has become so great that bridging it will require a major sustained effort.

Will the new African states have the requisite determination to bring about the revolutionary transformation required? Will they be able to induce the African cultivators to make the extra effort needed? Will they be able to forestall the impatience of those who want immediate discernible results?

Whether the new independent African governments, commanding popular support and laboring under a compulsion to develop their economies, have the will and the ability to organize, mount, and sustain the effort required to modernize their agriculture remains to be seen. The fragmentary evidence at hand is inconclusive. The infatuation with major development schemes to effectuate industrialization in one bold stroke is obviously a serious danger. Nevertheless, to the extent that a clear trend can now be discerned, the obvious awareness of the importance of agriculture on the part of the new African leaders, the increasing allocation of resources in the development plans of the newly independent states to agricultural development, and the potential political responsiveness of the new governments to the needs and aspirations of the largest part of their electorate, the rural and agricultural populations, suggest that in a good many areas of newly independent Africa the trend will be more and more to attempt the modernization of agriculture which is so essential to the development and growth of the new states.

If Dr. Hastings Banda, the leader of the principal party in Nyasaland, the Malawi Congress Party, and the first Prime Minister of the territory, should prove to be typical, there is every reason to believe the determination and willingness in requisite degree and intensity exist. Dr. Banda deliberately assumed the portfolio of Minister of Natural Resources and Local Government before the post of Prime Minister was established in preference to others with more apparent glamor in order to translate the Malawi Party platform on agriculture into reality, i.e., that the first necessity for economic development is "the commercialization of agriculture on a massive scale." [27] Dr. Banda has a favorite phrase which he uses to describe his goal in his new ministerial post—to make Nyasaland into "a central African Denmark." [28] His words and his actions on this score carry conviction. Mr. R. Kettlewell, the outgoing secretary for natural resources in the Nyasaland government, for one, accepts them. He has said, "I hope Dr. Banda and company will succeed where they caused us [the colonial administration] to fail. I think they will succeed before it is too late." [29]

Chapter 5

AFRICANIZATION OF THE PUBLIC AND PRIVATE SECTORS

Definition and Dimensions of the Problem

Along with modernization of traditional agriculture, as the root source from which the wherewithal to finance economic and social development will be derived, Africanization of the public and private sectors of the new states, as a concomitant of political decolonization and economic and social development, shares first place in the agenda of African priorities for nation-building. In some instances where the colonial preparation for self-government and independence has been totally or largely lacking, Africanization is the crucial requirement for the newly independent state. This has certainly been a lesson of the Congo debacle.

Originally Africanization of the public sector was thought of as referring only to the staffing of the public service of the state with African personnel in substitution for expatriates, i.e., nationals of the colonial power. In Nigeria (where its local application was called Nigerianisation) it was first defined in 1953, seven years before independence, as the reduction and ultimately the ending of expatriate predominance in the higher levels of the Civil Service.[1] Then in practice, in Nigeria and elsewhere in Africa, the term quickly came into common usage to mean the eventual re-placement of all expatriate personnel by Africans throughout the public service. But in the context of the conditions widely pre-vailing in many of the new African states even the broadened Nigerian definition proved too limited to describe the scope of the staffing change-over implicit, if not always recognized in timely fashion, in the assumption by Africans of the powers of self-government and independence. In the Congo, where with inde-pendence the administration of government collapsed and in sig-nificant areas disappeared, the lack of Africans trained to operate the government at all levels—national, provincial, territorial, and local—demonstrated in the most extreme way that it was not merely replacement of overseas personnel in the public service but the training of African political cadres which was the number one need of the new state. The Congo reflected in its most acute form the situation obtaining in one degree or another in many parts of Africa. The process of Africanization must be thought of, then, as embracing for most of Africa not only the replacement of foreign personnel in the public service but also the political training and experience for Africans to operate their new political structures.

In many areas such training and experience must and will be obtained on the job in the rough and tumble of the political arena. Where there is an adequate core cadre, Africanization in the sense of producing more and more qualified Africans to man the political mechanism can proceed in a more or less orderly way. Where the core cadre is inadequate some degree of strife and violence is likely to accompany its development; and where, as was the case in the Congo, it is totally lacking, chaos must be expected.

The Congo debacle, starting with the July 1960 mutiny of the Congolese army, the former *Force Publique*, highlighted an-other, and in the particular instance critical, area involving Afri-canization. The failure of the outgoing Belgian administration in the Congo and the incoming Lumumba government to recognize the need for a rapid program for Congolese replacement of Belgian officers of the *Force Publique* was certainly a key element in the disaffection and mutiny of large segments of the *Force Publique*.

The continuing lack of discipline and the erratic behavior of Congolese troops can be attributed in large part to the fact that corporals were made colonels and sergeants were made generals, on the assumption that somehow the change in title and rank would magically confer on the new battalion, division, and army leaders the ability to lead troops, plan and execute logistical and combat operations, and give military advice to the civilian government leaders.

The tragic course of events in the Congo ever since, with first one and then another army detachment committing atrocities, has thrust to the forefront the critical nature of the military cadre dimension of Africanization. Fortunately, it is a factor of considerably lesser proportions elsewhere in Africa. With a general stiffening of political posture among Casablanca powers in late 1961, Ghana dismissed British General Alexander and several dozen other British officers from the Ghanaian army (although some have returned and others have been replaced by Canadians). Although the United Kingdom had been training Ghanaian personnel for assumption of officer ranks, it seemed most unlikely that there were sufficient Ghanaian trainees on hand to take over the vacancies. Nevertheless, on this occasion Dr. Nkrumah's Pan-African political posture, rather than availability of replacements. determined the tempo of Africanization.

In addition to restaffing the public service—civilian and military—and staffing and to an extent restaffing the political structure in the new African states, another important dimension of Africanization is the need to staff and, to an extent, restaff the structure of the country's economy. This is so irrespective of the country's choice of growth model. Both the private sector of the economy and the public sector, where it performs economic functions, need African staff.

We shall consider some of the details of the process of Africanization later. Here we are concerned with its over-all importance in the African mind and with some of its special aspects.

Africanization of the public sector is a paramount objective of African states. One of the things the nationalist forces most resented in the colonial period was the exclusion of Africans from the higher and middle categories of the territorial civil services; and the right to man their own civil service has become one of the fruits of independence most sought.

On the eve of Nigerian independence, in 1959, the report of the Parliamentary Committee on the Nigerianisation of the Federal Public Service quoted with approval the following statement:

One of the fundamental rights and privileges of a self-governing country is that it must have control of its public service. No outside authority must be in a position to determine, even in the last instance, what appointments, promotions and disciplinary action are taken in respect of the civil service.[2]

The report carried the matter even further when it concluded:

Nigerianisation politically, must demonstrate in no uncertain term a clear break from the Colonial regime and reflect the dawn of [the] era of freedom and Independence . . .

The concept of Nigerianisation must be viewed in terms of Independence and independent status. This must involve the maintenance of the prestige of a nation and the desire to feel and assert the reality of Independence and not the shadow of it. For, to any national of any independent state, the Independence of such a state will not be meaningful if he [sic] should retain the same foreign Colonial Civil Service machinery with the same Colonial Civil Servants and personnel. . . . Independence will not be real to Nigerian nationals and would indeed appear to be a sham if after Independence the newly born Nigerian nation would have Nigerian Ministers and Nigerian Parliamentarians but with expatriate Permanent Secretaries and principal advisers.[3]

If these sentiments are to be found so eloquently articulated in Nigeria, where probably more had already been done than anywhere else in Africa to Africanize the public service, then certainly one must expect them to be held by all territories and new states in the independence procession. Africanization of the public service must be viewed as a *sine qua non* of self-government and independence in African thinking.

The development of adequate political cadres, in part to replace the departing colonial officials who acted as ministers, governors, commissioners, judges, etc., and in part to staff the new political structures—executive and legislative positions, not to mention the special category of judicial positions—is certainly a vital aspect of the Africanization process. But there is little more to add to what we have already said, other than that much of what follows in the chapters on the search for political stability relates and derives from the state of the political cadres—size, training, and experience—at the moment of independence of the new states.

A special aspect of Africanization of the public service which has generally escaped attention, even of the Nationalists, before independence is the question of Africanization of the military forces of a territory as it approaches the final stages of dependency before accession to independence. As we have already noted, the Congo, with the mutiny of the *Force Publique*, provides the extreme illustration of total non-Africanization. Ghana came to independence with Africanization of the officer corps initiated, but its troops with the U.N. Special Force in the Congo some three and one half years after independence were led by a British major-general and many of the officers were British. And, as we have noted, political pressures from Ghana's Pan-African associates to do away with this situation led Ghana to Africanize its officer corps abruptly by replacing all British officers with Ghanaians in late 1961, long before the planned change-over was due. Nigeria came to independence among the best prepared in this category of Africanization as in the others, with fifty regular Nigerian officers and others in training at Sandhurst.

It is not surprising that Africanization of the officer corps in African defense or military forces did not proceed very far in the colonial context. The nature of the colonial relationship tends to militate against it. Nevertheless, there are degrees, as already illustrated, and these degrees define the problem confronting the new states on the day of independence. The sentiments in the Nigerianisation Committee report expressing the need to Africanize the civil service as a manifestation and prerequisite of independence undoubtedly apply equally for the armed forces. Natural desire aside, failure to Africanize the military force has laid new African states open to embarrassing attack by their neighbors. Guinea and Ghana seem never to tire of pointing out that the

military force of the Federal Republic of Cameroon (formerly
the Republic of Cameroun) is led and officered by the French,
and inferring therefrom that the government of President Ahidjo
is a "puppet of France," overlooking the fact that Czech officers
led the Guinean troops in the Congo and that British and Cana-
dian officers are still serving with the Ghanaian armed forces.

Although Africanization of the private sector has attracted
considerably less attention than Africanization of the public sector,
its importance has been recognized by two such ideologically contrasting states as Guinea and Nigeria.

Guinea has recognized the need to "re-Africanize" the Guinean economy as part of its total doctrine of decolonization, which
means the "recapture" of all wealth and power in the country
from the "colonial exploiters." In the words of President Sékou
Touré:

When we say: "Decolonisation," we mean we want to destroy
the habits, conceptions and ways of conduct of colonialism. We are
determined to replace them with forms that are Guinean forms, conceived by the people of Guinea, adapted to the conditions, to the
means, to the aspirations of the people of Guinea.

Decolonisation consists in detecting all that remains of the
colonial system and finding a Guinean solution for it. . . . Decolonisation is the reconversion of colonial habits into national habits, the
reconversion of colonial mentalities into Guinean mentalities.[4]

At the other end of the political spectrum, the report of the
Nigerianisation Committee makes these significant references to
Nigerianization of the private sector, even though the report is
explicitly concerned only with the federal public service:

174. In every modern independent state to-day, at least three things
must be present[;] otherwise such a state is not truly independent:

(a) The Government must be wholly and solely under the control
    of its nationals,
(b) Its Public Service must be in the hands of its nationals, and
(c) The control and direction of her economic and other develop-
    ment policies must be in the hands of its nationals.[5]

Although the Commission is concerned only with training and
recruitment for the Government Service, it has very much in mind

the urgent need for highly qualified [Nigerian] men in . . . private enterprises. . . . It is also becoming increasingly clear how much Nigeria suffers from the lack of highly qualified and skilled men in private enterprises. The Commission takes the view that although the need to train . . . Nigerians for the Government Service is so important . . . it would be a disservice to the country if it overlooks these facts or if its recommendations had an adverse effect on the work of non-Government organizations.[6]

The federal and regional governments of Nigeria are aware of both the importance of Africanization of the economy and the critical need for trained Nigerian personnel with which to accomplish it. In contrast to Guinea's doctrine of the state taking over most economic activity as the way to development and Africanization, Nigeria's regions have all made significant bids to attract foreign private investment to further development and have emphasized the education and training—including in-service and on-the-job training—of Nigerians as a way of Nigerianizing the economy. In addition, the creation of a stock market and the introduction of stock issues are intended to expand Nigerian participation in ownership as well as management of private enterprise.

Ghana has tended to follow a course somewhere between Guinea and Nigeria, although as it evolves, it seems to grow closer to the former. Africanization of the private sector has been undertaken by enlarging and Africanizing the functions of the public sector, attracting private investment in selected areas of the economy, attempting to up-grade Ghanaian personnel to more responsible positions, and by official restrictions or requirements with respect to foreign staff and Ghanaian staff. Other African countries have followed variations of these patterns, although few have gone so far as to emulate fully Guinea's.

Irrespective of the pattern and the starting point, all of the African states have come to appreciate the importance of Africanization of their private sectors, some sooner and some later. Nigeria, whose path was laid out quite clearly some time before its actual accession to independence, was in a position to concentrate on economic development and the problem of Africanization of the private sector sooner than most. Other states which came to indepence in a more abrupt fashion, such as Guinea, the Republic of Cameroun, and the Republic of the Congo, had to begin coping with the problem as a matter of government policy after the achievement of independence. This is not to say that in these areas and elsewhere in Africa individual private enterprises did not undertake some limited programs to train African staff for technical, administrative, and lower management positions.

Aside from the political importance obviously attaching to Africanization in the public and private sectors, certain of its economic aspects must be noted before proceeding to a consideration of the present state of Africanization in representative areas. The dual nature of the problem of Africanization—its near critical impact on political stability as an end in itself and as a base for economic growth, as well as its direct impact on the total capacity of the new states to mount their new economic development plans—requires at least a brief look at a few of the more important aspects of the problem.

One aspect derives from the increasingly systematic approach to economic development in large parts of Africa, starting with the adoption of territorial development plans generally in British, French, and Belgian Africa as an aftermath of World War II. As a result of such plans, public services and private investment and trade expanded and required more trained personnel. Thus, unless the African were to be deliberately excluded and the existing top-heavy European layer in government and business augmented beyond economic limits, Africanization of both the public and private sectors had to be begun. It was not economically feasible—either for the public service or for private enterprise—in attempting to build a staff pattern which would be responsive to the dynamics of growth to plan for European personnel in positions below the most senior technical, administrative, and management levels; the cost would have been prohibitive. Moreover, the supply of Europeans (which generally meant nationals of the colonial power, and in the British areas also included nationals of other Commonwealth countries, for example, Australia and New Zealand) was not unlimited. Inability to recruit first-class European staff was increasingly reported. As early as 1948 an official inquiry in Nigeria complained that "it had proved impossible in recent years to recruit from overseas the minimum staff required to man the [Public] Service."

A second economic aspect of the Africanization problem derives from the expanded educational push to be found throughout Africa, which is considered in detail in the next chapter. Africans who have completed various levels of education, particularly secondary and university education, are increasingly candidates for middle- and upper-level positions in the public service, the public corporations, the university teaching field, and private enterprise. More and more suitable jobs will be required to satisfy the increasing number of educated Africans. Unfortunately the type of educated personnel becoming available does not always coincide with the professional, technical, and specialized needs of the public and private sectors. In time this type of problem is lessened, as supply attunes itself more and more to the demand of the society. There generally is a time lag, however, in reaching the adjustment, and tensions and dissatisfaction of a potentially dangerous type may build up and there may be economic waste resulting from trained but unused manpower resources. In the restrained language of Professor Frederick Harbison's study on "High Level Manpower for Nigeria's Future," underlying the report of the Ashby Commission on Post-School Certificate and Higher Education in Nigeria, we find the observation:

In Nigeria there may be a tendency, as in India and to a lesser extent in Egypt, to over-invest in education in the law and arts and to under-invest in engineering, agriculture, and science. As stressed earlier in this report, Nigeria is fast approaching a stage where it may have a surplus of university graduates seeking to enter the administrative ranks of the civil service. The same situation may soon be evident in commerce and private industry. This factor needs to be given serious attention in planning higher education in Nigeria as well as in the counselling of young people regarding future career opportunities within their country.[7]

Other economic aspects of the push for Africanization, particularly in the private sector, are inextricably involved with the state of Africanization in public and private life and are discussed in the following paragraphs.

Africanization—1960's

The Public Sector

Africanization of the public sector in Nigeria exemplifies in many ways the top level of programming and achievement of Africanization on the continent. The only close parallel is the program in Sudan. Hence it would seem appropriate to examine at the outset the state of the Nigerian program at the advent of independence so as to get a sense of the task confronting independent Nigeria, and in order to put in perspective the situation confronting other newly independent African states which, though they be smaller countries with smaller requirements, will find the task generally greater because of less pre-independence preparation.

In 1956 the government of Nigeria declared in a white paper: "The first need of the Federation is for the training of a sufficient number of Nigerians to man the whole Public Service"; the problem is "to give post-secondary training to at least 1900 Nigerians in order to fill posts which are now vacant or which are held by expatriates. . . ." [8] But in its final report, rendered in 1959, the Parliamentary Committee on Nigerianisation of the Federal Public Service records little or no achievement with respect to these and other conclusions and recommendations of the 1956 white paper.[9] In fact, the Parliamentary Committee went even further back, referring to an official report made in 1948 and complaining: "That was 11 years ago, and yet today we are confronted with the same problems of finding sufficient number of Nigerians trained and skilled enough to man the public service." [10]

In terms of numbers the Parliamentary Committee concluded, with respect to the federal civil service:

Of these 73 superscale posts [the principal posts in the federal administrative service], 10 are held by Nigerians and other West African Officers, and 63 by expatriate officers. . . .

There are 14 posts in the grades of Permanent Secretary and all but one are held by overseas officers. . . . There are 20 posts in the various grades of the status of Deputy Permanent Secretary and all but two are held by overseas officers; 34 officers are in the grade of Senior Assistant Secretary and of these only six are Nigerians or West African Officers. . . . It is in this situation that Nigeria will find itself in the year of Independence.[11]

These numbers take on increased significance when it is realized that the administrative service is to be distinguished from the technical professional services, for which the training period for specialists is necessarily rather long.

In 1959 in the Western Region of the Federation there were 117 overseas officers, 70 Nigerians, and 43 vacancies in the superscale category; in the Eastern Region there were 90 overseas officers, 43 Nigerian, 41 vacancies in the superscale category; and in the Northern Region there were 161 expatriate officers, 59 Northern Nigerians, and 1 non-Northern Nigerian [12] in the Senior Staff category.[13] If one is to accept the response of the federal government one year later to the 1959 report of the Parliamentary Committee, there was some amelioration of the situation in the federal service at the zero hour before independence.

There is another problem of which the federal government is fully aware—the risk of losing expatriate officials before trained Nigerians are available to replace them. Although it applies primarily to the professional and specialist areas rather than to the lay administrative areas, this risk should not be minimized. It exemplifies the magnitude and nature of the Africanization problem facing all new African states. On the one hand, there is a political urgency to Africanize the public service with all speed; on the other, there is a need to retain the confidence and services of the expatriate civil servants until the African cadres are sufficient in number and specialties to take over. Within these alternative requirements, it is essential to differentiate between administrative and technical cadres and to recognize the different political importance attaching to the two categories. The senior administrative service, going up through the post of permanent secretary, disposes of considerable decision-making power and is in a position to influence policy. Because of this the expatriate officers in senior administrative posts are vulnerable to political criticism. In Nigeria the case of the Personal Secretary to the Federal Prime Minister is most revealing. Although the Prime

Minister sought to retain the services of this key British officer on his staff, he had to bow to a sustained, vituperative campaign by many segments of Nigerian society, including some who were otherwise agreeably disposed to the Prime Minister. Nigerianization required that the incumbent of so vital a post be a Nigerian, and since late 1961 a young Nigerian has occupied the post.

In commenting on the Nigerian government's 1960 white paper on Nigerianization the well-informed journal *West Africa* declared: "The Parliamentary Committee has done its job; but Nigerianisation should never again become a political issue." [14] True as this may be, the fact remains that the Africanization task confronting the federal government (and also the regional governments), although improved over what it was at the time of the 1959 Parliamentary Report (and as indicated in the Younger Study), still remains a serious and politically sensitive one. The 1960 white paper emphasizes, quite rightly, an aspect the Parliamentary Committee tended to play down: the danger of an expatriate exodus before it could be coped with, especially in the technical and professional fields. It would seem that the task of Africanization is by nature a political issue. It may be that it will be limited to an issue among Nigerian political parties, but even here there is room for doubt. The judgment of a British colonial correspondent writing from Lagos on independence day seems an apt one:

Meanwhile frustration through lack of enough skilled posts faces a mass of ambitious school-leavers. Britain in a single year could squander the complicated love she has earned here if "Nigerianisation" of the civil services at least in the South, is not rushed ahead, leaving only the most efficient Britons.[15]

The issue of Africanization has also arisen across the continent, where the former British-administered U.N. trust territory of Tanganyika also moved to independence in scheduled steps, although somewhat more accelerated than Nigeria. But even here, where the all-inclusive, multi-racial Tanganyikan African National Union (TANU) peacefully negotiated its timetable for independence with the United Kingdom, willingly included two Europeans in its last pre-independence government as well as its first totally representative government headed by an African Chief Minister, and deliberately retained a European in the key ministerial post of Minister of Finance in its first independent government, the issue of the pace and scope of Africanization has created an open conflict between the government and labor unions. The issue came to the fore in late 1960, a year before independence, when the then Minister of Labor Derek Bryceson declared that the policy of the government was "localization" and not Africanization.[16] The Tanganyika Union of Public Employees, it was reported in the London *Times:*

. . . demanded that the Government embark on a full-blooded policy to fill the senior posts of the Civil Service with Africans. The letter said that the new Government had been in power one month, but so far no changes had been made in the Civil Service. "We therefore demand that the opportunities we have been refused should now be given us" said the union. "Certainly a great number of posts held by expatriate officers can be taken over by us." [17]

The Tanganyika incident illustrates how easily the pace and scope of Africanization can become an internal political issue even where the formal metropolitan-territorial relationship is very good. It also suggests that there is little room for complacency in Nigeria. If Africanization can agitate the relations between the government and labor unions in Tanganyika, which is at present a one-party state for all practical purposes, how easily can a storm blow up in Nigeria, with its three large parties, essentially regionally based but diversifying, and its divided labor movement. The program of Northernization in Nigeria even has some of the elements of the Tanganyika issue of localization. In the multi-tribal federation of Nigeria it would not be any more surprising for Eastern and Western regional tribes to take exception and protest against "Northernization" as a retrogressive and anti-federal practice than it is for Europeans and Indians in multi-racial Tanganyika to demand localization rather than Africanization, i.e., substitution of local people irrespective of race for overseas expatriate officials.[18]

An examination of the Ghanaian experience illustrates the time-consuming nature of Africanization as well as the size of the problem which confronted the new state upon achievement of independence in 1957. In the five years preceding independence the number of expatriate officials in responsible public service positions remained almost constant. The total was 1360 in 1952 and 1123 in 1956, whereas the total of Ghanaians in such positions grew from 620 in 1952 to 1553 in 1956. The Africanization program from 1952 to 1956, was thus largely a program of holding the line insofar as replacement of expatriates by Ghanaians was concerned. The European expatriate cadre was not to be expanded to fill the new and growing needs of a government embarked on an economic development plan and evolving through the stages of representative and responsible government to independence. Africans, by and large, took up the expansion. The key positions in the public service remained largely in the hands of expatriate officers. Of the 355 key administrative positions (implementing, decision-making, and managerial) in the Ghanaian civil service 74 per cent were in expatriate hands at the time of independence. At the end of 1959, after about three years of independence, this percentage had fallen to 42 per cent.[19] Educating and training senior civil servants takes time, especially if standards of performance are not to suffer too much. In the technical and professional services, where more special education and training may be required, the time lag between independence and substantial Africanization is likely to be even greater than in the administrative areas.

Compared to former British West Africa territories, former French West and Equatorial African territories have lagged far behind in Africanization of both the public and private sectors. There can be little doubt that the difference is attributable to differences in colonial policy between the two leading colonial powers in Africa. Self-government and independence for the people of its non-multi-racial African territories became settled policy for the United Kingdom much earlier than it did for France. More difficult to assess is the possible—and more likely the probable— counter-productive effect of the initiative of the African Socialist Leader Lamine Guèye, who as early as 1948 succeeded in having incorporated in Franco-African law the principle: "A travail égal, salaire égal." In the *Loi Lamine Guèye de 1948 sur l'harmonisation des conditions de traitement de salaire et de travail* the basis was laid for equal pay for equal work in the public service, which over time was to be extended to the private sector.

It is hard to believe that this principle, used so effectively by the European Mineworkers Union in Northern Rhodesia to frustrate African advancement in the copper mines, did not have something of a comparable effect in French Africa. In the absence of an existing cadre of trained Africans, insistence on equal pay for equal work means that there is little incentive to employ and train inexperienced Africans because they will have to be paid the same wage as their experienced European colleagues. It also means no fragmentation of existing categories of jobs into several separate jobs, each with more limited functions, and scaling of salaries accordingly, so that Africans can proceed up an employment ladder to increasingly responsible positions. Finally, since it means no lowering of standards and qualification, it militates against possible African replacement of Europeans as a realistic matter for some time to come. Nevertheless, juridically the *loi Guèye* was an important turning point in French Africa for the African's campaign to achieve the liberty, equality, and fraternity so intimately associated with the mystique, if not always with the actuality, of the French Presence.

Only with the *loi cadre* of June 23, 1956, which introduced important advances in African self-government, did Africanization of the public service for the first time achieve a recognized and serious position in French Africa. Under the *loi cadre* the practice of reserving a percentage of positions in the civil service for Africans was introduced with the objective of facilitating the promotion of Africans to all levels of the civil service. A further step in Africanization was taken when the *École Nationale de la France d'Outre Mer*, which trained Frenchmen to become overseas officers in the French African colonial service, was transformed in early 1959, as part of the Gaullist decolonization thrust, into the *Institut des Hautes Études d'Outre Mer*. The Institute is devoted to training African from Franco-African Community states and other states of *l'expression française* on friendly terms with France for the senior levels of the public services in these states.

The French effort came late in the day—too late to benefit Tunisia, Morocco, and Guinea. The situation at the time of Guinea's "secession" is a measure of just how late the French initiative was. When Guinea opted for independence in the September 1958 referendum on the constitution of the Fifth Republic and the creation of the Franco-African Community, a scorned France retaliated by denuding the Guinean public service of its French officers, and revealed how little the public service in French Africa had been Africanized at the end of 1958. The view of the government of Guinea is that it was most adversely affected by lack of technical cadres to man the public and private sectors. The *Parti Démocratique de Guinée* had basic political cadres ready to take over from the French. Since then some part of the deficiency of technical cadres has been filled by personnel from friendly countries, but the shortage has continued to be serious, particularly in the private sector.[20]

Even later and even less than the French did the Belgians turn to the problems of Africanization of the public service of the Congo. By expanding the Congolese economy, Belgium was creating a growing need for the very Africanization that it did so little to bring about; and its small effort came so late that it cannot be considered to have really got under way any program for Africanization of the public service of the Congo. The results of that failure have been all too evident to need restatement here. It was only in mid-April 1960 that Belgium, having agreed to Congolese independence on June 30, 1960, began a brief training course for 109 trainees who were to take their place in the senior public service two and one-half months later. The unpreparedness of the Congolese was dramatized by this hastily and almost hysterically mounted effort to provide African cadres for every important ministry, including foreign affairs. A typical result was the important and extravagant roles assigned to a handful of young and inexperienced college graduates in running the country. One of them, Justin Bomboko, served as Minister of Foreign Affairs successively in the Lumumba government, in the rival Kasavubu-Iléo government and (for a time simultaneously) in the Mobutu "commission of administration of students and technicians," in the second Iléo government, and at the time of this writing is in the Adoula government.

The Private Sector

There was, if anything, even less initiative in Africanizing the private sector than the public service. The nature of the relationship was such that colonial administrations were not prepared to insist on Africanization;[21] private interests felt little pressure to Africanize the administrative, management, and higher technical echelons of business and industry until the last few years, and then generally only after self-government or independence came within reach of African territories. To make this observation is not to ignore the difficulties and expense involved in recruiting and training local personnel. It is merely to record the fact and indicate the scope of the present problem; for, even more than in public service perhaps, actual on-the-job experience in business and industry, where the very concepts of a modern economy have to be learned, is vital. Professor W. Arthur Lewis put it simply:

If no one will employ the local people above the level of clerks, they cannot learn how to manage industrial businesses for themselves; their economic affairs will then always be dominated by foreigners, and economic growth will be held up by the costs and shortages involved in dependence upon foreign enterprise.[22]

African attention is sharply focused on this issue. Of the former French-West African territories none are more contrasting in their economic structure and political outlook than the Ivory Coast and Guinea, the former remaining closely related to France through the EEC and the franc zone, whereas the latter has completely disrupted all such connections. Yet in their estimates of the extent of Africanization of the private sectors of their economies on achieving independence they are one; and their shared criticism of that situation can be taken as representative for all fifteen of the independent African states of *l'expression française* south of the Sahara.

Of the Ivory Coast, the director of the cabinet of the Ministry of Technical Instruction has written:

> Existing industrial activities have contributed very unevenly to the increase in per capita income of the various population groups in the Ivory Coast. Almost all industrial enterprises are controlled by Europeans, and the principal staffs are also largely European.[23]

Of the Republic of Guinea, the Minister of Information has written:

> The training of Africans for technical and economic staff positions was practically non-existent, and employment opportunities for the very few who did receive training were limited not only by the country's low level of economic development but also by the preference given to Europeans in employment.[24]

Not only is there a background of failure to encourage African participation in business and industry at the intermediate and higher administrative, management, and technical levels. Also, the policies of private investors and colonial administrations frequently created wage structures which, when Africanization became inevitable, could only aggravate the difficulties and expense. The gap between the wage floor for unskilled workers and the wage ceiling for skilled labor is tremendous. The base wages for unskilled workers reflected a complete indifference to the quality of work performance. The ceiling for skilled workers reflected the high inducement wage necessary to attract Europeans from abroad. Closing the gap has become a formidable task. The temptation for African trade unions to urge building up the floor rather than lowering the ceiling has been a strong one.

One result has been that as semiskilled and skilled African cadres emerged they sought the elevated European wage standards as a matter of right, irrespective of the ability of African economies to establish across-the-board a "European expatriate wage level" for everybody and irrespective of the ability and experience of the newly trained African worker to perform at the same level as his European counterpart. Another result has been a growing inflationary pressure by the unskilled workers to close the gap now that some of their African compatriots have scaled the heights and have achieved or are close to achieving the higher levels of the wage and benefit structure.

These two drives have greatly complicated the Africanization process, particularly in the private sector, and have augmented costs markedly, and perhaps prohibitively, if African industry is to be competitive within Africa and in the world market generally.

As early as 1941 Félix Eboué, Governor of French Equatorial Africa, expressed serious misgivings about the foundation stone being laid for the African wage structure in the private sectors of equatorial and central Africa:

Too many laborers are employed and are employed inefficiently. Low salaries have created and continue to create an illusion; manpower appears to cost less than machine power, a concept which, in particular cases, may be open to discussion, but which remains as a general proposition fallacious.[25]

Moreover, although the overwhelming bulk of African laborers in industry and mining have been unskilled, with little or no training, the productivity of such African labor has been a subject of little or no concern until fairly recently.

In the Federation of Rhodesia and Nyasaland, which along with the Belgian Congo has been the leading industrial and mining area in tropical Africa, a recent experience in constructing the Kariba Dam is both illustrative and instructive. At one point in the construction the total African labor force, 5700 strong, went out on strike for an increase in the hourly wage from 4 pence (4¾ cents) to 1 shilling (14 cents). The Italian contractors issued an ultimatum—an increase to 6 pence (7 cents) per hour for underground workers or "release from contract," i.e., dismissal. Two thousand Africans did not return to work. "This episode," writes the author of a recent study of the dam construction, "taught the employers a lesson. African labor had been so cheap that they had been using far more men than they really needed. Although 2000 left, only 800 more were ever recruited. So the rather pathetic 50 per cent increase in basic pay hardly cost the employers anything; and a month later, without being asked, perhaps in remorse, the Italians increased the underground pay to 7d. and the surface pay to 5d." [26]

Another illustration is the Belgian Congo, where also large numbers of unskilled laborers were employed with little regard to their productivity. Congolese low wages and low productivity became part of an emerging pattern. As groups of semiskilled and skilled workers developed, the industrial évolué had for their goal the wage rates and benefits of the Belgian workers imported into the Congo, rates which, in order to attract Belgians away from the metropole, were necessarily high and were supplemented by a variety of allowances and perquisites. But despite pressure and the passage of time, only a small group of skilled African employees attained levels approximating the wages of Belgians. In 1954 in the important metallurgical industry in the Congo only 0.6 per cent of the Congolese were earning 70 to 80 per cent of the wages of Belgian workers in comparable positions in Belgium; the remaining 99.4 per cent were earning 45 to 55 per cent, with the largest number of Congolese at the lower level of the range. The ratio of wages of unskilled to skilled workers in the metallurgical industry in Belgium in 1954 was 1 to 1.38, whereas the same ratio in the Congo was 1 to 3.54 at Union Minière du Haut Katanga, the huge mining complex in Katanga Province, and 1 to 4.75 in Leopoldville.[27]

Today, as a heritage of colonialism, the spread in the wage structure between skilled and unskilled labor presents a formidable social and economic problem for the newly independent states. The need to augment the wages of the large mass of unskilled workers and at the same time restrain or even reduce the wages or prune the fringe benefits of the skilled industrial elite so that a relative improvement in the status of the unskilled workers can be achieved raises difficult and delicate economic, social, and political issues. A policy of general undifferentiated wage increases for all skilled, semiskilled, and unskilled labor would fail to alter the proportions of the wage gap and the social tensions implicit in such a gap. Such a policy would also fail to solve the problem of the African industrial elite's attempts to achieve the artificially high wage and benefit rates built into the wage structure by the European wage-earner—that temporary bird of passage (and in some contexts a special category of settler). The impact of an upward spiral of wages and benefits for the African industrial elite on the competitive position of African industrial output, and on the prospects for new investment, could only be disastrous for African economic development aspirations.

The wage-gap problem, although most clearly seen in the Belgian Congo and the Federation of Rhodesia and Nyasaland, has in no sense been a phenomenon confined to those areas.[28] It is a fundamental one for economic and social growth in divergent areas of Africa. The concern expressed by the East Africa Royal Commission in its report in 1955, reflecting the less industrialized status generally of East Africa, emphasized the dis-incentive effect of narrowing the wage gap too much. The Commission cautioned:

We do not minimize the importance of having regard to the wages of unskilled labour, but we are also concerned with industrial development and the prospects for African skilled labour. A relatively high natural minimum wage for unskilled labour is liable to lead to a narrowing of the differentials for skilled labour and thus to a weakening of the advantages which accrue to the African from whatever training in industrial skills may be available to him.[29]

In view of the difficulties involved in structural reforms, colonial powers by and large tended to limit their reforms of the wage structure generally to wage or cost-of-living awards. The fundamental issue of structural reform still remains in most parts of Africa and confronts the new states with a serious problem not only in the context of Africanization but also in the larger context of economic and social development. This is one area in which the solution of a growth problem has as many, if not more, implications for political stability in the new states as for economic development. Achievement of restricted wage scales is fraught with political dangers. As we have already noted in Chapter 3, Guinea, as a matter of ideological doctrine, has dealt with the problem of the inflated expatriate-type wage levels setting the pace for Africans, and President Senghor of Senegal has flagged it as a major one for African development.

In this connection we would again note the Congo experience. In 1952 Governor Pétillion of the Belgian Congo announced that thenceforth statutory provisions requiring increased wages and supplementary benefits would be tied to increased productivity,[30] and there are indications that this policy had been accepted by an increasing number of para-public and private corporations in the Congo prior to independence as part of their wage policies. Increased productivity, however, often carries with it the need for a whole range of readjustments, particularly in the transitional period between indifference to productivity and conscious attempts to achieve it, which are likely to result in a series of problems of considerable difficulty and of great risk for a colonial administration or for the successor independent state that falls heir to the structural problems. So long as the Congolese economy was expanding, unemployment did not loom too ominously on the political and economic horizon. However, with the break in world commodity prices in 1957, industrial unemployment, augmented by technological unemployment of Congolese industry in transition, and by the growing movement of rural population to urban centers without reference to employment opportunities,[31] created serious problems. In fact, according to the Belgian Parliamentary Commission of Inquiry, one of the principal causes of the Leopoldville riots of January 1959, which played a dramatic part in instigating the series of events which led to the Belgian withdrawal from the Congo, was the large number of unemployed Africans concentrated in the city and ripe for the political picking. In a frenzied attempt to do away with the visible evidence of the unemployment problem the Belgian colonial authorities spread the virus by deporting many of the unemployed to their tribal areas. The unemployment remained; it was merely dispersed, with the net effect that unemployment became an unsettling force in areas of the Congo where it had previously been successfully disguised. Also, in time, the unemployment problem coalesced again in the larger urban centers. Unemployment, which has been an isssue ever since the achievement of independence, remains a difficult problem for the Congolese.

Finally, note must be taken of the fact that the states of Africanization of the public and private sectors tend to interact upon one another. The structural imbalance to be found in the

Congo and elsewhere could have the effect of drawing off the best qualified African personnel for the private sector, or forcing up wages *pari passu* in the public sector. In Nigeria the opposite effect has been in evidence and has been the source of complaint from private employers.

The report, late in 1959, of the Mbanefo Commission to Review Salaries and Wages in Nigeria raised this point:

> We have received strong representations from the Nigeria Employers' Consultative Association against the principle of fixing wages and salaries of Government servants by Public Commissions. . . . The Association also points out that as the Governments [Federal and Regional] are the largest employers of labour any action by them is bound to have serious repercussions on private employers. We are doubtful if an increase in Government wages and salaries as a result of a Commission is necessarily more embarrassing to commercial employers than an increase in Government wages and salaries arrived at by some other means. . . . We feel that the Nigeria Employers' Consultative Association is more justifiably concerned with the effect of Government granting large increases at somewhat infrequent intervals.[32]

President Senghor of Senegal, writing about his own country, could have been referring to all tropical Africa, and certainly all French-speaking tropical Africa, when he linked modernization of agriculture with reforming the wage structure of the country as part of its Africanization program, and both with building the nation. M. Senghor wrote:

> The living standard of our government employees should be higher than that of the peasants; but we cannot do less than to fix a relationship between the living levels of our quasi-classes. As the standard of living of the peasants rises, in the same proportion we would raise that of the government employees and of salaried workers in private employment. However, to raise peasants' standards of living, it is indispensable that we invest productively in agriculture. This implies an increase in our budgets and, accordingly, a temporary freezing of salaries.
> . . . To renounce productive investments would place us in a vicious circle and make us beg France to balance our budgets; this would in fact mean renunciation of all political autonomy. The gov-

ernment workers will understand their role in the building of the
nation and will accept the sacrifices asked of them. The peasants are
already enthusiastic. . . .

This general enthusiasm must help the . . . State to build
the nation but it must first help us to realize our *Development Plan*.[33]

Thus the problem of Africanization in the private sector is
not only one of developing trained cadres of Africans to replace
Europeans. It is also intimately related to the problem of reforming the wage-benefit scale originally set up for an industry
and commerce dependent on significant cadres of Europeans to
conform to the realities of African economic life,[34] and, to the
extent that the doctrine of egalitarianism is a reality of African
political life, to conform to it. Also, in the words of President
Senghor, "It could not serve the public interest to increase the
disproportion between the living standards of the classes now in
process of formation." [35] And, as we have already seen, the competition for personnel and the conflicting pull of wages and benefits between the public and private sectors have already become
issues in several African contexts, and they may well become so
in many more as the private sectors expand. Finally, as President
Senghor has so clearly demonstrated, this multi-dimensional problem of Africanization, in its political as well as economic aspects,
is intimately related to the total tasks of nation-building and
economic development.

Prospects

The magnitude of the Africanization problem as set by the
colonial experience—state and size of the administrative, technical,
political, and military cadres, the skewed wage structure, etc.,
at independence—is perhaps the clearest indication of the task
ahead for the newly independent states, a task created, then, in
the main by events beyond African control. There are also, however, aspects of the ongoing process of Africanization which are
reflected by the policies and ability of the new states themselves.

For one thing, the whole problem, as we have seen in connection with our discussion of economic decolonization by the new states earlier in the chapter, has become inextricably intertwined with the general tendency in the new African states to enlarge in some degree the public sector at the expense of the private. In Guinea there is an ideological motivation, expressed in the totality of government policy aimed at "reconverting" the social and economic structure of the new state. Elsewhere in Africa both doctrine and a shortage of private capital are responsible for the public sector being significantly enlarged by taking over functions ordinarily thought of in the metropolitan countries as belonging to the private sector. This enlargement of the public sectors means finding and training more African staff for a greater variety of functions by the government at public expense; it means enlarging the size of the public service; it means even more intimate connection between wages in administrative and overhead sectors and in productive sectors; it means complications for restructuring the wage scale to link wages to productivity, given the nature of the ordinary public service salary scale; and it makes Africanization of staff, but one element, which can be lost sight of, in a much larger program to induce major social transformations.

The lesson of history is that any social transformation such as Africanization by itself or as part of a larger objective must be orchestrated with the over-all political and economic objectives of a country, and more specifically with the educational and training programs and facilities, experimental pilot projects and demonstration schemes, and information or propaganda programs. Failure to recognize this point, or having recognized it, to take account of it, presents the gravest threat to the ability of the independent African states to achieve Africanization. Such failure may be induced by pressures from below, from Africans anxious to fill the desirable public service and private company jobs of the expatriates. Or it may be induced by doctrinaire considerations or party politics communicated from above to the African population generally.

In the first case—pressure from below—the question becomes for the most part one of the strength and determination of the independent government. Where these are sufficient, Africanization is likely to proceed more or less systematically with intensified and accelerated educational and training programs and a rapid expansion of facilities. There is also likely to be the adoption of government policies requiring private investors to conform to certain standards, which might range from conducting programs of on-the-job training to limiting the number of foreigners who may be employed. The latter type of policy may be implemented by law or by administrative techniques relating to visas and residence permits. The new states should be able to find any number of precedents to emulate in this regard among the practices, past or present, of the former colonial powers.

Where the independent government is not strong or determined enough there is the risk of submitting to popular pressures for jobs, or to xenophobia, or anti-colonial influences. Here the ability to Africanize in the sense of developing qualified cadres of Africans not only to replace expatriates but also to take up new jobs engendered by independence and growth will be seriously compromised. The experience in the Sudan has some relevancy here.

In the two years immediately before independence the Sudanisation Committee, established and operating under the Anglo-Egyptian agreement of February 12, 1953, granting full internal self-government to the Sudan, reduced the British cadre in its public service from about 1200 to just over 150. The technical services suffered most. The administrative, policy-influencing, and defense services apparently fared better. However, some observers believe that the serious revolt in the Southern Sudan shortly before independence in August 1955 "had as one of its contributory causes the hasty replacement of British officials in the South by northerners who knew neither the area nor its language." [36] By 1958 the Sudan was again employing large numbers of British personnel, primarily in the technical services and for teaching posts. The Sudan had also in 1958 started to employ British advisors in "important senior posts." The conclusion of Kenneth Younger on the Sudanese experience is that the "Sudanese themselves would probably not now recommend to others a policy as drastic as the one which their exceptionally tense political situation led them to pursue." [37]

In the second case—of pressure from above—the question of the ability of the newly independent governments to transform the cadres of the public and private sectors by developing qualified Africans to replace Europeans revolves around political patronage, political tactics, and ideological drives. As in older states, political parties in new states are subject to pressure for jobs by the faithful. In primarily pragmatic one-party states such as Ghana, the Ivory Coast, and Liberia there are signs that the Convention People's Party, the *Parti Démocratique de Côte d'Ivoire*, and the True Whig Party, respectively, have used their monopoly over access to public office to reward the faithful and to entice the opposition. In primarily ideological one-party states such as Guinea the drive for doctrinal purity may override other considerations, such as technical qualifications, training, and experience, in staffing the public service. The probability is that:

Enthusiasm and devotion to public affairs are more important factors than technical and professional qualifications.[38]

In all one-party states in Africa with any significant ideological strand in their make-up there is likely to be a tendency for the party to dominate the government and its public service, with a resultant emphasis on party dogma rather than professional and technical qualifications. The view that "Le parti . . . est l'autorité morale suprême de la Nation" [39] is likely to be the controlling precept in this context rather than the production of cadres of impartial, objective, and professionally trained Africans.

If the ideological test is additive to the others relating to qualifications, the public services of new states with one-party structures need not suffer too much. If, as may tend to be the case in the primarily ideological one-party states, the ideological test is the chosen alternative to qualification tests, then the public services are likely to suffer. The risk is that the party mechanism, in insisting on doctrinal purity, may at once so rigidly proceed with Africanization that standards and performance of the public service will be sacrificed.

And finally, even where a strong government is in a position to resist pressures from below, it may for tactical political reasons decide to submit as a way to enhance its mass following or intensify its mass support. In the private sector of the new states Africanization may be subject to one restraining influence which could operate to avoid the excesses which could develop in Africanization of the public service. The fear of going too far and driving out all foreign investors, where this is not the purpose of the new government, could lead, as it has in Guinea, to negotiated arrangements on Africanization with selected foreign enterprises, e.g., the large foreign aluminum combine, FRIA (*Compagnie Internationale pour la Production d'Alumine*).

Thus the problem of Africanization remains a critical one for the new states. They generally have the will to Africanize. Their ability to do so is subject to the political pressures to which the new governments are exposed. As for the financial resources and the knowledge necessary to bring about Africanization, the resources are in one way or another likely to be forthcoming, and the knowledge is likely to be imported. In no event, however, will the training of new cadres be easy or quick. It will take time to establish training institutions and develop cadres. It will take time to acquire skills and experience. It will take time and hard work to develop a professional spirit and code of ethics for the public service. Standards and performance are likely to suffer; the challenge is to prevent them from falling too much, and to prevent deterioration and collapse.

In the words of a special conference report devoted to problems of cadres in underdeveloped countries, particularly to those of new states:

The problem of cadres [of the new states] . . . is governed by three principal factors:
  I. Decolonisation and the establishment of new relationships;
  II. Social conditioning connected both with a particular sociological inheritance and with the sudden changes of to-day;
  III. The demands of development and of political evolution.[40]

Chapter 6

THE PUSH FOR EDUCATION

What has aptly been called a "thirst for education [which] grows stronger year by year among Africans" [1] is largely the result of three related phenomena of the postwar period: the attempts by the leading colonial powers to induce economic development in their African areas; the political change resulting from the interplay of African nationalism and European political decolonization; the social ferment involving growing social mobility for increasing numbers of Africans as economic development and political change have made their mark on the already significantly impaired subsistence structure of traditional African society.

It goes without saying that in any setting the absence of educated and trained manpower is one of the principal limitations on economic growth; and it follows that the common objective of economic growth has provided one of the strongest impetuses to Africans to obtain more and better education. At first there were the ambitious few who saw in primary education an open sesame to white-collar employment in junior clerical positions and minor civil service posts. Now increasing numbers seek secondary and higher education and, most recently, technical education at all levels. In fact African professional men, teachers, and techni-

cians have already started to make their appearance in many of
the developing African areas; and there is every evidence that the
realization of the need for education and training of African
cadres for both the private and public sectors of the African
economies has been intensified wherever Africans have attained
independence.

It is also axiomatic that the rapid political advance of
Africans on the wave of nationalism and political decolonization
has brought with it a desperate need for educated political leadership. The education and training of political elites has already
advanced at varying paces, but the problem of education for the
political area does not end with the elites if there is to be any
general participation in political processes and decision-making in
the new states. This aspect of the educational function was for
the bulk of the colonial period given scant attention. Thus, in the
words of a leading Indian diplomat writing about the problems
of the new Afro-Asian states, the attempted transfer of democratic
European political institutions and systems with independence
"has made the problem of universal education an urgent one. A
democratic system based on adult franchise inevitably postulates
universal education. It creates an irresistible demand for education which the government is compelled by circumstances to
accept as a first priority; and yet no state is able to realize it." [2]

The social problem implicit in the widespread movements
of economic growth and political change in developing Africa is
fundamental. New social structures and new types of social relationships based on achievement rather than status, and responsive
to the impersonal forces of change, growth, and development, are
being thrown up by events or imposed by political elites. Education is seen by many of the leaders of new African states as the
means for welding together into a national unity disparate populations with tribal, regional, and religious differences, for creating
a national consciousness, and for disseminating the knowledge and
the doctrine necessary to modernize their countries. Education has
also become for more and more Africans caught up in the transition from tribal existence to nationhood the touchstone of their
new status as citizens of a nation-state and participants in a market
economy. Education, once widely thought of as white man's

magic beyond the reach of all but a few Africans, has suddenly—with the approach of self-government and the advent of independence—become available for ever increasing numbers. It not only means better jobs and improved standards of living; it also means a new social status and acceptance. Education in this sense becomes not only a long-term economic investment but also a most desirable consumer good. This almost visionary African view of the value of education reveals not only the importance attached to education by growing numbers of Africans; it also emphasizes the importance of avoiding the disillusioning let-down that comes when there are no jobs available commensurate with the dignity acquired with the education.

Thus we come full circle. If there is to be economic growth, political development, including the development of an efficient and Africanized public service, and social cohesion, "a reasonably large class of highly educated and trained people . . . is . . . the primary necessity for every new state." [3] Yet even the training of the indispensable lay cadres is dependent on an adequate level of economic growth. Hence, in the words of a British report on its overseas dependencies: "Education has to take its place not only within the structure of social services as a whole but within the general framework of economic development." [4]

The Current Scene

The présent state of African education, like that of African agriculture and African participation in the structure of the public and private sectors, implies both an index of colonial performance and a task list for the new states. The strengths of the former period are the growing points for the new; the inadequacies are the problems. Of necessity, then, the ensuing discussion, which is primarily concerned with the challenge of the push for education confronting the new states, will stress the problems involved rather than the assets bequeathed from the colonial period. The latter are implicit in the very existence of the formal educational frameworks and educated elites to be found anywhere in Africa, which in any event must be the points of departure for the present discussion.

A recent study on the role of science and technology in the development of Africa south of the Sahara, conducted under the auspices of the United States National Academy of Sciences, reached this sweeping conclusion:

> Even though the existing educational systems and institutions vary widely in kind and quality, *in toto* they are entirely inadequate to serve the present, still more the future, educational needs of the region. This situation cannot be changed radically within a short period of time, since educational advances can only be deliberate, at best.[5]

The systematic examination of the educational situation in large areas of Africa provides ample support for this conclusion. At all levels of education there are striking deficiencies, and in the total structure there are critical gaps, both magnified as one goes from the primary school base up the African educational ladder.

If universal compulsory free education is taken as the goal (and it is not exceptional to find it the aim among the leaders of the new African states—and even foreseeable in some areas, such as the Western and Eastern Regions of Nigeria, where primary education is close to universal now, though not compulsory and not entirely free) the magnitude of the primary school problem can be grasped by comparing the percentage of African population enrolled in primary schools with the estimated percentage of African children of primary-school age.

The population under 15 years of age in Africa is frequently estimated to be about 40 per cent of the total population.[6] The percentage of the total population which normally would be primary-school age where 40 per cent of the population is below the age of 15 has been estimated to be 25 per cent.[7] Table I shows a primary school enrollment high of 17.9 per cent of the African population in Southern Rhodesia and a low of 0.4 per cent in the Northern British Cameroons. The average enrollment tends to be in the lower half of the scale, with 27 of the 36 areas represented in the table having less than 8.5 per cent of their total African population in primary schools. It is also significant to

Table I

Primary School Enrollment in 36 Countries Expressed in
Percentages of Total African [a] Population, Listed in
Sequence of Percentage Magnitude

Area [b]	Year	Maximum Length of Course in Years	Total Enrollment	Percentage of Estimated Total African Population
Southern Rhodesia	1958	8	354,854	17.9
Eastern Nigeria	1958	8 [c]	1,221,271	15.4
Western Nigeria (Lagos included)	1958	6 (Lagos 8)	1,037,388	14.6
Belgian Congo (Leopoldville)	1957	7	1,558,972	11.8
Northern Rhodesia	1957	8	230,963	10.5
Congo (Brazzaville)	1958	6	78,962	10.3
Nyasaland	1957	8	263,390	9.9
Gabon	1958	6	39,763	9.7
Cameroun (French)	1958	6	293,977	9.8
Kenya	1958	8	595,850	8.3
Uganda	1957	6	418,179	7.3
Ethiopia	1957	8	135,642	6.7
Togo (French)	1958	6	70,618	6.4
Malagasy (Madagascar)	1958	6	321,518	6.3
Zanzibar and Pemba	1957	8	16,188	5.6
Ruanda-Urundi	1957	7	240,032	5.1
Mozambique [d]	1956	3	293,723	c. 4.5
Dahomey	1958	6	75,406	4.2
Tanganyika	1957	8	346,532	4.0
Central African Republic	1958	6	45,774	4.0
Ivory Coast	1958	6	125,727	3.9
Senegal	1958	6	80,473	3.5
Somaliland (French)	1958	6	2,214	3.4
Southern Cameroons (British)	1958	8	54,844	3.4
Sudan	1958	8	c. 240,000	2.4
Guinea	1958	6	42,543	1.6
Chad	1958	6	32,610	1.3
Northern Nigeria	1958	7	244,838	1.2
Somaliland (Italian)	1957	7	15,047	1.1
Upper Volta	1958	6	38,143	1.1
Soudan (French)	1958	6	42,052	1.1
Angola [d]	1956	3	40,142	1.1

Table I (Continued)

Area [b]	Year	Maximum Length of Course in Years	Total Enrollment	Percentage of Estimated Total African Population
Mauritania	1958	6	6,493	1.04
Somaliland (British)	1957	7	c. 4,822	0.7
Niger	1958	6	13,459	0.5
Northern Cameroons (British)	1958	7	6,060	0.4

Tables I–IV; compiled from official country and territory reports, are taken from an unpublished study prepared by Dr. Hedwig Schleiffer for the Center for International Studies, M.I.T.

Table I was constructed from the latest published statistics available in 1960, generally for the years 1957 or 1958. Since the reliability of the statistics varies considerably by area, they are not fully comparable. The main difference, the length of the educational course, is, however, indicated in the table. No attempt has been made to weight the statistics to reflect the variations in content and quality of the primary curricula, teaching, facilities, etc. The estimated totals of the populations in primary school at any one time do not of course represent the number of children who will complete their courses.

[a] Figures for the French Territories and for Zanzibar and Pemba, refer to all ethnic groups; figures for other British territories refer only to Africans.

[b] Statistics not available for all African areas.

[c] Since reduced to 7 years.

[d] Refers to Portuguese category, "uncivilized" Africans in "rudimentary" primary courses.

note that the relatively high rating in southern Nigeria, 15 per cent for the Eastern and Western Regions, is comparatively recent, 1958. It coincides with self-government and the approach to independence and contrasts drastically with the 1.2 per cent for the Northern Region, which has half the population of Nigeria and attained self-government only in 1959. It is also interesting to note that the Republic of Guinea in the year of its independence, 1958, had only 1.3 per cent of its total population in primary school, one of the lowest percentages in all of French Africa. The heavy emphasis on primary education in independent Guinea is certainly a response to this extremely low rating. The Congo (Leopoldville) ranked relatively high, fourth in the listing in Table I, with 11.8 per cent of its African population in primary school in 1957. Across the Congo River, the Congo (Brazzaville) was close behind, ranking sixth in the listing in Table I with 10.3 per cent in primary school in 1958, whereas its near neighbor, Chad, ranked twenty-seventh on the list, with only 1.3 per cent in primary school in 1958.

Table II indicates the percentage of candidates taking the

Table II

Primary School Leaving Certificate Examination Results [a]

Area [b]	Passes	Percentage of Candidates	Percentage of Estimated Total Population
French Territories (1957) (6-year course)			
Ivory Coast	2,113	36.4	0.08
Dahomey	1,898	38	0.1
Upper Volta	927	51.1	0.02
Mauritania	435	72	0.07
Niger	218	43.6	0.009
Senegal	3,109	51.8	0.1
Soudan	1,445	45.1	0.03
Guinea	1,293	47.8	0.05
Central African Republic	874	54.6	0.07
Congo	980	36.4	0.1
Gabon	644	42.9	0.1
Chad	492	61.5	0.01
Somaliland	77	38	0.1
Malagasy (Madagascar)	4,187	38.4	0.08
Cameroun	4,979	38.5	0.1
Togo	1,572	28.1	0.1
British Territories			
Western Nigeria (1957) (6-year)	37,170	62.6	0.56
Eastern Nigeria (1957) (8-year)	23,462 [c]	49.5	0.3
Southern Rhodesia (1958) (8-year)	6,848	65.8	0.2
Northern Rhodesia (1957) (8-year)	2,452 [d]	57	0.1
Nyasaland (1957) (8-year)	1,892	58	0.07
Southern Cameroons (1958) (8-year)	773	36	0.05
Tanganyika (1957) (8-year)	4,607	82	0.05

[a] French figures include all ethnic groups; British figures refer only to Africans.
[b] Statistics not available for all areas.
[c] Including 1803 girls. Of the girls alone 66.7 per cent passed.
[d] Including 278 girls. Of the girls alone 39.7 per cent passed.

primary school final examination who passed and earned the certificate qualifying them for secondary school, the lower ranks of the civil service, and some positions in the private sector. It also shows the percentage of the total African population represented by the successful candidates. The table reflects the remarkable attrition or wastage in the primary school population. In 1958 in Southern Rhodesia only 0.2 per cent of the total African population earned school-leaving certificates. In Western Nigeria, which had the largest total, only 0.56 per cent of its African population in 1957 earned school-leaving certificates. Thus, although in Southern Rhodesia and Western Nigeria there are relatively large enrollments in primary school at any one time, the percentage of children actually completing primary school is pitifully small.

Table III

Secondary Schools' School Certificate Examination Results

Countries	Year	Passes	Percentage of Candidates	Percentage of Estimated Total African Population
Southern Rhodesia	1958	92	76	0.003
Northern Rhodesia	1957	87 [a]	78.3	0.003
Nyasaland	1957	41		0.001
Tanganyika	1957	149	99.3	0.001
Zanzibar and Pemba	1957	2 (Afr.)	22.2	0.0007
Sudan	1957	484	52	0.004
Kenya [b]	1957	363	90.7	0.005
Uganda [c]	1957	491	70.1	0.008
Southern Cameroons (British)	1957	63		0.003
Western Nigeria	1958	1,124	72.3	0.01
Eastern Nigeria [d]	1958	1,182	73.8	0.01
Northern Nigeria	1958	317	73	0.001

[a] Including 7 girls.
[b] Including 22 girls, who all passed.
[c] Including 35 girls.
[d] Including 141 girls.

However, the number completing primary school is on the increase. The value of the education received by children leaving primary school after two or three years, particularly when the tendency in the early years is to give instruction in vernacular languages, is highly questionable.

Tables III and IV demonstrate the major gap in African education, the very small number of secondary school students and the even smaller percentage of secondary school graduates. Secondary school certificates (Table III) are roughly equal to

Table IV

Higher School Certificate and Baccalaureate Part 2 Examination [a]
Results Listed in Sequence of Magnitude of Percentage of
Estimated Total Population [b]

Countries	Year	Passes	Percentage of Candidates	Percentage of Estimated Total Population
Lagos (Nigeria)	1957	16	89.1	0.049
Senegal	1957	362	59.8	0.01
Dahomey	1957	49	59	0.003
Malagasy (Madagascar)	1957	151	48.5	0.003
Congo (French)	1957	29	33.3	0.003
Ivory Coast	1957	66	61.1	0.002
Gabon	1957	10	32.2	0.002
Cameroun (French)	1957	79	53.3	0.002
Togo (French)	1957	32	62.7	0.002
Western Nigeria	1957	41	89.1	0.0006
Guinea	1957	15	71.4	0.0005
Southern Rhodesia	1958	10	62.5	0.0004
Northern Rhodesia	1957	8 (boys)	38	0.0003
Eastern Nigeria	1957	29	76.3	0.0003
Upper Volta	1957	11	68.7	0.0003
Soudan (French)	1957	38	67.8	0.0001
Niger	1957	3	50	0.0001
Tanganyika	1957	6	50	0.00006

[a] The examination is conducted after 13 to 14 years of schooling.
[b] French figures refer to all ethnic groups, British figures refer only to Africans.

junior high school diplomas in the United States and are earned at about sixteen years of age. They may provide entry into a preparatory or intermediate university course, to middle civil service ranks, and higher clerical jobs in private business. Higher school and baccalaureate certificates (Table IV) are roughly equal to junior college diplomas in the United States and are earned after thirteen or fourteen years of schooling. These certificates usually qualify the holder for university education and better paying jobs in the civil service and private business. The comparisons are rough approximations, intended only to place the various African certificates on an educational scale analogous to that used in the United States, not to suggest that they signify equivalent academic achievement.

The small number of secondary and higher school certificate holders shows the gap in the educational pyramid. Although there is a long way to go in most African areas to achieve universal primary education, there are increasing numbers getting some primary education. However, the number of those going on to and completing secondary school is extremely small. This means a lack of qualified students to feed into technical and vocational education, into college and university education, and into the intermediate positions in the economy which are so critical in supporting the university-trained professional categories of personnel. The nature of the gap in the educational pyramid is dramatized by the fact that, despite the weakness in the middle of the structure, an increasing number of the new African states are putting in place the top of the pyramid—colleges, universities, and even professional schools.

The report of a conference of African states on the development of education in Africa in mid-1961 stated:

> The scale of the problem can be seen from the following: today for the African States as a whole, only 16 per cent of the children of primary and secondary school age combined are enrolled in school. The situation varies, ranging from 2 per cent of the school age group in several States to nearly 60 per cent in others. In the majority of cases, the proportion of children out of school exceeds 80 per cent of the school age population.[8]

What emerges from the foregoing is that the inadequacy of secondary school education in all African countries is the major problem in their education structures. Professor Arthur Lewis estimates that, although countries at the level of development of West Africa "could probably absorb as much as 5 per cent of each age group in secondary school training," and those "of the more rapidly developing countries" as much as "10 per cent of each age group," most of the African countries "have provision for only one per cent or less in secondary school." [9] The conclusion reached by the Conference of African States on Education with respect to priorities to be assigned the various needs of the new states sheds further light on this point. In the words of the *Report* under the section on "priorities":

(a) *Secondary and higher level*
It was noted that some African countries have unduly neglected secondary and higher education in proportion to primary education. Economic development is highly dependent on skills of the sort which are taught in institutions to students of 15 years of age and upwards. It is of the highest priority to ensure that an adequate proportion of the population receives secondary, post-secondary and university education; this should be put before the goal of universal primary education if for financial reasons these two are not yet compatible. Plans for economic and social development depend upon an adequate supply of teachers, technicians, agricultural assistants, nurses, book-keepers, secretaries, medical technologists, clerks and other secondary level skills. Whereas the numbers required at the university level are so small that deficiencies can be met by external recruitment at relatively small cost, the numbers required at the secondary level are so large that deficiencies seriously handicap development.[10]

And again, the *Report* declares in its "Outline of a Plan for African Educational Development":

. . . the following needs are given priority status for the next five years:
A. *Secondary education.* The past decade has witnessed a marked growth in primary school places, but the increase in secondary school places has been insufficient to absorb a fair proportion of eligible primary school leavers. Current demands for manpower possessing at least a secondary school education cannot be met and all projections of future manpower needs at this level point toward a widening of the gap between supply and demand unless drastic action is taken. Further, the required increase of students pursuing higher education in Africa and abroad in preparation for posts of major responsibility calls for a larger production of secondary school graduates.[11]

Nothing would therefore seem more urgent than large-scale expansion of secondary education.

This need plainly conflicts with the priority of universal primary education to which many of the leaders of the new Africa are committed, sometimes as a matter of doctrine, sometimes as a method of indoctrination, and sometimes as a matter of redemption of "campaign pledges" given by the nationalist leaders in their push toward independence. For whatever reason, many and probably most African leaders would share the view expressed by Dr. Nkrumah:

> The Government attaches great importance to educational advancement as one of the means of transforming the society of Ghana to a higher standard. Our goal is to achieve a free universal primary and middle school education within the shortest possible time. A commission is being appointed to investigate and report upon university education and the Government intends that a University of Ghana will be created which will not only reflect African traditions and culture but will also play a constructive part in the programme of national awakening and reconstruction.[12]

Should less be spent on primary education and more on secondary, at least until the existing gap is somewhat reduced? In terms of economic development the allocation of increasing amounts to secondary education to produce the required corps of intermediate technicians and administrative personnel required by an expanding economy, and to insure an adequate flow of students to the university level—at the expense of primary education, if need be, in those areas where a substantial part of the primary school population is in school—would seem imperative. The same might be said in the interest of achieving Africanization of the middle and technical positions of the public services. Moreover, the heavy expenditure on higher education in British Africa, more recently in Belgian Africa, and most recently in French Africa—university education in Ghana, Nigeria, Sierra Leone, Uganda, Kenya, Tanganyika, the Federation of Rhodesia and Nyasaland, the Belgian Congo, Senegal, and the Ivory Coast —underlines the need for an adequate feed-up of secondary school graduates to make full use of the university facilities. Finally, the very expansion of primary education on a sound basis depends on turning out a sufficient number of trained teachers with secondary school education. In the words of the *Report* of the Conference of African States on Education:

The need for increasing secondary school enrolment was urged since the training of primary school teachers at the secondary level is the *sine qua non* for the extension of primary education. Effort at the secondary level is also essential for the training of the administrative and technical staff required for the economic expansion which would make possible the increase in national income necessary for the purpose of introducing universal primary education. Further, secondary schools are necessary to produce youth eligible for higher institutions which will supply the urgently required high-level manpower. That viewpoint was particularly expressed by representatives of countries which have already attained a satisfactory primary school enrolment rate, together with a level of economic development likely to provide employment for supervisory staff trained at the secondary level.[13]

However, the political currents in the direction of universal primary education are flowing strong. It may prove extremely difficult, if not impossible, for the African leaders to redirect them.

Similarly, the prestige value of universities is so high among Africans that one of the first acts of the leaders in many of the new African countries which had none was to create them or, as in Nigeria, to increase their number by creating at least one in each of the regions. Even accepting without qualification the desirability of many of the newly planned universities (the Ashby Commission in Nigeria recommended three universities be built in addition to the University College at Ibadan),[14] it is in order to question whether it would not be more effective to use existing facilities in Africa and elsewhere, particularly in view of the mounting scholarship offers from abroad, until the secondary school gap is reduced to more manageable proportions. Such a question would seem particularly appropriate with respect to the establishment of graduate schools. Regional universities or regional graduate schools in some faculties, e.g., medicine and engineering, would seem particularly worth consideration.

Also related to the secondary school gap is the prevailing lack of facilities for educating and training technicians and technical personnel generally, which applies both to vocational education at the secondary school level and to technical education and training for one to three years after secondary school. The modernization of traditional agriculture requires agricultural extension workers with this level of education. Africanization of the public and private sectors requires African medical assistants, laboratory technicians, and nurses; practical accountants and engineers; office and clerical personnel with knowledge of management, bookkeeping, and statistics; junior research personnel; and primary, secondary, vocational, and technical school teachers.

Looking behind the deficiencies in technical and vocational education at the secondary and post-secondary level, a major cause is one almost universally found in countries in the early stage of development: a lack of qualified teachers for all types of schools up to the university level. The lack of teachers and institutions for training them is in many areas of Africa the principal bottleneck to the expansion and the improvement in quality of primary and secondary education.

Turning to the university level, there is obviously a need for more qualified students, particularly in many of the professions such as engineering, medicine, dentistry, veterinary and agricultural sciences, the sciences generally, architecture, and economics. Partly, the short supply is attributable to the inadequate educational base. Some is due to the fact that during the colonial period Africans were not encouraged to pursue many of these professions.

In many instances using existing facilities to capacity, taking advantage of existing scholarships for study abroad, and expanding the number of such scholarships as the need grows would probably suffice for most areas of Africa for some time to come. The immediate need is to plan for expansion of capacity within Africa on a country and regional basis for the likely requirements of university graduates some ten to fifteen years hence—assuming that the secondary school deficiency is remedied, which is essential not only to fill the pipeline to the universities with qualified students but also to provide qualified secondary school students to work as technicians, aides, and clerks in support of university graduates. Professor Lewis has estimated that the number of qualified secondary school graduates should be at least five times the number of university graduates in order to effectuate the work of the university graduates and enable them to make a full contribution to the economies of their countries.[15]

The specific educational needs outlined above point up one set of formidable tasks confronting the African states. There are also three broad issues of educational practice which should be mentioned here.

Throughout Africa there are serious language problems. There is considerable controversy as to the number of years vernacular and tribal languages should be used as a medium of instruction, if at all. The practice now varies considerably, both being frequently employed in the early primary grades. Because most students drop out before completing their primary education, large numbers of Africans have inadequate command of English and French, the national languages adopted by most of the new African states, and this is most unfortunate in view of the lack of serious linguistic nationalism generally in Africa. English and French, properly taught and widely learned, would be forces for national cohesion, preventing the kind of internal conflict along language lines which, for example, plagues India. There are some pressures to teach important African languages and to make them second official languages as part of the general trend to restore or revivify African culture and history. Not too much emphasis, however, has been placed on the language point because of the multiplicity and diversity of African languages frequently found in small geographic areas. Some of the North African states have made Arabic their official language, and it is the language of primary school instruction, although French is also common. Swahili, a *lingua franca* along the coast of much of East Africa, is widespread in Tanganyika and is the language of instruction in primary school, along with English in the upper grades. Both Arabic and Swahili could in fairly significant areas serve, as do English and French, as unifying forces. Amharic, the official language of Ethiopia, occurs nowhere else. English and French, however, are fairly common in official circles.

In the language context there is also a serious problem for intra-African communication and Pan-African movements generally in the almost total lack of knowledge of English in French-speaking Africa and *vice versa*. There can be little question that this situation has proven a formidable barrier to the consummation of the Ghana-Guinea "nucleus of a union," to the effectiveness of English-speaking African countries in the Congo crisis, and to the coalescence of African states in West Africa. Ghana and Guinea have perceived the need for language instruction in each other's official language if their union is to coalesce and prosper and have launched language programs in French and English, respectively. Nigeria, which is surrounded by French-speaking states—Dahomey, Niger, and the former French Cameroun—has launched a French language teaching program. Other states are slowly following suit.

The second broad issue, crucial everywhere in Africa, is the Africanization of the curriculum and of the direction of the schools at all levels. As one educator has observed:

> The relationship of the school to the environment is a question which has stimulated the most frequent and impassioned controversies. To adapt education to the environment seemed to the African elite, only a short time ago, to be refusing Negro children the benefits of French ["English" could be read equally well here] programs of study, to be introducing intolerable racial discrimination, to be hindering the output of an elite which might be capable of taking the place of their white colonizer.[16]

The winds have shifted and the leaders of the new African states are now more than ever concerned to develop educational systems and curricula suited to the recently propagated African personality. On the one hand, functional and utilitarian subjects fitted to African needs are beginning to be stressed; on the other, African history and case material in economics, law, politics, etc., drawn from the local environment are beginning to be emphasized. The interest of many of the new African leaders in American secondary vocational and technical training schools, in American schools and institutes of engineering and technology, and in American land-grant type colleges and universities is one important indication of the African search for new educational patterns and institutions responsive to their needs as they conceive them. The new University of Nigeria at Nsukka in the Eastern Region is an interesting attempt to blend the traditional British university concept and structure which is typified by the University College at

Ibadan (in the Western Region) with an American university concept and structure.

In addition to Africanization of the curriculum, there is the two-fold problem of Africanizing the direction and structure of African education as well as the institutions themselves. The appointment of an eminent Nigerian historian, Dr. K. O. Dike, in 1960 to be principal of the University College at Ibadan indicates the trend at the top administrative and management level. The limitation here in many African states is likely to be the availability of qualified personnel.

Africanization of the structure and institutions of the educational system means in most instances a revolutionary transformation—the nationalization of the school system. In almost all independent African states the schools are directed, operated, staffed, in part financed, and in many instances owned by private missionary and other voluntary organizations and bodies. This is particularly true of primary education. There are also secondary schools, trade, vocational, and technical schools, and even higher educational institutions which are operated by missionary societies. The University of Louvanium in the Congo (Leopoldville) is the outstanding example of an institution of higher education operated by a religious group. Its long-term future is uncertain and has been at times an issue in the internal politics of the Congo. Clerical and anti-clerical Congolese have differing assessments and views of the past and future role of the university.

Africanization or nationalization means either the organization of a state-owned- and -operated school system alongside the existing private ones, which have been financially aided by the colonial governments and by the governments of the new states since independence, or the taking over and expansion of the facilities of the private schools by the governments of the new states. In some of the new states at independence there were, in addition to large numbers of mission and other privately operated school institutions, smaller but growing numbers of government-operated schools, particularly at the secondary and technical school levels.

The likelihood is that the trend will be toward government-operated school systems at all levels accomplished over varying periods of time in the different states. Financial resources, facili-

ties, staff, administrative and organizational difficulties, the growing demand for education, augmented by growing populations,
and the competition of other demands for scarce resources—all
are likely to impose limitations on the pace at which the independent states can nationalize education. Many will be hard pressed
to expand their educational structure enough through government
schools to keep abreast of the growing demand and to fulfill the
commitment of many of their leaders to universal primary education, more secondary education, and more university education.

In any event, though, governmental supervision and regulation of private educational institutions with respect to curricula,
standards, types of facilities, staff, types of certificates awarded, and
so on, is likely to increase considerably. It is also likely that secondary, technical, and higher education will increasingly come
within the scope of government systems. And probably most, if
not all, of the new primary schools will be government schools.

The Republic of Guinea is likely to be the first of the independent African states fully to Africanize and nationalize its
school system. In addition to the shared motivation of all African
states to transform their more or less heterogeneous mission, de-
nominational, and privately-operated school systems into government-operated systems with a common nation-building function
and dedication, Guinea brings to the educational sector, as to all
other sectors of national life, an ideological motivation. It is therefore appropriate to examine Guinea's program for Africanization
of education, which is well along.

The program, designed to nationalize education within three
years, starting in 1959, appears to be on schedule. President Sékou
Touré announced in the autumn of 1961 to the national conference of the *Parti Démocratique de Guinée* that "the Government
deemed it essential for all private teaching establishments to close
before the school year opened." [17] The plan, which now seems to
have been carried through, provided that private schools continue
to receive state support for the three-year period 1959–1961. They
could not, however, register any new pupils during this period. All
new pupils had to be registered in government schools, which were
to make use of the classrooms which became available in the private schools as their students graduated. At the end of the three

years the pupils then in private schools would be expected to take the competitive entrance examination for scholarships to the more advanced public schools, "and after these three years there [would] be no pupil not belonging to the public sector." And President Touré added: "Public education will then have its true character as a State organization put at the disposal of the people not only for its learning, but also and especially for its complete education." [18]

The third broad issue can only be mentioned here. It is the problem of education for girls. As an outgrowth of both African tradition and custom and colonial indifference, education of girls has lagged badly behind education for boys. With independence most African states are concerned to redress this imbalance, partly in response to the general trends of nationalism and modernization, and partly in response to pressure from women, who frequently in West Africa have played a not insignificant role in helping to finance nationalist movements with their earnings from trading and operating "mammy wagons" (passenger- and produce-carrying trucks). Once again it is appropriate to quote briefly the *Report* of the Conference of African States on Education on this point:

> Great need exists to increase the number of girls receiving education at all levels. Research indicates that girls make up less than 30 per cent of the present total African primary school enrolment and about 22 per cent of the secondary school enrolment. . . . The need is urgent for the increased use of educated "woman power" in the working life of the community. . . . [19]

The push for education can be said to be an insistent and universal problem for African development, the source of many important and sensitive issues. The institutional structures being established involve decisions with implications for the evolving growth patterns and poltical systems. The allocation of funds among the different levels of education—primary, secondary, post-secondary, and university—will impose different cost burdens on the economy, and produce different manpower availabilities for the economy. Timing manpower availabilities to the needs of an expanding economy is at best a difficult calculation; without adequate data, particularly statistical series on the performance of an economy, it becomes a hazardous calculation, more like an informed guess. Nevertheless, this is a condition characteristic of underdeveloped economies for which due allowance must be made in making manpower projections, and in relating the educational structure to the manpower projections.

In addition to the institutional problem, we have also explored briefly the problems of language of instruction, Africanization of the content and administration of the school system, and the problem of education for girls. All of these are important manifestations of the broader problem or objective of modernization of African society. The ambivalent urge to modernize, as a passport to the new dignity and status associated with freedom, and at the same time to preserve and restore customs and traditions, as the hallmark of a great and ancient past, afflicts many African leaders. Thus, while all recognize the desirability of retaining English or French as national languages, there is an impulse to develop indigenous languages. Similarly while there is a political drive to emancipate women, there is a traditional urge to retain some of the old restraints. While the universal movement to Africanize the content and direction of education emphasizes the shaping of education to African needs and is responsive to African aspirations to modernize, there are pressures looking backward, seeking to recreate the glories of the past by developing national myths, symbols, and histories. Nevertheless, the trend is toward retaining European languages, advancing the status of women through increasing educational opportunities, and viewing Africanization of the curriculum and management of the school system as primarily an aspect of the broader Africanization of the public and private sectors we considered in the preceding chapter.

Some Unanswered Questions

There is already compelling evidence in southern Nigeria, Ghana, and Guinea that Africans are likely to have the necessary determination to tackle the vast educational problem. One questions not the will but the ability of the new states to finance and staff dramatically enlarged and diversified educational systems.

How many states will be able to allocate over 40 per cent of their ordinary budgets to education as the Western and Eastern Regions of Nigeria have? And even if they could, or try to, should they? At this state of their growth how much of their scarce financial resources could and should they pour into education, especially primary education? How much could be justified as long-term capital investment, and how much must be viewed as an expenditure on a consumer good? To what extent should manpower be channeled into teaching, educational administration, and related tasks?

There are no clear-cut answers. The likelihood is that more will be allocated to education by all new states than the colonial powers ever spent, and more than the budgets of most of the new states can effectively carry. An evident danger is that a disproportionate amount of the national wealth may be allocated to primary education, leaving a gap at the secondary level and in the technical fields. This has certainly been the problem in the Western and Eastern Regions of Nigeria. The Eastern Region, in an attempt to cope with the serious drain on its resources attributable to primary education, has cut back on the number of years of schooling from eight to seven, reimposed fees originally removed for several grades of primary school, and raised the fees for other primary grades. Both the Western and Eastern Region are confronted with the need to expand secondary and technical education and are hard pressed to find the resources. Another danger is that an excessive amount of educational funds will be lavished on showplaces at the university level.

In addition to having limited funds, the new states are likely to find it difficult to staff expanded school systems. It will take considerable time to train adequately qualified Africans; and it is too costly and probably not possible to employ sufficiently large numbers of overseas staff for expanding educational systems, especially for primary- and secondary-level schools. School teachers are the principal category of personnel African countries have requested from the United States Peace Corps. The bulk of the program in Ghana and Nigeria, for example, is composed of school teachers.

Moreover, the recurrent cost problem, once money has been

found for facilities, will be a major one for the new states. External assistance may be forthcoming for the establishment of some facilities, for initial staff, for training new staff, for acquiring books and developing new teaching materials, and generally for launching expanded programs. However, it seems hardly likely that external aid can be relied on to meet annual recurrent costs for maintenance and staff over the years. And this consideration brings us to the interlocking facts of economic growth.

The shaping and timing of the response of the new states to the irresistible push for education must take account of existing resources; education must expand *pari passu* with the growth of resources, which, in turn, will be intimately tied to the success or failure of the new states in achieving transformation of traditional agriculture and the Africanization of the public and private sectors. Completing the circle, too much emphasis on one or another element in the educational structure—for instance, the disproportionate expansion of the primary level of education—could result in retarding economic growth. Failure to produce trained manpower at the secondary, post-secondary, and university levels at the time required could create—as we have suggested, and actually is creating in the more developed economies—bottlenecks, gaps, and weaknesses limiting the growth of the economy and its ability to finance just such programs as universal primary education.

In addition, the production of larger and larger groups of primary school graduates without adequate secondary and technical schools available and without a sufficiently developed economy to absorb them could only encumber any economy and threaten the stability of the political system. Disillusioned young people without sufficient qualifications to make a contribution at the technical, administrative, and professional levels, and in many instances too young to, but with more qualifications than there are equivalent jobs to absorb, could constitute a major source of instability in the new states. Ghana is already confronted with this problem, and its answer so far has been the questionable one of the Workers' Brigade, a semi-regimented youth corps with political overtones more or less effectively carrying out public works projects. The Western and Eastern Regions of Nigeria are also confronted with the problem. The Western Region's answer is an experimental one, an interesting attempt to adapt the Israeli *kibbutzim* and *moshavim* to the problem of launching primary school graduates on an agricultural career. The Eastern Region is also experimenting with various types of "farm settlement" schemes. Both the Ghanaian and Nigerian remedies are expensive. Although they may have other purposes and may meet other problems, to the extent that they are directed toward meeting the problem of educational programs out of joint with the absorptive capacity of their economies they are an unfortunate drain on the scarce capital resources of the two countries which the latter can ill afford.

In Nigeria the Dynamic Party, a radical splinter party in the Eastern Region which split off from the ruling National Council of Nigeria and the Cameroons, now the National Convention of Nigerian Citizens, has made political capital out of the growing disaffection of unemployed primary school-leavers. And in the Western Region particularly, but also in the Eastern Region, Chief Awolowo, leader of the opposition at the federal level and head of the Action Group party, has been making a special effort to cater to the discontent of the growing body of unemployed school-leavers. They are becoming a recognizable political factor. The school-leaver problem illustrates the direct link between the economic growth and political stability of the new states. Formulation of suitable educational policies and resolution of the school-leaver problem not only would enhance and reflect economic growth; they would also reinforce the political stability of the new states at a time when they are still concerned with building and consolidating their nascent political structures and systems.

One wonders, then, if the new African states will decide to allocate resources to a balanced educational system producing the needed trained personnel and still satisfying as much as possible the craving for universal primary education. In the end this is more likely to produce the desired goal of universal primary education·on a continuing basis than a quick plunge with little regard to the balance of the education structure and the consequences to the economy—and the political system—of serious imbalance.

Chapter 7

THE ROLE OF WELFARE STATE CONCEPTS

The desire to have something to show for independence creates a nearly irresistible temptation for the leaders of the new states in Africa to allocate resources to social welfare services and facilities on a scale which commits their countries to living beyond their means. The degree of pressure the new leaders feel themselves to be laboring under is already evidenced by their willingness to divert resources from productive investment and allocate them in their ordinary budgets to defray the cost of social welfare services and in their extraordinary budgets to finance social welfare facilities. It reflects a trend toward enlarged state welfare programs, with the danger of soon reaching a point of diminishing returns; for economic growth may be seriously impaired and even aborted if too large a share of resources is dissipated and too heavy a burden of recurring costs incurred.

It is a trend frequently—some would say inevitably—accompanied by the growth of the public sector at the expense of the private sector. Whether inevitable or not, it is often the case that with the expansion of public-financed social welfare services and benefits the profit incentive or personal gain motive is lessened and the scope of its operation circumscribed. In the view of an eminent British authority on welfare economics:

It is ironical that what is coming to be called the Welfare State is a state in which much is provided free, and in which the personal gain motive is weakened, but not apparently replaced—with the result that the sphere within which the theory of welfare can be applied is smaller.[1]

Even if this secondary effect is disregarded, the fact remains that a disproportionate or premature allocation of resources to social welfare may inhibit economic growth to such a degree that maintenance of the social welfare services and facilities already installed is jeopardized and improvements in their level and diversity precluded. The possibilities are only too easy to visualize— schools without teachers, hospitals without staffs, and universal primary education without commensurate jobs, all of which not only imply a misallocation of initial resources but also mean carrying charges beyond the capacity of the economy. Then there must be a choice in each successive budget of abandoning some portion and eventually all of the investment already made, as deterioration and wastage cannot be indefinitely postponed, or diverting even more resources from productive investment to salvage something from the investment already made. And here lurks the ultimate disaster from an economic and social development point of view. Once started down the road of salvaging existing non-productive investments, it is a complicated and difficult task to reverse gears and return to the starting point. Aside from the many vested interests in the new institutions, contracts, jobs, and so on which resist change, no politician, and Africa is not different in this respect from other areas of the world, likes to admit blunders and publicly retreat. Pride of position and saving face are not absent from the African scene.

The importance of welfare state concepts in the new African states goes far beyond their intrinsic national merit. It is to be found in their attraction for African independence leaders who want independence, in contrast to colonial status, to signify a new deal with immediate tangible payoffs for their people. It is also to be found in the inability of such leaders to retreat either from their own earlier promises given in the heat of anti-colonial campaigns or from levels already established in some areas by the departing colonial power. It is to be found too in the competition for Pan-African leadership, with Ghana, for example, seeking to hold itself out as a model of social advancement for others to emulate or to achieve in political union with Ghana. Finally, it is to be found in the vanishing context of colonialism, as in Kenya, where the two leading political groups—the Kenya African National Union and the Kenya African Democratic Union—vying for power as independence approaches have been engaged in attempting to win popular support by outpromising one another with respect to educational and other welfare benefits. The same phenomenon, to a degree, is discernible in some of the politics of Nigeria. It existed, as in Kenya, before independence, and continues currently as a concomitant and cost of a competitive democratic political system. Clearly the successful resolution of the problem of proportions is a crucial one for all the new African states.

Present State of Social Welfare

In many ways a description of the present state of social welfare services, benefits, and facilities in the newly independent states must be a survey or inventory of the departing colonial powers' policies and programs inherited by the new states, and to an extent the response of the new states to their legacy.

In the development plans they sponsored in their African territories, and in the assistance they provided to carry out the plans, all of the principal colonial powers gave some degree of emphasis to social welfare. All were confronted with the same issue now confronting the new states, the proper allocation of resources, and with pressures roughly corresponding to those at work on the new African leadership. From the point of view of the temptations of welfare state practices the self-generated pressure of a colonial power's paternalism is not unlike the reformist drive of an African independence leader. The external pressures associated with the revolution of rising expectations have also acted to induce comparable welfare actions by colonial powers and independent states.

The legacies of British, French, and Belgian Africa are very different; the responses of the new states have tended to be similar although for different reasons.

The British succeeded, for the most part, in their attempt to have their African colonies live within their means—certainly insofar as social welfare benefits were concerned. They failed, however, to enlarge those means sufficiently to expand the social welfare benefits in important areas which the new independence morality has been emphasizing as appropriate—primary and secondary education, adult literacy, housing, urban amenities, recreational facilities, rural development, and general wage and fringe benefit standards.

The response, insofar as it is discernible in Ghana and Nigeria, is a tremendous thrust in favor of expanding educational and literacy programs, with all the risks of disproportionate allocation within the sphere of education (noted in the preceding chapter); a growing issue on wage levels and fringe benefit standards with pressures to assimilate European expatriate standards in the public and private sectors (noted in our discussion of Africanization); and a general tendency in all the other neglected or relatively neglected social welfare areas to expand facilities, improve services, or initiate new programs. One important element of the building boom, for example, which has afflicted Accra—and some of the signs are to be found elsewhere—is government-financed construction of public buildings for meeting halls; exhibition centers; headquarters for cooperative, labor, agricultural, trade, and other quasi-governmental associations; community centers; recreational facilities; studios, and the like.

In short, the reaction in the former British West African territories on independence seems to have been characterized by a drive to redress a balance between European-exhibited standards and those available to the Africans. Their problem has not been one of keeping up inherited facilities and standards so much as expanding a limited base or building new facilities and adopting new standards. Their compensation, and perhaps overcompensation, for gaps and weaknesses in the colonial inheritance is a not unexpected response to the *laissez-faire* policies long pursued by the British not only in colonial economic affairs but also in social welfare matters.[2]

The Belgians in many ways present far and away the most striking contrast to the British with respect to African colonial economic and welfare policy. The Belgians were interventionists in all spheres of Congolese economic and social life. Their vigorous policy of active state participation in economic development and a long-standing policy of paternalism contrast sharply with the British *laissez-faire* doctrine and attitude. However, although they pursued a vigorous policy of ever-expanding social welfare facilities and services in the post-World War II period, contrasting markedly with the British practices, the Belgians failed to relate the scope of the welfare policies to the capacity of the Congolese economy. Hence in 1960, when the Belgians withdrew from the Congo, the lack of correlation contributed to the serious financial position of the new state. The Congo Republic inherited a heavy debt service and charges for recurrent costs for the elaborate social welfare installations as well as widespread popular expectations not only that the network of social welfare facilities and services inaugurated by the colonial administration would be preserved and continued but that it would be enlarged and scaled to the style of the retiring European rulers.

The crisis of political instability which afflicted the Congo immediately after independence makes it all but impossible to discern the response of the new government to their legacy and the expectations it has created. However, a relatively weak compromise or coalition government, which appears to be as much as the Congo can now aspire to, is not likely to be able to withstand pressures; and it is likely to want to do almost anything to gain popular acceptance. This bodes serious difficulties for the Congo with respect to the allocation of resources. One straw in the wind was the action of the crumbling government of Prime Minister Lumumba in early July 1960. In the face of independence and accompanying widespread industrial unrest in Leopoldville it decreed an increase in the legal minimum wage of a flat 30 per cent irrespective of all other considerations. One consideration overlooked or disregarded was the impact of this across-the-board increase on the personnel of the *Force Publique*, not included in the increase, which was certainly a factor in the discontent which led to their July mutiny. Although an extreme example, that mutiny demonstrated the critical dimensions of wage and benefits policy in the new states. An increase in family allowances for civilians and not the *Force Publique* or a decrease for the *Force Publique* and not for civilians might have had a similar impact. In fact the mere rumor of the latter occurrence led to reports of grave disorders in the already mutinous but at the time apparently reorganized *Force Publique* in Leopoldville in September 1960.

French development and welfare policy in Africa fell somewhere between the British and Belgian policies, probably closer to Belgian with respect to the transfer of welfare state concepts from the European context to Africa. Looming larger in the French African areas than in the Belgian, which also introduced the practice in the Congo, was the payment of *allocations familiales*. In metropolitan France the practice was related to a population crisis resulting from heavy World War I manpower losses, whereas in French Africa, with improved health and related programs contributing to the pressures, the oft-heralded population explosion has long been in the offing. This paradox engendered serious controversy in France, in the course of which an interesting aspect of the transfer of modern welfare state concepts to Africa was revealed.

The following exchange illustrates the nature of the problem confronting the new states and introduces the issue of external aid as a source for financing welfare state programs:

As B. de Jouvenel has noted,[3] the introduction of the family allowance system in the overseas territories is truly an economic paradox. The scheme is peculiar to France (it does not exist in any of the countries which are industrial competitors of ours). The scheme is a result of the demographic crisis which has plagued France for a century. It would therefore be paradoxical to institute the scheme in countries where the rate of population growth is four to five times that of France.

Generally speaking, de Jouvenel added, the general concept that institutions of the metropole must be extended to their overseas territories is a mistaken one. What can be done in the social welfare field depends on the state of the economies concerned, and these are totally different in France and its overseas territories. If, at the outset of the industrial era in Europe, employers had been required to bear obligations comparable to those borne today, few manufacturing enterprises would have come into being. It is certain that if the overseas territories were left to themselves the application of social measures of this sort would be economically impossible. . . . But the overseas territories are not left to themselves. The principal role of external economic aid is to avoid the pauperization of the population during the period in which the foundations for economic growth are being laid.[4]

Thus into the structures of the economies—and in a larger sense, of the societies—in former French Africa is built an assumption of substantial French aid for the public sectors and for social welfare generally. The abrupt independence of Guinea and the equally abrupt French withdrawal have upset this assumption in Guinea. But it is more than likely that the original adherence of all the French African territories other than Guinea to the new Franco-African Community in the September 1958 referendum was significantly influenced by the existence of this assumption. As independent states these former French areas have continued to look to French assistance from its various economic and social aid funds for African countries of *l'expression française* and from the EEC Overseas Development Fund, which has allocated from its inception about half of its funds to "social development" projects, to help maintain and expand the welfare state facilities and services of the Associated African States. What would happen if these sources were cut off is of course not possible to say. It seems most unlikely, however, that the initial capital expenditures and recurrent charges for maintenance and staffing could be sustained by these new states at their expected state of development over the next five to ten years.

Investment of Labor

The various responses of the three leading colonial powers in Africa in the social welfare field suggest the broad lines available to and apparently being followed by the newly independent states.

One aspect of the response of independent African states calls for special attention. Human labor was available to the colonial powers, but only on a diminishing scale as a means of providing social welfare facilities and, to a lesser extent, services. During the post-World War II period a growing aversion to anything approximating forced or compulsory labor developed in colonial Africa. As a practical matter this aversion acted to circumscribe large areas of community labor which, although voluntary, had to be induced, generated, or inspired by colonial governments or native authorities responsible in the last analysis to the colonial governments. The use of human labor—*l'investissement humain*— has now been reintroduced into Africa as a principal means to provide social welfare facilities, some maintenance and service thereof, and to bring social development to rural areas.

Although Ghana has encouraged human labor in its community development programs and developed the Workers' Brigade, it is with the independence of Guinea that Sékou Touré provided a philosophical justification and model for other African areas. In the words of Touré *l'investissement humain* is a policy which was adopted when the Democratic Party of Guinea "unanimously decided to make use of human resources through the voluntary use of human energy, collectively placed at the service of the common interests." M. Touré went on:

> The use of human resources has become one of the standing activities of the Guinean society, as a means of improving the conditions of life of the communities. . .
> Through the use of human resources, our peasant brothers have realized that they were more important than money, since they have fulfilled a large part of their programme of cultural and social development without the help of money. . . .
> This is how the Party must launch ideas, use our values, look for forms of mobilization of the masses, must call forth, organize and direct the creative action, the source of the happiness, of the prosperity and of the greatness of the peoples.[5]

This type of exhortation of voluntary human labor apparently becomes acceptable with independence, which seems to purge it of coercive overtones. *L'investissement humain* goes some way to supplying physical plant for welfare purposes. The question of whether the labor employed is always surplus to other economic needs or might be more fruitfully used in other ways does not arise. It is assumed to be a new resource—unused or under-used labor. To the extent that it is a resource diverted from other uses which might be more productive to the economy its diversion is likely to be less serious than that of capital resources in the same circumstances. This is the new dimension involved in the resuscitated programs of human investment in the newly independent states insofar as welfare state programs are concerned.

In the final analysis welfare state concepts depend on the strength and growth of the economies of the new states for their translation into being, with the condition that precipitous or lavish indulgence en route to self-sustaining growth may well impair the achievement of the desired social welfare standards. The human investment asset of the new states may enhance their ability to satisfy their welfare state aspirations, but it may also divert attention and interest from the key tasks of economic development through propagation of the doctrine that human investment can permit dispensing with capital, in large part or entirely. M. Touré comes close to this when he talks of "cultural and social development without money," and almost as an alternative to development with money. There is no doubt that labor-intensive projects, in M. Touré's phrase "mass labor methods" (to build the Konkouré Dam, if necessary), can be an important element in development schemes. There is also little doubt that even labor-intensive schemes require capital, and that much development is impossible without substantial amounts of it.

Mobilization of manpower to build social welfare facilities with a religious zeal can also lead to a lack of emphasis on agricultural development, which likewise requires in the first instance considerable manpower; on basic infrastructure, which requires manpower as well as capital; and on secondary, servicing, and processing industries, all of which require trained manpower as well as capital. The problem is not so much one of diverting manpower as of creating an impression of solid achievement which does not rest on the firm basis of a growing economy able over the long run to maintain and staff, as well as expand, social welfare programs.

Human investment need not, of course, go to this extreme. It is a risk, however, to be recognized—particularly if things do not go well in the productive sectors of the economy. Public works and busy work are, like external adventures, age-old distractions used by leaders the world over.

The Outlook

Thus, the ability of the new African states to mount successful economic development plans will vary directly with their ability to keep in check the strong pressures at work within their bourgeoning societies for heavy social welfare expenditures as the visible and tangible fruits of the much sought-after independence which has now been achieved. The needs for productive investment, particularly, as we have seen, for agricultural and manpower development, are primary, and enormous in nature. The many other claimants on the limited resources of the new states, although they have not been identified as critical growth problems in this study, nevertheless exist. In varying degrees, in Africa as elsewhere in the underdeveloped world, the needs for transportation and communication networks, power grids, etc., are important, and will require significant expenditures. In this context, then, of growing needs and as yet all too limited resources, policy on social welfare expenditures becomes central to the capacity of the new states to achieve their goal of growth. It will be necessary to hold a tight rein on welfare expenditures, but not so tight as to curtail incentive for individual performance. The balance at best will need to be a delicate one, varying in each case with the level of development, the colonial social welfare heritage, and the social and economic development philosophy and politics of the new states.

PART THREE

Search for Stability

The safest thing to do in Africa is to have a one-party state. . . . . Here in our own traditional way of government, in our own traditional concept of society and governmental organisation, we know of the council of elders, elected or whose nomination has been approved by the masses, all sitting together with one of them who has either been elected chief or been agreed upon to lead them. There is no question of a deliberate division of that group. . . .*

> HON. KOFI BAAKO
> Minister of Defense
> and Leader of the House in Ghana

Speaking for my colleagues, for my Party, and myself, I categorically disavow the so-called African way of conducting public affairs. There is only one way of conducting public affairs in the interest of the masses, in the interest of the people, in the interest of the electorate, and that way is the democratic way, which is popularly known in the British Commonwealth of Nations and the British colonies as the British way of life. This way of life is the human way. As a political animal, man is the same everywhere, no matter his race or colour. There are, therefore, only two forms of government, the democratic form of government and the undemocratic form of government.†

> CHIEF OBAFEMI AWOLOWO
> Chairman of the Action Group and Leader of the
> Opposition in the Federal Parliament in Nigeria

* As quoted in *Africa Today* (London), Vol. 6, No. 7, 1962.
† *Towards Independence*, Ibadan, Nigeria, 1958.

Chapter 8

STATE STRUCTURES AND POLITICAL SYSTEMS

Since in almost every instance the new states of Africa have inherited state structures derived from those of the former colonial powers, the tendency has been for former British, French, and Belgian territories to emerge with governmental institutions reflecting those of their respective former metropoles. In fact, more often than not, the critical decisions on state structure were reached in the final stages of pre-independence negotiations between the metropole and the about-to-be independent territory.

Thus agreement at that point on the institution of a unitary structure has frequently paved the way for the emergence of authoritarian political systems, whereas the rare agreement on the adoption of a federal structure has provided the opportunity for development of a democratic system. Similarly, the adoption of a parliamentary system with unlimited power concentrated in the parliament has frequently paved the way for authoritarian political systems, whereas the rare adoption of a system wherein the parliament is subject to constitutional restraints on its exercise of power by an independent judiciary has provided the opportunity for the development of one of the few democratic political systems on the continent. The colonial legacy has also exerted influence at other levels in the political organization of the new states—significantly, for example, in determining the role and structure of local government, the recognition and preservation of regional differences based on cultural, tribal, or economic grounds, the continuing role in one guise or another of district or provincial commissioners in regulating political activity, and the acceptance and use of preventive detention acts, restrictive citizenship and nationality statutes, and restrictions on press and assembly as techniques for regulating political behavior.

However, it would be wrong to assume the wholesale unqualified African acceptance of existing models. Quite the opposite of any such process, the leaders of the new African states, once they become masters in their own houses, have utilized their colonial heritage to implement their own concepts of political stability and frequently to achieve such stability in their own interests or in the interest of their political parties. Thus we are concerned here not with the colonial heritage itself but with the principal aspects of the resulting structures of the new states as they shed some light on the different ways that African leaders have sought to achieve stability for their countries through the choice of governmental institutions and the development of political systems to operate the institutions.

State Structures

Federal Structures: The Unique Case

The rare case, and for practical purposes the only case, of the establishment of a federal structure for a newly independent African state is the Federation of Nigeria.[1] Here, after prolonged consideration and much controversy, the British agreed to the formation of a federal system as the price for creating a unified independent country. It is more than likely that a single Nigerian state would not have been possible if agreement had not been reached on a federal system which recognized the cultural, tribal, and economic diversity of the colonial territory. Although there continues to be agitation in Nigeria for the transformation of the federal system into a unitary structure, it would seem much more likely that Nigeria will undergo the almost universal experience of federal systems, which has been the growth over time of power at the federal level accompanied by a proportionate decrease at the regional or provincial level.

In any event, the distribution of power among the regions in Nigeria and between the regions and the federal government has resulted in one of the few vigorous multi-party political systems in Africa. Although the regional governments tend to be dominated by one party, there is no absence of political activity and political contest in all of the regions by the competing political parties. The NCNC (National Convention of Nigerian Citizens), the controlling party in the Eastern Region, constituted the opposition in the Western Region parliament until recently when it became part of a two-party coalition government with the United People's Party (UPP); and the Action Group (AG), until recently the controlling party in the Western Region, has been the opposition in the Eastern Region parliament. In the regions there is also intense competition among the principal regionally based parties and a few small parties for election of members of the federal parliament. There is also sharp competition between the NCNC and the AG for control of the local government of Lagos, which like Washington, D.C., is a federal area.

Although in many ways the strongly centralized unitary government of Ghana rather than the federal system of Nigeria is the prototype for the structure of most African states, it may be that Nigeria will become the prototype for the association of independent states into larger units. In fact, federal structures may offer the only practical way to associate new states in larger units, since such structures would seem most suitable to accommodate differences and absorb the political leaders of independent states. This was certainly the case in the Federation of Mali. In fact, one of the reasons assigned for the dissolution of the Federation is that, in the words of a noted French authority, Mali was *"plus proche d'un Etat unitaire décentralisé politiquement que d'un Etat fédéral."* [2] Apparently not enough flexibility was built into the Mali federation. It was also the only basis on which President Ahidjo of the Republic of Cameroun and Prime Minister Foncha of the trust territory of Southern Cameroon could compromise a wealth of differences, not the least of which arose from the differing colonial heritages of a former French and a former British territory, and bring their respective countries together within a unified political framework, the Federal Republic of Cameroon.

Reflecting the traditions and practices of the European metropoles, most of the new African states have come to independence with parliamentary systems; and almost as a first order of business the newly independent states have transformed their parliamentary systems into strong presidential systems. Thus Prime Ministers Nkrumah, Olympio, and Ahidjo of Ghana, Togo, and Cameroun, respectively, became presidents of their countries. Only the Nigerian parliamentary system, within a federal structure and subject to constitutional safeguards, has not been transformed into a presidential system; and even if it should be so transformed, it is not likely to be a strong presidential system without constitutional and political restraints. The very nature of a federal structure dividing and allocating powers to the different levels of government, the constitutional definition of individual rights as well as regional rights, and the existence of the rule of law and an independent judiciary to administer it all militate against a single strong executive power of the type provided for in the Ghanaian constitution, for example. The Nigerian constitution has all of the suggested self-limiting provisions. Finally, it is interesting to note that the suggestions so far made in Nigeria by leading political figures for transforming the country from a monarchy, headed by Queen Elizabeth of Great Britain, into a republic have not envisaged a strong president. The most recent and most detailed suggestion made by the Governor-General of Nigeria, Dr. Azikiwe, envisages a moderately weak presidential power. In a speech of national importance late in 1961, Dr. Azikiwe stated:

> My optimism is based on the fact that an equitable distribution of power between the Head of State and Head of Government in a republican government would make it possible for man to exercise power over man in a manner that would insulate those who exercise such power from becoming victims of temptation to succumb ultimately to excesses in exercising power which goads one not only to continue to seek for more power but to become power-drunk and ulti-

mately emerge into a full-fledged dictator. Events in certain parts of
Africa point to this direction.

Should Nigeria decide to become a republic, then a reorientation
of attitude towards this moot issue will be inevitable; in which case,
we should avoid the concentration of power either on the Head of
State or on the Head of Government. Other things being equal, a
diffusion of power between the two would appear to be a satisfactory
compromise.[3]

Chief Awolowo, leader of the Action Group and the opposition at the federal level, has invoked the Indian model of a weak
figurehead president and a strong prime minister responsible to
parliament as the ideal Nigeria should strive to emulate. The
Northern People's Congress (NPC) and the National Convention
of Nigerian Citizens, the coalition government parties, have just
raised the question of altering the structure of the state to transform Nigeria from a monarchical structure into a republican one.

In this connection it is pertinent to note that in all instances
where the transformation from a parliamentary to a presidential
system has occurred the form of state structure has been unitary
rather than federal.[4] It is also pertinent to note that in all of them
the restrictions on the exercise of parliamentary power, to the extent they existed, were largely predicated on unwritten custom and
tradition, which unlike the institutions could not be transferred
readily by the metropoles to the territories, rather than as in Nigeria on explicit constitutional provisions safeguarded by an independent judiciary.

With respect to local government also Nigeria presents
something of an exception to the general African trend toward
strongly centralized unitary governments in the new states. In
the Northern Region, as the result of Lord Lugard's principle of
indirect rule, the traditional Fulani-Hausa emirates and other
traditional local government units have not only retained their
significant governmental powers but also reinforced them. The
power of the local governments in the Northern Region is so
formidable that the Native Authorities, as they are called, are
often referred to as "states within a state." In the other two regions
of Nigeria the traditional local government institutions which the
British found in existence at the turn of the century were far less

developed, and at the time of independence they had still not achieved anything of the power of those in the Northern Region. Nevertheless, they do exercise some powers, and the trend since independence is towards the devolution of increasing regional powers on the local government units.

Lastly, in terms of the phenomenon of retaining but improving on the political control mechanisms of the colonial era, which has been repeated time and again in many of the new African states, Nigeria presents a different picture. An entrenched Bill of Rights interpreted and applied by an independent judiciary operating under the concept of the rule of law has produced in Nigeria the most democratic political system in Africa. In fact, in an interesting court case in early 1961 a leading federal minister was found guilty of illegal seizure and made to pay damages. It would be hard, if not imposssible, to name another African state where a minister could be held to account in so public a fashion for trespassing on the private rights of an individual.

Unitary Structures: The General Trend

Turning from the unique case of Nigeria to the prevailing trend of African political development, the outcome of the controversy in the Gold Coast preceding its accession to independence has become the classic case and the controlling precedent for African nationalists seeking to establish wholly centralized unitary governments. Prime Minister Nkrumah and the Convention People's Party vigorously opposed every attempt by opposition groups and parties in Ghana to establish a federal government structure. They contended that a federal structure was a type of organization that a new state of the size of Ghana with its problems of cultural and tribal diversity could ill afford; they viewed such a federal structure as divisive. The British government, with its own tradition of a unitary state, accepted this position.

Since independence in 1957 Prime Minister Nkrumah has used the unitary state structure to build, and some would say force, national cohesion. Dissident or recalcitrant tribal, regional, and economic groups have been brought into line through the use of the machinery of the central government. Trade unions, farmers' organizations, cooperatives, women's organizations, youth groups, newspapers, and so on have all been brought under the control of the central government or the party in a one-party state.

His belief in the unitary structure of the Ghanaian government has become a principal tenet in Nkrumah's philosophy of Pan-Africanism. It was one of the principal determinants of his all-out pro-Lumumba position in the early days of the Congo crisis, when he supported Lumumba in the latter's insistence on the consolidation at all cost of the equivocal and somewhat uncertain unitary governmental structure bequeathed to the Congo by the Belgian government, even to the extent of achieving it by force of arms. Preoccupied with his view that only a unitary state means unity, Dr. Nkrumah seemed blind to the various possibilities of compromising the Congo crisis on the basis of a federal solution. Even President Tshombé of the break-away province of Katanga, after a prolonged exchange of cables with Nkrumah in which he raised several times the possibility of a federal solution, almost in despair cabled Nkrumah:

It appears to me that you do not very well understand the Congo problem. It is just an institutional problem. The political structures imposed by the Belgian colonialists have proved in practice to be incompatible with the realities of Congo life. Katanga supported by the other regions and provinces of the former Belgian Congo wished Congolese unity to be restored on the basis of a federal union.[5]

The general pattern in almost all of the new African states has been to follow the Ghanaian precedent. Even in the vast heterogeneous Belgian Congo, in the face of considerable opposition, the Belgian government and the then leader of the *Mouvement National Congolais*, Patrice Lumumba, pushed through the Belgian-Congolese Political Round Table Conference in February 1960 a compromise and somewhat equivocal constitutional provision providing for a central unitary government, with provincial governments authorized to exercise certain designated powers. With independence the meaning of this constitutional provision and the opposition to a strongly centralized unitary government became a principal factor in the separatist movements which developed and have continued to play an important part in

Congolese affairs. It has taken a long series of conferences during the first two years of Congolese independence—Tananarive, Coquihatville, Leopoldville, and Kitona—to find a way back from the political wilderness which the Congo plunged into over the struggle for power, epitomized by the issue of the form of the state structure. From Lumumba's insistence on a tight unitary structure, after his death in early 1961 the pendulum swung at Tananarive to the ideal of Tshombé, a weak confederal structure with a multiplicity of sovereign states. By early spring of 1961, at Coquihatville, the pendulum swung back again to a federal structure. And by the summer of 1961 a relatively strong federal structure started to emerge at Leopoldville, beginning with the session of the reconvened Congolese parliament. However, by the end of 1961, another conference, this time between the Premier of the central government, Cyrille Adoula, and the head of the break-away province of Katanga, Moïse Tshombé, became necessary to deal with this issue. Tshombé agreed to recognize the unity of the Congo and the *Loi Fondamentale*, the provisional Congo constitution bestowed by Belgium. He also agreed that the Katangese parliamentarians would return to the National Assembly. They did, and they carried a mandate to participate in the work of a special commission to prepare the draft of a revised constitution and to argue for the adoption of a federal system for the Congo. Discussions between Adoula and Tshombé continued intermittently well into 1962, but without concrete results. U Thant, the Secretary General of the the United Nations, intervened and proposed a package deal for the reintegration of Katanga into the Congo under the terms of a new federal constitution prepared by a special United Nations' commission. Tshombé agreed in principle but equivocated; hostilities broke out late in December 1962 between the Katangan and United Nations military forces and as a result Katanga was forcefully reintegrated into the Congo. The status of the U Thant federal constitution and the constitutional terms controlling Katanga's position, as well as the other provinces, in the Republic of Congo, remain somewhat uncertain. The issue, federal versus unitary government, still persists. And Dr. Nkrumah persists in his initial anti-federalist position to the extent of entering into a bitter exchange with U Thant over the terms of Katanga's reintegration into the Congo. Nkrumah has denounced the proposed federal constitution notwithstanding the fact that the Adoula government has approved it.

How much of the Congo's trial by ordeal might have been averted by the initial adoption of the Nigerian state model can only be a matter of speculation. What does seem clear is that in view of the obvious lack of national political parties, of a sense of nationality, of any and all of the attributes of a nation-state in being or in the making, the choice by the Belgians and the radical nationalist Congolese of a unitary state model ensured that, even if there were no other reason, political strife and fragmentation would afflict the Congo. It is one thing to conciliate and dissipate local and regiqnal fears and interests; it is another to deny and repress them.

The unitary states have, as we already noted, almost uniformly transformed themselves soon after independence from parliamentary systems to strong presidential systems. Once again Ghana has set the precedent. Prime Minister Nkrumah at the earliest convenient opportunity became a strong executive—head of state and government—with a proportionate decrease in the power of the reorganized Ghanaian parliament.

In the former French African territories, as a result of the special history of the French Community, transformation from a parliamentary system to a presidential system has generally coincided with the achievement of independence. When Sékou Touré led Guinea to "independence by secession" in the 1958 referendum, he set the pattern by becoming a president who was head of both state and government. The Gaullist constitution of 1958 in France has also served as a model for strong presidential systems in the newly emergent states of l'expression française. The American presidential system is also said to have served as a model, especially in Togo.

Thus the structure of the state apparatus has both reflected and influenced the search for stability. In the more typical case, exemplified by Ghana and the former French territories, the unitary state apparatus after independence made possible the complete centralization of power in the hands of the unitary government without restraint. In the rare case, exemplified by Nigeria, the state machinery established a distribution of powers within the society, which makes similar centralization extremely unlikely if not totally impossible. In the Ghanaian concept the achievement of stability must be sought through the ever-increasing concentration of power at the center; in the Nigerian concept, through protecting diversity and guaranteeing constitutional channels for the expression of such diversity.

Local government in former French and Belgian Africa and in large parts of British Africa never developed during the colonial era into a source or repository of effective power. As already noted, Nigeria was something of an exception to the rule. In the Gold Coast and Tanganyika some of the traditional rulers retained and even enhanced their power during the colonial period; but there the British, by building up strong governmental institutions at the center, counterbalanced the growth in power of the local traditional rulers and at the same time created the institutional framework for the eventual destruction of their power by the central government. Thus in most African states the inherited absence of strong local governmental institutions has contributed to or made easier the concentration of power at the center, and there has been little tendency since independence to build up local government through the devolution of power from the center. In Ghana, Nkrumah to a large extent broke the power of the remaining islands of traditional power based on local tribal areas soon after independence by use of the machinery of the central government.

The general paraphernalia of the colonial system for controlling political activity has also by and large been transferred, retained, or emulated by most of the newly independent African states as part of their state structures. Nkrumah, stung to the quick by British criticism of repressive political measures sponsored by him in Ghana, has been quick to reply that he learned his lessons well at the feet of successive British colonial governors and has merely continued to make use of the concepts and machiney bequeathed to him by the colonial overlords. Dr. Nkrumah had particular reference to the Ghanaian Preventive Detention Act and the new citizenship and nationality legislation under which long-time residents, unable to prove the nationality of their parents and grandparents in a country without vital statistics, could be expelled.[6] He could also have been referring equally, however, to the acts and practices which control the press and circumscribe political and trade union activity in the country. The Rule of Law has little scope in Ghana with respect to the political rights of the individual.

In the context of former French Africa, Guinea has taken over much of the colonial mechanism for control of political activity but has given it an efficiency and an ideological twist associated with its doctrine of a one-party state which exceed anything the colonial power attempted in this field in recent years. Other former French African states have in one degree or another retained colonial political control devices and adapted them to their own purpose. The Rule of Law has limited scope with respect to the political rights of individuals in a good many of the former French African states, ranging from a Communist-type conceptualization of the Rule of Law in Guinea which places all those opposed to the régime outside the law (i.e., they are by definition not covered by the law and not entitled to its protection) to pragmatic infractions or disregard of the Rule of Law in order to achieve immediate political objectives. For almost all of the new African states the right of the opposition to agitate for turning out the incumbent government is a relatively sophisticated concept either not fully understood or not accepted.

Once again, Nigeria, with its carefully evolved federal structure, written constitution with provisions to guarantee the powers of the regions and the rights of individuals, and independent judiciary, has made little or no use of this particular colonial heritage. By and large Nigeria has foregone this range of colonial practices or confined it to use only in cases of national emergency, and then only under specified constitutional and legal safeguards.

Nor is the Nigerian experience totally unexpected. K. C. Wheare, one of Britain's most eminent experts on federalism, "assumes it to be axiomatic that federalism is inseparable from liberal democracy. . . ." [7] Furthermore, in the words of another British authority:

> Federalism is essentially constitutional government. It rests on respect for constitutions, the rule of law, and an independent judiciary.[8]

The foregoing should not be taken to equate federalism with democracy. What it does equate is successfully operating federal systems with democratic political systems. In the absence of the latter the federal system is likely to fail. And on the other hand, the opportunity for a democratic system to work successfully in the new African states is considerably enhanced by a federal system, and diminished in the highly centralized unitary governmental structures emerging in many of the new states. In short, federal state structures and democratic political systems seem to need one another and to reinforce one another. We shall examine this connection more closely in the following section.

Political Systems

The political systems of the new African states tend to be authoritarian and to be identifiably either left or right. On the extreme left, Guinea verges on being a totalitarian state. Somewhat more typical of African authoritarian states, although moving in the direction of Guinea, is Ghana, Guinea's partner in the Ghana-Guinea unit. Mali, the most recent adherent to the Ghana-Guinea union, and the United Arab Republic also belong to the left-authoritarian group. The UAR has special characteristics deriving from the origin of the Nasser régime in a military *coup d'état* and the nature of Middle Eastern politics. The right-authoritarian states tend to cover a greater range and reflect to a greater extent local variations. Such diverse one-party states as the Ivory Coast, Mauritania, the Central African Republic, Liberia, and Katanga (if one were to consider Katanga for this limited purpose as a separate state) are right-authoritarian states.

Authoritarian Systems

The left-authoritarian states are characterized by a one-party system with a monopoly on the government apparatus and the channels of communication, the cardinal tenet being supremacy of the party over the state. This has been the case from the outset in Guinea, where the single power is the *Parti Démocratique de Guinée* (PDG). In Ghana, after some five years of independence, the Convention People's Party (CPP) has achieved much the same status as the PDG in Guinea by a series of pragmatic steps involving a bitter struggle between principal ministers and a group of MP's on the one hand and the party hierarchy on the other.

In Guinea the PDG neutralized a good deal of the opposition, actual and potential, in the twilight period between the enactment of the *loi cadre* in 1956 by the French Parliament and the achievement of independence in October 1958. The remaining opposition was liquidated after independence in a way now traditional with one-party authoritarian states the world over, including the use of the country's legal apparatus to impose criminal penalties for all sorts of "political crimes." The most heinous of these are "conspiracies to subvert the government," i.e., everything from mild but effective overt political opposition to actual plots to use force to overthrow the government.

In Ghana, under British administration the CPP could make life difficult for the opposition but was not in a position to eradicate it; however, since the achievement of independence in early 1957 opposition groups have been systematically nullified. First the trade unions were brought under control of the government through the Industrial Relations Act, which coerced unions into membership in a National Trades Unions Council controlled by the government. The same fate awaited the opposition farmers' organization, the independent press, the significant independent cooperative movement with its international affiliations, and the independent women's organizations. All of the recognized organizations, trade unions, farmers' councils, cooperatives, newspapers, and women's organizations have been put in the hands of the party's faithful. The Workers' Brigade operated by the government takes care of unemployed youth. The Preventive Detention Act takes care of opposition political leaders, non-conformists within the CPP, and other politically troublesome people. In short, the government apparatus of a centralized unitary state was used on behalf of or put at the disposition of the CPP, which in turn used it to liquidate all opposition.

The next step was accomplished in early 1961 when principal ministers seeking to exercise the authority of their ministries without recourse to the party hierarchy found themselves dismissed or demoted. At this juncture President Nkrumah, already Life Chairman of the CPP, assumed the position of General Secretary and Chairman of the Central Committee of the CPP, concentrating in his own hands the control of the party bureaucracy as well as the government bureaucracy in keeping with what has now become a tradition in Communist bloc countries.[9] President Nkrumah also became at various times over the next several months acting Foreign Minister, Minister of Defense, Minister of Economic Planning and Development, and Minister of the Interior. Finally, by the end of 1961, Dr. Nkrumah dismissed from his cabinet his two comrades-in-arms in the struggle for independence, Messrs. Gbedemah and Botsio, who went into hiding or exile (although Botsio has since made an adjustment and comeback); appointed a new ministerial team completely dependent on him and the party; became head of a new state control commission and new planning commission which are responsible for economic development, budgetary matters, and the economy generally; and became chancellor of the newly reorganized University of Ghana and the Kwame Nkrumah University of Science and Technology. Also during this time, after uncovering an alleged plot against his life and arresting in preventive detention forty-nine opposition and strike leaders [10] (who led a strike of port, railroad, and other transportation workers against Dr. Nkrumah's new austerity budget and forced savings measures which would take at least 5 per cent of wage-earners' salaries), Dr. Nkrumah sponsored and pushed through the rubber-stamp Ghanaian Parliament, now bereft of most of the opposition, who were being held in preventive detention or were in flight from the country, a bill establishing special new courts which could impose the death sentence, without the right of appeal, on those adjudged guilty by these courts of serious "political crimes," including the mounting number accused of conspiracy to subvert the government, destroy the state, or assassinate the Osagyefo (frequently translated to mean "Redeemer") Dr. Nkrumah, as he now officially styles himself. The concentration of authority in President–General Secretary Nkrumah's hands of course means that total power in the country is invested in the party hierarchy—which, Nkrumah has said on various occasions, with growing insistence, is as it should be. However, as a result of a series of assassination plots on the life of Nkrumah during 1962, two ministers and the Executive Secretary of the CPP have been placed in preventive detention, and the party hierarchy has been purged of "unreliable elements."

Thus in Guinea and Ghana we have two models of left-authoritarian régimes. The PDG in Guinea started with a considerable body of ideology, particularly with the ideas of the supremacy of the party over the state and the state over the individual.

In the words of President Touré to the children of the party faithful at the PDG headquarters:

Individualism is damned, because we have chosen the freedom, the right, the power, the sovereignty of the people, and not of the individual. . . . Before this people you should have no individual personality; your personality becomes a part of the personality of the nation, a part of the personality of the people. You cannot have any interest which is opposed to that of the people, for your interest must be an element which cannot be disassociated [sic] from the interest of the nation.[11]

The CPP in Ghana was largely devoid of ideology despite various pronouncements by Dr. Nkrumah of his "Christian-Marxist" beliefs, his fragmentary references in speeches and writing to "African socialism" and the supremacy of the party, his use of communist organizational tactics in building the CPP, his concept of the African personality, and his view that there is only one African ideology. With the exception of the organizational tactics none of these has been given precise definition.

The PDG has from the outset proclaimed its adherence to the principle of democratic centralism. Policies could be debated within the party apparatus but once decided were binding on the party and through the party's Politbureau on the government. Deviations would not be tolerated. It is only recently that the CPP has apparently reached much the same result, symbolized by the party's victory over the ministers.

The elaborate mechanism of the PDG for formulating party doctrine, including party conventions at the national level working down toward cells at the village level, exists more on paper than in fact in Ghana. There is no equivalent in Ghana of the annual party conference which adopts a national program and establishes party doctrine which then controls party policy and government action. There is no equivalent of the PDG Politbureau in Ghana. The analagous body provided for in the CPP's constitution, the Central Committee, has been a dead letter from the time that independence was achieved. Dr. Nkrumah has tended to keep party policy-making a personal preserve, admission to which he grants from time to time to those in personal favor. Increasingly these came from the left side of the CPP, and increasingly there were signs that the party machinery was becoming more powerful, aside from Dr. Nkrumah's manipulation of it, in response to the ministrations of the small group of young radicals on the party's left, headed by Ghana's then Minister of Information, Tawia Adamafio, who were the new intimates of Dr. Nkrumah. However, Adamafio and his associates either grew too strong or became too ambitious. They have now been purged; Adamafio and other leaders of his faction are being held in preventive detention accused of plotting against Nkrumah's life. The party machinery is now apparently safely in the hands of faithful adherents of Nkrumahism, as the new Ghanaian way of life is called.

In Guinea the PDG from the outset has tolerated no independent channels of communication. With independence and the expulsion of foreign newspapers and newsmen, Guinea was left totally without newspapers except for an irregularly produced PDG mimeographed broadsheet. The only radio station in the country was controlled by the government. Thus the PDG had the only effective channel of communication—namely, its own party apparatus which provided a network reaching out from Conakry to the most remote hamlet in the country.

In Ghana it has been necessary for the CPP to liquidate the independent or non-CPP press. With the capitulation of the last independent newspaper, *The Ashanti Pioneer*, in 1961, the job was completed. The radio has been in government hands and has been expanded to cover the country as well as large parts of West Africa and areas of East and Central Africa.[12] One British-owned newspaper, which continued to operate in Ghana within the practical limitations arising from the authoritarian political context, recently was taken over by a government-supported trust. No independent press remains in Ghana.

Both Guinea and Ghana invoke the police powers of the state to regulate, control, and repress political activity. The state structure provides all the necessary mechanisms. Arbitrary arrests and a severe circumscription of political rights are the rule in both states. Guinea has gone the whole way in this regard, with one-party lists and published results of 99 per cent in favor of the one-party lists and government policies. Ghana has still retained some of the external manifestations of free elections, but the trend is increasingly clear. Stability, it is said, requires continuity, and continuity precludes change. Thus power must be retained in the hands of the CPP. It is only a matter of time therefore before the token opposition which still exists in Ghana is likely to disappear. Against this background both states go to great lengths to conduct plebiscites and elections with universal adult suffrage, displays which have no greater meaning in African countries than in one-party states elsewhere.

Ideologically President Touré conceives of Guinea as a totalitarian democracy. The PDG is thought of as the custodian of the popular will and in this sense the only permissible voice in the country. All others are deemed counter-revolutionary or anti-democratic and therefore illegal. The PDG can do no wrong; it determines what the general will is, proceeds to give it expression, and safeguards it against "betrayal." Opposition to the PDG becomes betrayal of the people and treason to Guinea. President Touré announced immediately after independence that Guinea "will be the first African government to institute forced labor":

Forced labor will be imposed. . . . Rigorous measures will be taken for we shall not be influenced by electoral considerations. . . . This is why you should not even ask questions when you hear of harsh measures striking any person, no matter who; simply know that he or she has betrayed the nation, betrayed Guinea.[13]

The PDG is entrusted with total power because it claims to represent the totality of the people; and it is in this sense that it conceives of itself as democratic. There can be no argument about the fact that it is largely totalitarian.

Sékou Touré has described Guinea as a "popular dictatorship." Kwame Nkrumah has not yet gone this far. The CPP in
Ghana subscribes to some of the same tenets or theories as the
PDG, but not in the comprehensive and integrated sense that one
finds in the writings of Sékou Touré, and not in the systematic way
that one finds the PDG applying and administering party doctrine.
It is only in the last year that the CPP has openly activated some
of the tenets and theories it shares with the PDG. It is only now,
with opposition either liquidated or intimidated, that the CPP
has begun to put into practice on a significant scale its theories
about the key role of the party as "the vanguard" of the people
and its only true representative, about certain aspects of "African
socialism," e.g., state trading on a limited scale, and about "Africanization" of the officer corps of the country's armed forces. Also,
until mid-1961 the revolutionary jargon was more restrained, in a
lower key, and on the whole less meaningful as a guide to action
in Ghana than in Guinea.

It is more difficult to characterize the right-authoritarian
régimes than their counterparts on the left. They tend to have
less doctrine, and they tend to be less articulate about such doctrines as they do have. They tend to grow out of special local conditions and circumstances to a greater degree than the left variety.
For example, the one-party systems in the Ivory Coast, Mauritania,
the Central African Republic, Liberia, and Katanga tend to be
primarily the organizational response of the controlling groups in
the respective areas to the exercise and retention of power, although in the Ivory Coast the *Parti Démocratique de Côte
d'Ivoire*, the local section of the regional *Rassemblement Démocratique Africain* (RDA), for long the leading political and social
reforming party in French West Africa, has a mass following. In
each instance a group achieves power and, without conscious reference to such matters as relationship of party and state, democratic
centralism, the general will, and channels of communication, almost instinctively attempts to preclude or nullify opposition in
order to perpetuate its power. In Liberia and in the Ivory Coast
the practice has been to absorb individuals in opposition, or likely
to be in opposition, into the single party through patronage, jobs,
contracts, and all of the other techniques so familiar to political

parties in most parts of the world. This does not mean that from time to time other pressures, including exhortation, coercion, and force, have not been used to still opposition. The efficiency, the ideological motivation, and the institutionalized nature of such pressures in left-authoritarian states, however, have not often been a feature of right-authoritarian states, with the possible exception, at an earlier date, of the Ivory Coast and more recently of Katanga. With respect to the latter there has been more of an air of improvisation and even desperation rather than long-term policy and established routine about the repression of opposition, particularly on doctrinal grounds.

Tunisia and Senegal are essentially one-party states that cannot be placed in either of the foregoing two groups. Although left oriented in political philosophy, and although the party machines are among the best organized from top to bottom, Tunisia and Senegal have so far, under the leadership of Presidents Bourguïba and Senghor, respectively, escaped a good deal of the xenophobia and closed-society mentality of the authoritarian systems at work in Guinea and Ghana. One does not get the same sense of political fear, tension, and insecurity in Tunisia and Senegal that one does in the left-authoritarian states. Nevertheless, the *Néo-Destour* Party in Tunisia is perfectly capable on the one hand of dealing out summary political punishment to internal political opposition, e.g., prison and exile, and on the other of mobilizing thousands of Tunisians on short notice for all sorts of massive public demonstrations, including such violent affairs as the pocket war with France which occurred in Bizerte in July 1961. And although from time to time small splinter parties appear in Senegal, their life is not an easy one.

There is thus a clear preference among African leaders for authoritarian political systems, which are combined with unitary state structures, to produce strong one-party systems of the left or right. Most frequently, the one-party system is headed by an unchallenged leader. It is not always clear whether the leader controls the party or *vice versa*. One suspects, with the exception of Guinea, perhaps, that the situation generally starts out with the leader controlling the party, and that with time he either entrenches his control or finds that he must share it with new forces which arise, and which he may in large part be responsible for, e.g., the probable situation evolving in Ghana prior to the purge of Adamafio.

Democratic Systems: Nigeria and Sierra Leone

Nigeria has the most democratic political system in Africa. As already noted, it operates within a federal structure under an entrenched Bill of Rights. Power is shared by the regional governments and the federal government, and in varying degrees by the regional governments with local authorities. Political activity, except in the Northern Region, where there have been repeated allegations by the Action Group of interference by the Native Authority's police with their political campaigns, has been open, relatively free from governmental interference, and widespread. Most recently the Western Region, which in many ways has been most advanced in political and economic development, has been having a rough passage, which has put in question not only its capacity and willingness but that of the entire country to operate successfully a democratic political system.[14] The governmental crisis (described in detail in note 14 to this chapter) has not yet run its course. What may be ventured at this point is that the rule of law has been much in evidence and although subjected to considerable pressure has not yet been impaired.

The principal political parties in Nigeria up to now all have had access to the public press and, in fact, all publish party newspapers. The Action Group, which was in control of the Western Region government, is in opposition at the national level; nevertheless, in the Western Region it has had access to radio and television facilities as well as newspapers.

The whole atmosphere of Nigeria, including that obtaining locally in the three regions, has been drastically different than that found anywhere else in Africa. Stability here has not meant consolidating the power of one party or one leader as in the authoritarian states; it has meant established and recognized channels and processes for expressing opinions and advocating change, with the expectation that change would be brought about in a peaceful way through the orderly and largely unhindered use of the constitutional political processes. For example, the Dynamic Party, a splinter party in the Eastern Region, has been able to organize itself and campaign on a platform of violent criticism of the coalition federal government with particular reference to corruption in the federal government. It was also able to campaign in the Eastern Region in the autumn of 1961 against the controlling National Convention of Nigerian Citizens, in a free-swinging fight on a range of issues, including alleged corruption, and win five seats in the Regional Parliament. This is in sharp contrast to Ghana, where President Nkrumah took to the radio in his now famous dawn broadcast in which he inveighed against corruption in public life. Nkrumah's was a type of auto-criticism reminiscent of the practice in Iron Curtain countries where the leadership lashes out against bourgeois corruption before launching charges or liquidating personalities. The Nkrumah dismissal and demotion of ministers, already referred to, coincided with or subsequently relied on the dawn broadcast or allegation of conspiracies against the security of the state or his person by opposition forces seeking change. The Dynamic Party action in Nigeria has been much more suggestive of political opposition in a western democratic country, where it is unexceptionable for an opposition party to campaign on the subject of corruption and inefficiency in government.

Of the multi-party unitary states, Sierra Leone perhaps has the most democratic political system. Opposition groups and parties exist and operate with fewer restrictions than in most other unitary states in Africa. Nonetheless, the accession of Sierra Leone to independence in early 1961 was marred by the action of the government in seizing the leaders, among them Siaka Stevens, of the opposition All Peoples' Congress and imprisoning them during the independence period and for a short period thereafter. The opposition had been involved in acts of minor violence and had threatened more on the eve of independence, and the government acted in response to these provocations.[15] Subsequently Sir Milton Margai, Prime Minister of Sierra Leone, invited into his government most of the leaders of the opposition and constituted a coalition government, dominated by his party. There were still, however, individuals in opposition, notably Mr. Stevens, who from time to time coalesced in opposition parties. Most recently, in the 1962 elections for the Sierra Leone parliament, a coalition of opposition parties led by Mr. Stevens scored a significant victory, winning twenty seats in parliament against twenty-eight for Sir Milton Margai's party. By contrast, in the multi-party unitary states in former French Africa frequent recrimination over the government party's use of the government machinery to the disadvantage of the political opposition has been the rule. For example, in the Congo (Brazzaville) Abbé Youlou, the President, more or less effectively disposed of the opposition party through use of armed force, and in Upper Volta the governing RDA party banned opposition parties and exiled their leader, M. Nazi Boni. In many instances the result has been the growth of *le parti unifié*, which is in fact basically *le parti unique* (the one-party system).

Some Conclusions

Despite the promise of Nigeria and the importance of its potential for influencing developments in other African states, it remains very much the unique case on a continent beset by an authoritarian trend. Centralized unitary governments have proven to be much more consonant with the development of authoritarian systems than with democratic systems. They generally provide a structure which concentrates power at the center and more readily allows for one-party control and manipulation, in contrast to the inevitable dispersion of power in a federal structure which makes it more difficult to control all the levers of power and to manipulate them with ease. They also allow for the concentration of the leadership elite at the center to the exclusion of the rest of the country, in contrast to a federal structure which at least keeps open the opportunity for leadership elites in the regions. Authoritarian systems are numerous and increasing.

Remaining multi-party unitary states, particularly among the former French territories, as we have noted, are tending toward the one-party system. Here Sierra Leone presents something of an exception. The dominant party, through use of the governmental apparatus, tends to harass and circumscribe opposition parties. At the extreme, armed force has been used to break the back of opposition strength.

The left-authoritarian states tend to emulate the organizational techniques and tactics of the Communist bloc. Guinea seems to be moving toward a totalitarian pattern, and Ghana now seems to be following closely behind. The drive toward unity has become the central impulse in the left-authoritarian political system, and unity is taken to mean uniformity, rather than "unity in diversity" as Nigeria's goal has been described.

Right-authoritarian models on the African scene, with the possible exception of the Ivory Coast, seldom achieve the same level of unity *cum* uniformity as the left versions. They seldom have the same ideological compulsion to achieve unanimity. Ordinarily the absence of effective opposition and the acceptance, albeit reluctant, of the government's role and positions are sufficient. Participation by the masses is not generally thought to be as important by right-authoritarian states as by those of the left.

If the first conclusion is valid and the trend toward authoritarianism is as strong as the foregoing analysis would suggest, then it becomes important to understand the rationalization for the trend given by the leaders of the new African states—particularly if one is going to deal effectively with the situation.

The choice of authoritarian systems by African leaders has been rationalized on the ground that political stability for its own sake and as a necessary precondition of economic growth precludes debate, difference, and dissent, all of which are equated with disorder. They are enjoined as luxuries which an underdeveloped state with a largely illiterate population living at the subsistence level can ill afford, or, worse, as part of a colonialist plot to divide the people and sap their strength. Opposition parties are viewed as "stooge" parties for neo-colonialist forces. Stability in this view requires uniformity, unity, and unanimity, all of which are equated with order. Order is solidarity behind the one party and its leader, which gives them the strength to achieve "jet-propelled" national development and resist colonial and neo-colonial conspiracies. Thus departures from the Rule of Law with respect to the political and civil rights of individuals are justified as necessary to maintain the order which is indispensable to stability and growth.

This view holds that tribalism must be suppressed in order to build national cohesion and national loyalties. If incidentally all the forces of traditional power and local power are destroyed in the process, that is said to be an unavoidable sacrifice at the altar of national unity. All traditional religious institutions and bodies which stand in the way of the drive toward national unity must give way. And so everything from traditional religions to Christianity, to the extent they represent independent or alternative sources of power or persuasion, must be dealt with at arm's length as potential or active adversaries. Cultural characteristics which deviate from the newly adopted or rediscovered traditional national norms must be viewed with suspicion, and even be suppressed where they tend to create a basis for non-conformism. Economic power must be tamed. Foreign economic power must be circumscribed and controlled; indigenous economic power must be brought within the governmental orbit through state ownership or regulation or through state favors and corruption. Only thus can economic development be achieved in a hurry, and, the left-authoritarians would add, free from imperialist interference. A free press and free assembly tend to cause diversity; political opposition creates unrest and disunity. Thus regulation, control, and suppression are indispensable to still these disruptive and anti-cohesive forces.

Uniformity must be forged; unity of the party and the state must be achieved; and unanimity of opinion must result. Then, and only then, democratic order and rule can be said to prevail. For example, Guinea can point to mass participation in government. Everybody supports the PDG; everybody votes for the one-party list; everybody casts his ballot for Sékou Touré. This unanimity, now identified with "popular democracy" in Guinea, must be maintained at all cost. The instruments of authoritarianism—coercion, force, social pressure, rewards, education, indoctrination, propaganda, external enemies and internal plots, and external adventures—must all be invoked to this end. All individual and group interests must be sacrificed to unanimity, which means strength and stability. The rationalization of the right-authoritarian models is substantially the same except that they would arrive at the same place—unopposed support for the one party in control—without the ideological baggage. Strength and stability are still the goal, and they can best be obtained by suppressing or dissipating differences and opposition.

In the frank but relatively modulated and non-ideological words of the head of a state which does not belong either to the radical nationalist bloc of African states or to the right-authoritarian category, Habib Bourguiba of Tunisia:

> If they accuse me of dictatorship, I accept. I am creating a nation. Liberty must be suppressed until the end of the war in Algeria —until the nation becomes homogeneous. . . . The state and its existence are essential before anything else. All this preoccupation with liberty is not serious.[16]

Looking ahead Tanganyika has one predominant party, the Tanganyika African National Union, and weak scattered opposition: the outlook is for the development of a one-party state. On the other hand, Uganda, which is already independent, and Kenya, which is approaching independence, are likely to have multi-party systems for the present. Nyasaland, with the overwhelmingly strong and well-organized Malawai Congress Party under Dr. Banda, and given the history of the bitter struggle against Nyasaland's inclusion in the Federation of Rhodesia and Nyasaland, seems well on the way to a left-authoritarian one-party model. In view of the strife and violence Northern Rhodesia has been exposed to, and Southern Rhodesia is now exposed to, authoritarian one-party systems would seem to be looming on the horizon there, notwithstanding the existence of several parties at the present in both territories. Thus one must conclude that among the crop of recent states and those in the offing will be a number which will reinforce or redirect the trend toward authoritarianism.

The pattern of authoritarianism we have outlined here has an ominously familiar shape. The model of the Communist state seems to loom large in the minds of African leaders. Yet the rationale offered for use of this model is not the aim of achieving a communist society or building a Communist satellite but rather that it is necessary and even inevitable for the creation of a social revolution in a compressed time period, a revolution distinctly African in nature and growing out of African conditions. In fact, many of the new leaders have gone out of their way to demonstrate that the uniformity called for in their democracy grows out of ancient tribal tradition and custom, by which tribal chieftains relied on the advice of elders and a final decision was never taken until the advisers had endless "palavers" leading to unanimity.

There can be little doubt that the divisive forces of tribalism and religious differences are widespread throughout African society. And there is little doubt that differences in economic wealth, as we shall see, have been a strong motive for separatism on the part of those states or areas that are in the "have" category. One approach to coping with differences long imbued and still dominant in many areas in the absence of other more prevailing or attractive forces is to dissipate and suppress the differences. This will, if successful, forge a type of cohesion, as has already been observed, and establish a type of stability in which forces for change from the prevailing norms of the incumbent group are apparently absent. For many of the African leaders committed to authoritarian political systems, particularly those on the left who are committed to "social mobilization of the masses" behind their parties, the divisive elements of African society are undoubtedly a significant factor in the choice of political systems as well as of unitary political structures. By contrast, federalism is generally thought of by its adherents as responsive to difference and as containing separatist pulls by recognizing them and giving them an outlet within larger and newer concepts of a federal structure and an accompanying federal nationality, and thus conducive to democratic political systems.

It is difficult if not impossible, as we have already intimated, to distinguish the motives of African leaders making the choice of authoritarianism. As we have suggested, many believe it is the most effective way to cope with centrifugal forces, which obviously exist and are potent. Other African leaders, a small group to be sure, characterized by the leadership group in general in Nigeria, have in the face of similar divisive forces opted for "unity in diversity," banking on the centripetal effect of forces deriving from the promise of political harmony and economic development within the larger federal union of Nigeria, which could not have come into being without the tolerance of difference implied in a democratic system, and political importance and leadership abroad.

There can be little doubt that among ideologically oriented African leaders the authoritarian route is also preferred for doctrinal reasons which may have obtained even in the absence of the tribal and other divisive factors. Then, too, there can be little question that for party or personal reasons deriving from little more than ordinary power drives some African leaders have chosen the authoritarian way. And one suspects that in so complicated an individual as Dr. Nkrumah all of these aspects are present in one degree or another, plus the all-consuming drive he has to be a Pan-African leader. Stability at home, at one's base, as we shall see, is obviously a key precondition to carrying on a Pan-African crusade on the large continent of Africa. Thus the rationalization offered for authoritarianism by African leaders undoubtedly reflects African conditions and the judgment of the leaders as to how best to deal with them, as well as concealing ideological and power motives of parties and men, which are frequently inextricably commingled.

Therefore all we can do is be aware of the rationalization, what it means and what it conceals, and put the following queries in every African context where the authoritarian trend is manifest.

Can and will the trend mark a step, as many African leaders characterize it—a step on the way to modernized, stable, economically developed societies which can afford the luxury of liberal democracy? Or will authoritarianism become a permanent condition, leading in some instances to development, and in others concealing stagnation, but in all instances entrenched and resistant to change except by force? And once the "national liberation" movement occurs and the authoritarian structure and system is created, to what extent has the stage been set for a change at the top—a substitution of one authoritarianism for another, of Communism for the local African brand?

These are the imponderables which the continent-wide trend toward authoritarianism contains for the African states and for the outside world. The answers and their implications for African economic and political development are likely to vary considerably in the various African contexts. Only in the unique non-authoritarian case of Nigeria thus far is there substantial promise of economic development in democratic circumstances; Nigeria initially accepted this goal and has developed a happy combination of federal structure and democratic political system working toward this end. Much is at stake in Nigeria—for the country itself, in its growth and development; for Africa, in producing a vivid example of development and democracy existing together for economic growth and political stability; and for the free world, in the emergence of an important state with a system and interests compatible with those of other free-world states. As for most of the authoritarian states, it is much too soon to discern their ultimate position, and prediction is beyond the purpose of this essay.

Chapter 9

FOCUS OF STABILITY: NATIONALISM, PAN-AFRICANISM, AND EURAFRICANISM

We have seen how the search for stability, strength, and growth is reflected in the African rationale of internal development—in the shape of state structures and in the emerging political systems. And we have seen that, although there are conflicting African views of the correct path of internal policy, there is a major and increasing trend toward the authoritarian state and the one-party system. The search for stability is, of course, bound to be reflected also in the African assignment of relative priorities to internal development and external relationships and in the rationale developed for external relationships, especially those among the African nations themselves.

A principal phenomenon of the age is the emergence of blocs, unions, communities, and other groupings of nations—regional, religious, political, economic—all for the purpose of combining strength vis-à-vis the other actors on the world stage while assuring stability and growth at home. African leadership, which could hardly be unaware of or ignore this historical turn, has thus looked outward—to neighboring Africa, to neighboring Europe—as well as inward to internal circumstances; and already, in the context of the search for stability as it is reflected in the African emphasis on internal development vis-à-vis external affairs and in the related rationale of external relations policies, there can be discerned three distinct African movements—nationalism, Pan-Africanism, Eurafricanism.

All three are rooted in the African nationalism for which independence was sought and attained, and which all of independent Africa is now engaged in building. For nationalism in Africa does not start out with a hard core of unifying factors—common language, common religion, common cultural attainments, common history and mythology, and common symbols. African nationalism has been characterized by educated elites leading large inarticulate masses in anti-colonial movements toward the goal of independence. After the achievement of the legal status of independence—international sovereignty, in de Gaulle's phrase—the leaders of the new African states will have to build the nationalism they have long proclaimed, aspire to, need, and want but do not have as the foundation for the political and economic development of their countries. Hence the priority assigned to nation-building, and the rationalization provided for authoritarianism.

African leaders have chosen to follow different roads in building this all-important nationalism. Some have concentrated simply on building their respective countries into nations. Others have sought to merge the task into a larger task—of creating an African personality, an African ideology, and an African social structure in a union of African states. In short, they have replaced the building of nationalism in their own lands with the goal of a Pan-African nation. And still others have sought to develop their states' nationalism in conjunction with the forging of new or recasting of old links with the former European metropoles.

The African leaders who have chosen the Pan-African route may be characterized as radical nationalists. They tend to combine the thrust toward independence and the task of nation-building in a larger framework of integrated states with a social revolutionary mission: they seek to restructure society, the relationship of the individual to the state, and the state to the party—the one party in the left-authoritarian one-party state. As part of the social revolution they seek to develop an economic system called "African socialism" through use of authoritarian development models. Sékou Touré, Kwame Nkrumah, and Modibo Keita are the principal examples of the type.

Most of the remaining African leaders are nationalists committed to building their nation-states as an end in itself or as a precondition to the establishment at a later date of larger political groupings of African states. Of these a good many, particularly from states of *l'expression française*, are also Eurafrican in their outlook. In greater or lesser degree they seek to associate their nationalism with various extra-African ties or links ranging across systems of states, monetary zones, trading areas, defense systems, and a multiplicity of individual economic and cultural arrangements.

The purpose of this chapter is to look at the nature of and participants in these movements and particularly at the antagonisms and conflicts among them.

Individual Country Nationalism

Nationalism in Africa found its first organized expression after World War II. The relatively mature nationalism of Asia first swept the postwar scene; Indonesia, the Philippines, India, Pakistan, Burma, Ceylon, the new states in the Indo-Chinese peninsula, and others made their hasty appearance among the ranks of the world's independent states. Then came Africa's turn in the late 1950's and early 1960's. A thin layer of educated African leaders demanded independence and in many instances were surprised that the demand was enough. For independence followed the demand, frequently even before a minimal anti-colonial unity could be developed, let alone a sense of nation among the disparate population brought together within "frontiers which were drawn to suit the convenience of colonial powers," in the words of Dr. Nkrumah.

It was logical, then, that for the new African states which

emerged before Ghana—Libya, the Sudan, Tunisia, and Morocco —their national borders were their horizons. But with Ghana's appearance in 1957 African nationalism became intimately interwoven with vaguely idealistic concepts of Pan-Africanism current in some American and Antillean Negro circles to which Nkrumah was exposed as a student in the United States and England. Nkrumah at first held the Pan-African stage as a solo performer; with Guinea's appearance in late 1958 he was joined by Touré. These two leaders beat the Pan-African drums insistently and repetitiously. Their radical nationalism embraced a vague and somewhat mystical concept of African unity involving an African personality, an African ideology, and increasingly something called "African socialism" in a union of African states. They were more or less successful at the doctrinal level in investing African nationalism with an essentially supranationalist quality for the first wave of new national leaders. The original thrust of African nationalism, to drive the European colonialists out and to build new nation-states, seemed to have been merged into the drive for African unity. Almost by sleight of hand the merged doctrine of independence *cum* Pan-Africanism was substituted by the principal African actors on the stage.

The success of Pan-Africanism was not so complete as it seemed. While weaker opposing forces felt that discretion compelled temporary silence, President Tubman of Liberia sought to hold the Pan-Africanists in check until more of the expected African states emerged; and with the long-awaited emergence of Nigeria late in 1960 the original focus of African nationalism of building nation-states was reasserted. Nigeria, a federation of three distinct regions, each with a different principal tribal group, had in its very make-up a sufficient challenge as it set out to build its state structure and national cohesion as well as its underdeveloped economy and backward technology, particularly as the leadership of Nigeria set out to do this by voluntaristic means within a democratic framework. The Nigerian banner of nationalism at home rallied other of the new African states which shared the desire to focus first on their own development but were too weak or too young to challenge the Pan-Africanist wave. Nineteen of them joined with Nigeria in May 1961 at Monrovia in reasserting the doctrine of political independence for each African state, accompanied by interstate economic coordination, educational and cultural exchanges and cooperation, joiht health and social undertakings, and integrated transport and telecommunication grids.

When the Monrovia powers, twenty strong, rejected Pan-Africanism as a political goal for the foreseeable future, they were in effect proclaiming the doctrine of individual country nationalism. Moreover, they were proclaiming a doctrine immediately attacked as reactionary, as a defense of the "*status quo* in Africa," by the champions of Pan-Africanism, who called the advocates of the Monrovia principles "lackeys" of "the divide and rule policy of the imperialists." [1] What, then, is individual country nationalism in Africa?

The opening address of President Tubman, speaking for the host nation at the Monrovia Conference, put the philosophy of individual country nationalism in these words:

> Political union is attained by virtue of agreement. In the absence of free agreement any form of political union is but imperial domination. . . . History has clearly demonstrated that political union as opposed to political domination can be more readily achieved where there is a community of economic interest, cultural cross-fertilization, as well as free social intercourse and association.[2]

Sir Milton Margai, Prime Minister of Sierra Leone, responding for English-speaking Africa to the opening address, formulated it in this way:

> We have, from time to time, given open support to the principle of African unity which respects the territorial integrity of each state, the free choice of political ideology, and form of government. . . . We are willing to begin discussion as soon as possible in those areas where we believe that we can most readily apply these principles of co-operation, particularly in the fields of education, cultural cross-fertilization, and communication.[3]

And to make it unanimous, President Léopold Senghor of Senegal, speaking for the French-language African states, declared:

> . . . If we wish to succeed, we must emphasize cultural, technical, and economic co-operation rather than the co-operation of political

parties. We must advance step by step, keeping our feet firmly on the ground.[4]

The Monrovia Conference resolutions spelled out what its leading spokesmen had already said when they emphasized the equality of African states, reiterated time and again the principle of non-interference of African states in one another's internal affairs, proclaimed for each state the "inalienable right to existence and development of its personality," called for cooperation, advocated "the non-acceptance of any leadership," and rejected political unity and integration of African states and substituted the "unity of aspirations and of action considered from the point of view of African social solidarity and political identity" as the proper posture for African states.

The Monrovia Conference powers thus gave a doctrinal definition to individual country nationalism. For them there were to be as many roads to the promised land of political stability and economic growth as there were members. African states were to develop their own political structures and systems, their own national personalities. They would cooperate in those areas which lend themselves to cooperation in the mutual interest. Political cooperation would be by conferences and contact arranged by a standing secretariat, which should result in agreement on political positions where the African states have an identity of national interests. Eventually this type of cooperation, if successful and rewarding for its practitioners, might lead some to political grouping and unions. Thus the Monrovia powers would now and for the foreseeable future endeavor "to present a united front" on world problems which might confront Africa at the United Nations.

At the time of the Monrovia Conference the doctrine of individual country nationalism had twenty adherents with an estimated population of eighty-five to ninety million people, or about two-fifths of the people of Africa. This represents far and away the largest single bloc on the continent with almost one-fifth of the votes in the United Nations. The membership of the Monrovia bloc has fluctuated but has never dropped below eighteen, the number which constituted itself the Inter-African and Malagasy States Organisation in December 1962.

Pan-Africanism

One strand of Pan-Africanism has grown out of the experience and beliefs of Dr. Nkrumah, who is the active projector of it today on the African scene. As a student in the United States, Nkrumah became familiar with the history of the Garveyite Back-to-Africa movement for American Negroes, and later, as a student in the United Kingdom, he became an intimate of the late George Padmore, an early advocate of Pan-Africanism who until his death was to be Prime Minister Nkrumah's advisor on African affairs. Padmore's book, *Pan-Africanism or Communism?*, published in 1956, became a classic for the Nkrumah school of Pan-Africanism. Nkrumah distilled the mystique and philosophy of Pan-Africanism into one cogent sentence in his autobiography:

Its ideology became African nationalism—a revolt by African nationalism against colonialism, racialism, and imperialism in Africa —and it adopted Marxist socialism as its philosophy.[5]

As a political reality Pan-Africanism made its bow with Ghanaian independence in April 1957 and its formal debut with the first Conference of Independent African States a year later at Accra. The compressed time period between the political birth and adolescence of Pan-Africanism is about typical for Africa, a continent in a hurry to make felt its presence on the world scene.

Nkrumah's Pan-Africanism had little specific political content beyond anti-colonialism everywhere on the African continent. It was to be built around an African personality, which has never been defined. Like natural law, it was there to be discovered, and Nkrumah was, in his view, destined to discover it. An African ideology, which also has not been defined, has been added; and most recently "the Marxist socialism" element, which had been relegated to the back shelf during Nkrumah's drive to win friends and influence African leaders, has been revived as "African socialism" and has been blended in as an important ingredient. Essentially the guiding principle has been that in union there is strength, and that, after generations of subjection to predatory European colonialism, strength, security, and stability for Africa necessitate a union of African states.

Nkrumah's Pan-African movement made Accra a center of African political intrigue, a haven for disaffected or exiled African nationalists from independent as well as colonial areas. Ghanaian financing for nationalist movements everywhere in Africa became increasingly a feature of the African political landscape.

Nkrumah's movement also sought to turn the physical barrier of the Sahara into a political bridge between North and sub-Sahara Africa. First the United Arab Republic, and then Morocco, Libya, and Tunisia were drawn into the vortex of African politics.

Unity against colonialism and imperialism in Africa has been the cement of Nkrumah's Pan-Africanism. He rejected Nasser's early attempt to introduce Arab and Near Eastern politics into the African scene. He tended to ignore cold-war politics, and his early neutralism did not prevent him from refusing to allow the Soviet Union to establish an embassy in Accra for over eighteen months or from taking aid exclusively from the West during that period. The British remained relatively close. The French were cast in the role of colonialist villain.

But then a rival strand of Pan-Africanism appeared in late 1958 to challenge Nkrumah's Pan-African monologue—and alter its composition and mood. The second strand grew out of Sékou Touré's philosophy of African unity for doctrinaire purposes. Touré saw the triumph of the Guinean social revolution in a wider African context, much as the early Communists saw the success of the Russian revolution assured only in terms of world revolution. Socialism in one land alone was anathema to the early Communist, as is individual country nationalism to Touré and his followers. So long as political unity is not achieved, the social revolution which Touré sees as urgent for Africa, and political development on authoritarian lines which he sees as vitally necessary for Africa, are not attainable. The colonial heritage of contrived boundaries must be washed away in an ideological surge which will enlarge the stage for revolution and left-authoritarianism, and then and only then will economic development be meaningful. Only then could dependence on colonialist monetary and trading areas be overcome and be replaced by a continental African system. In the words of President Touré to the National Conference of Cadres of the *Parti Démocratique de Guinée* in April 1960:

> Guinea is not just an area of 250,000 square kilometers; Guinea is not just three million people; Guinea shares the interests of the totality of African peoples and, as may be required, shares jointly the destiny of all of Africa. This is why we shall never make any decision which would not be historically valid as a factor in increasing the liberating power of African peoples.[6]

To this end Touré has actively supported the formation of a Pan-African or All-African Trade Union Federation, an All-African Organization of Journalists, an All-African Military Command, an All-African Economic Union, many disaffected African political émigré and splinter movements, and, of course, basic and foremost, the Union of African States, to which Guinea, Ghana, and Mali belong, and which has been up to now ineffectual. Only the trade union movement has in any degree transcended the radical nationalist trio of states and their three North African associates in the Casablanca bloc in drawing its membership, but even so the major Casablanca-Monrovia bloc division is clearly reflected. The All-Africa Trade Union Federation draws its inspiration from the radical nationalist trio of states and emphasizes the African nature of the movement, rigorously opposing all extra-African ties. The broader African trade union grouping, the African Trade Union Confederation, founded at Dakar in early 1962, reflects the Monrovia power orientation, emphasizes labor issues *per se*, and allows for extra-African ties of its national members, which means essentially ties with the anti-communist International Confederation of Free Trade Unions.

In response to the impact of Touré's more radical brand of Pan-Africanism, and the series of frustrations experienced by Nkrumah in his attempt to envelop the new states with his Pan-Africanist wave, Ghana's Pan-Africanism moved closer and closer to Guinea's. It became sharper in its aims and more truculent in its means. The radical nationalist gospel became increasingly the political content of Pan-Africanism. To unity, social revolution was added as a goal. Then "national liberation," a doctrine emerging from the conference of Communist parties in December 1960, was added. Not only the colonial powers but also the so-called neo-colonialist "stooge" governments were to be ousted from power in Africa. "Free national development," the Communist euphemism for economic development along "non-capitalist" lines, i.e., along "socialist" lines, was also adopted and became the occasion for the re-emphasis of African socialism. The ideological view of African socialism in Guinea and the pragmatic view of it in Ghana have become clear enough, as we have seen in Chapter 3, to suggest what is meant by African socialism. Apparently Nkrumah now equates it with "free national development."

By the summer of 1961 the merger of radical nationalism with Pan-Africanism was complete. Ghana and Guinea had bridged and to a degree reconciled the differences in their brands of Pan-Africanism, motivated in part by the setback both received in their attempts to impose their respective ideas on the Congo through Prime Minister Lumumba. The Communist doctrines of "national liberation" and "free national development" were so largely accepted by the radical nationalist trio of Ghana, Guinea, and Mali and incorporated in the foreign policy outlook of the Pan-Africanist union that these three states launched in the summer of 1961 the reconstituted Ghana-Guinea "nucleus of a union" under the style of the Union of African States.

The accession of Mali to the Ghana-Guinea union represented the high tide of Pan-Africanism in 1961. The union remains largely a paper organization with few institutions and fewer special ties, and with no concessions of sovereignty on the part of the members to a central or supranational government. Such a government may come into being, but it can hardly be said to exist now any more than does an underlying common national interest uniting the three countries or their three leaders, Nkrumah, Touré, and Modiba Keita, President of Mali. As independence preceded the nationalism in the name of which it was achieved, so Pan-African groupings may precede the welding together of the interests of the constituent states.

There can be no question of the appeal of the Pan-African concept to many African leaders. In East Africa there has been a less intense and less doctrinaire movement toward a grouping of

African states. President Nyerere of Tanganyika has been in the forefront of a movement to associate the three British East African territories on their accession to independence. Nyerere's timetable had to be revised in view of Tanganyika's achieving independence in December 1961, well ahead of the other East African territories. In the summer of 1961 Nyerere was able to get the agreement of the African leadership of Kenya and Uganda and the approval of the United Kingdom to transform the East Africa High Commission, which provided some twenty common services for the three territories, into a body with the same functions but run by four ministers each from independent Tanganyika and the two remaining colonial territories, and to retain on an *ad interim* basis the customs union among the three areas. The stop-gap arrangements were to keep open the possibility of an East African federation, building on these essentially economic ties instituted originally by the British colonial administrations, with the advent of independence of Kenya and Uganda. Uganda became independent in October 1962, and its Prime Minister, Apollo Milton Obote, has joined Julius Nyerere in pressing the United Kingdom to grant independence to Kenya so that the leaders of three independent African states can take decisions to develop the East African Common Services Organization into something closer to a regional federation.

Eurafricanism

There are many degrees and variants of Eurafricanism. Common to all is a continuation of many of the economic, cultural, military, and political links between former European metropoles and former African territories in new forms and in new ways. The links have been rearranged and adapted to take account of the changed status of Africa. The accession to independence of the African territories has emphasized the need for mutuality in constituting the arrangements and sharing the benefits.

The British Empire has been transformed into the Commonwealth, and the British African territories, with independence, have uniformly sought Commonwealth membership. Ghana was first and, despite its Pan-African role, has retained its membership. Nkrumah has been able not only to reconcile Ghana's Commonwealth link with his Pan-African leadership but also to avoid the slings and arrows which his fellow Pan-Africanists have directed at African states associated with the Franco-African Community. Recently, however, there have been some disapproving murmurs. Associated with Commonwealth membership has been participation in the Imperial Trade Preference System, membership in the sterling area, participation in the Special Commonwealth African Aid Program, access to the British capital market, numerous cultural and education exchange programs, and a variety of economic, technical, and military assistance arrangements.

Through many, and for most through all, of these Eurafrican links Ghana, Nigeria, Sierra Leone, Tanganyika, and Uganda have maintained their relationship with the United Kingdom in the post-independence period. Ghana, however, would distinguish its Eurafrican links from those linking Nigeria and Sierra Leone to the United Kingdom. A veteran Pan-Africanist and radical nationalist state, as such things are measured in Africa today, Ghana escapes the suspicion to which more recent adherents to these doctrines are liable. In addition, Nigeria and Sierra Leone have negotiated defense pacts with the United Kingdom. Although the Nigerian–United Kingdom agreement has by mutual consent been abrogated, the substance of the arrangements under the agreement continue in effect. The fact that approximately the same *de facto* relationships have existed between Ghana and the United Kingdom is discreetly ignored.

The reconstituted Franco-African Community has provided for the former French Equatorial territories and some of the former French West African territories the famework for the renovated links with France. For the former French territories outside the Community the renovated links are, for the most part, not readily distinguishable from those within the Community. France continues its close economic, cultural, military, and political ties with Community and non-Community members alike. The trade and aid relationships continue both on a bilateral basis and on a multilateral basis within the framework of the European Economic

Community. The cultural and military links continue on a bilateral basis. And the close political links continue on a bilateral basis, and on a multilateral basis on the African side, through the Brazzaville bloc of twelve.

The association of African states with the EEC, the Common Market, represents the high-water mark of Eurafricanism. All the former French territories, except Guinea and possibly Mali, which has retained its association with the EEC but is still equivocating, Somalia, the Congo, Rwanda and Burundi, are closely and elaborately linked with their former metropoles and other continental European powers in preferential trade arrangements and in favorable aid arrangements through the Overseas Development Fund of the EEC. The EEC, taking note of the independence of all of its associated African members, is reconstituting itself under a new Convention of Association to accommodate the change. The African states have negotiated a status compatible with their sovereign status. If successful in its reconverted form, the EEC will strengthen the economic links of its European and African members and reinforce the Eurafrican outlook of its African members.

Unless the African membership of the EEC is broadened to include former British African territories, the Common Market is potentially a divisive factor for the Monrovia bloc, which, despite its essentially Eurafrican tendency, is composed of both EEC and non-EEC members. Moreover, the abortive British attempt to gain membership in the Common Market, if renewed and more successful than the original attempt, promises to create problems for Ghana and other African state members of the Commonwealth, such as Nigeria and Tanganyika, which have for the present decided against association with the EEC.

Ghana has carried its anti-Common Market campaign to such a high pitch that it is difficult to see any possible retreat. President Nkrumah has carried his message far and wide, and has gone to the length of getting the agreement of the Soviet Union that the Common Market is a European "scheme designed to attach African countries to European imperialism, to prevent the African countries from pursuing an independent neutral policy, to prevent the establishment of mutually beneficial economic ties among these countries, and to keep the African countries in a position of suppliers of raw materials for imperialist powers." [7] There could be little more that Ghana or the Soviet Union could add to this sweeping indictment. If the United Kingdom shall ever become a member of the Common Market, it will require extraordinarily adroit and fancy footwork for Ghana to stay in the Commonwealth and continue its violent attack on the Common Market.

By contrast, other African Commonwealth members, which have been hostile to the Common Market but primarily on the ground of economic discrimination against them as non-associated African countries, and more recently also on the ground that the Treaty of Rome has political goals unrelated to Africa, would have a much easier time of it if the United Kingdom ever joined the Common Market. They could probably choose Common Market membership if it was open to them or stay out of it and still remain Commonwealth members. In fact, in the view of the Nigerian Prime Minister expressed before the French veto of the British bid for admission, British membership in the Common Market might have a salutary effect. It could remove the "legitimate grievance" against economic discrimination of West African countries not associated with the EEC.[8]

There are many other Eurafrican ties and links. Language and culture are perhaps most important. English and French are the languages of most of Africa, and even where they are only spoken officially or among the elite they are becoming the national languages. There is little linguistic chauvinism in Africa. Although, as we have seen in the discussion of education in Chapter 6, there is an attempt to develop and teach the principal African languages in some countries, particularly at the early primary level and as an aspect of the revival of cultural tradition, there does not appear anywhere a serious attempt to substitute an African tongue for English and French. The cultural ties tend to have followed the language ones, but there is some resistance in the new states to continuing the European cultures in undiluted fashion. *Négritude* in some of the former French West African countries is one expression of the attempt to identify and evolve an African culture using European languages as the medium of expression.

Economic ties—trade, investment, and aid—also exist within

and without the institutionalized Eurafrican frameworks. Defense arrangements are frequently but not necessarily confined to institutional frameworks. The United Kingdom's defense arrangements in Africa relate to Commonwealth countries. The French defense relationships relate not only to Community countries but also to other countries of *l'expression française* which are members of the Common Market. The latter membership, however, is not the operative factor in the relationship. It is only one factor, albeit an important one, in the total posture toward France of the former French African states which are outside the Community.

Thus many of the new African states have sought stability for their fledgling state structures and political systems and support for their economies in Eurafrican relationships. This has been particularly true of former French African territories. These states have tended to reconcile their posture of individual country nationalism with Eurafrican ties. The then Prime Minister of Senegal, speaking about the Common Market, could have been talking about all Eurafrican ties of the former French Africa when he said:

We do not agree with Dr. Nkrumah when he says that association with E.E.C. would necessarily mean a form of neo-colonialism. It would depend upon the conditions but there is no reason why free co-operation between free and independent states should mean neo-colonialism or imperialism in Africa.[9]

For some, such as Nigeria, the commitment to internal nation building would seem to predominate, although reconciled with membership in the Commonwealth and special defense and other ties with the United Kingdom. For others, such as Senegal, the Eurafrican tie would seem, if not to predominate, at least to share equal honors with nationalism. And for still others, such as Gabon, the Eurafrican tie would seem most important, at least for the present.

Irrespective of the priority accorded nationalism and Eurafricanism by these states, all in greater or lesser degree are seeking stability and security outside or apart from a strictly Pan-American system of the types being sponsored by Nkrumah and Touré, although lately there have been indications that Touré is beating a

tactical retreat from political union now, and is seeking a reconciliation with the Monrovia bloc and its concepts. It is not without interest that these indications of a shift in external posture
have followed closely the deterioration of Guinea's internal economic position, and the liberalization of her state trading system,
already noted. As the cross-currents continue, and as newly emerging countries are carried one way or another, the Eurafrican tide
may recede before the Pan-African, or *vice versa*. What can be said
with some certainty is that the total posture—internal and external
—of African states will be considerably influenced and shaped by
the degree of commitment they have made to the alternative paths
to stability available to them: nationalism, Pan-Africanism, and
Eurafricanism.

Antagonisms and Conflicts

The three movements have already given rise to a host of
antagonisms and conflicts.

The basic clash has been between the nationalism of individual countries and Pan-Africanism: between the states which
want to emphasize their internal development and those which
want to merge their development into that of a larger bloc of
integrated states; between those who want ties and links with Europe and those who want to minimize, even sever, those ties in
favor of all-African ties and links.

President Tubman correctly assessed the African political
horizon when he undertook a holding action which restrained first
Nkrumah and then Touré in their drive to establish a Pan-African
hegemony under their own auspices in the Africa of 1958 and
1959. Tubman would not be pushed into a Pan-African union. He
wanted a broader spectrum of independent African opinion available on the scene before positions became frozen. He particularly
wanted any decisions on unions, federations, associations, and so
on to await the independence of the sleeping giant, Nigeria. At
the Sanniquellie Conference in 1959 in a personal *tour de force*

President Tubman got President Touré and Prime Minister Nkrumah (as he then was) to settle for nothing more than a loose,
informal, and ill-defined Community of African States. It held the
door open until May 1961 and the Monrovia Conference.

The Nkrumah-Touré strategy was to anticipate the outpouring of new African states by preempting the African political scene
for Pan-Africanism. Each new state would at its inception be confronted by a *fait accompli*, a political union of African states. The
new state could join the union or be relegated to the political limbo
for neo-colonialist stooges, dupes, and tools. The line of demarca-
tion was clear: pro-Pan-African or pro-European. The choice was
clear too: political stability and economic development as part of
a larger Pan-African union, or political weakness and economic
dependence on the colonialists and neo-colonialists.

With the advent of Nigerian independence in October 1960,
the Ghana-Guinea monopoly on African leadership was broken.
By May 1961 competitive lines were drawn. The issues between
the radical nationalist African states and the Monrovia powers
are many. The shadings within the Casablanca bloc—the grouping
of African radical nationalist states deriving from a conference
held at Casablanca in January 1961—are also many, for it is not
a homogeneous grouping of like-minded states. The shadings are
numerous within the Monrovia bloc, which then comprehended
the Brazzaville bloc of twelve states of *l'expression française* and
just about all the other independent states at the time outside the
Casablanca bloc, and which ranged from Somalia to Nigeria and
from Tunisia to Ethiopia. For the purpose of this discussion we
have been concerned only with the transcending importance of
the key differentiating factor between the Casablanca bloc—particularly the hard-core radical nationalist members of the bloc,
Ghana, Guinea, and Mali—and the then twenty-strong Monrovia
powers: the road to political stability.

By the end of 1961 the positions of the two major groups in
the field had hardened. The Monrovia bloc consolidated its beliefs
and structure at the second full meeting at Lagos early in 1962. The
Casablanca bloc became increasingly isolated and, as already noted,
became the sole exponent of Pan-Africanism.

The Monrovia road to stability, in the words of Mamadou

Dia, then Prime Minister of Senegal, commenting on the African personality, assumes that:

Each country has its own culture and before talking about co-operation, we should consider the personality of each of the different peoples.[10]

The Casablanca road to stability, in the words of Osagyefo Dr. Nkrumah, speaking of the Monrovia Conference, rests upon a quite different base:

I have advocated and will ever advocate an entirely contrary view. . . . In the new Africa we must be prepared to scrap outright frontiers which were drawn up to suit the convenience of colonial powers. . . . Africa cannot stand divided. . . . Imperialism has lost the fight for colonialism and cannot hope to win the new battle for neo-colonialism.[11]

As the *coup de grace* Nkrumah denounced the "so-called Monrovia Conference." He said: "When one speaks of a majority of independent African states meeting in Monrovia one must bear in mind that the majority is false and does not reflect the strength and power of the masses of the African people." [12]

The ominous note implied by the words of Dr. Nkrumah became explicit just a few months later when Nkrumah paid an official state visit to the Soviet Union. The rationale for interfering in the internal affairs of other states and subverting their governments is to be found in the judgment that the "majority is false and does not reflect the strength and power of the masses of the African people." In the same way that the CPP in Ghana and the PDG in Guinea are the sole custodians of the general will in their countries, so too in Africa at large they conceive of themselves as the sole custodians of the African personality, free to interpret it and duty-bound to defend it in their own ways according to their lights. Thus the joint communiqué issued at the end of Nkrumah's visit to the Soviet Union proclaims:

President Kwame Nkrumah and his party also noted that the heroic struggle for the peoples of Africa for their national liberation, as well as the aspiration of Ghana and of the other independent African states to unite in order to strengthen their sovereignty and to ensure free national development, meets with full understanding and sympathy on the part of the Soviet people.[13]

And again in the same communiqué:

The Soviet Government states that it profoundly appreciates the desire of African states and people to unite their efforts in the interest of the final liberation of Africa from colonialism and in the interest of ensuring the prerequisites for free national development and African unity.[14]

The Monrovia powers lashed out against "subversive activities" by "neighboring states" and made it abundantly clear that their accusation was directed at those who were missing from their conference—the Casablanca bloc vanguard states.

The most bitter antagonism of the radical nationalist Pan-Africanists has been reserved for the double devils—Monrovia powers who are associated with the EEC. The radical nationalist Pan-Africanists have cast the European Economic Community, the Common Market, in the role of arch-villain. And well they might, as it represents the most highly organized and institutionalized expression of Eurafricanism. The danger that the Pan-Africanists perceive in Eurafricanism is that it presents a positive alternative to Pan-Africanism and at the same time is consistent with developing nationalism in individual African states.

There are many degrees and variants of Eurafricanism. The Common Market, however, because it involves so many African countries (there are eighteen African "associated" countries), because the Eurafrican links involved are so clearly identifiable and important to the economic development of the African states, and because the leading radical nationalist states are all outside the fold, has drawn the bulk of the fire of the radical nationalist states. The reorganization of the Common Market, putting African membership on a footing consistent with the sovereign states' new status rather than one deriving from their former colonial dependency, should go a long way toward strengthening the Eurafrican ties within the EEC. The new status should also reduce the vulnerability of the associated African states to the Pan-Africanists' attacks based on the colonial origin and the second-class status of the African territories in the initial Common Market set-up.

Thus the struggle for leadership in Africa between the Casablanca bloc and the Monrovia bloc is multi-dimensional and involves all the principal routes to stability. If there should at any time be a reconciliation between the Monrovia bloc and the Casablanca bloc—unless the radical nationalist states jettison their total ideological baggage, which seems unlikely—the reconciliation is likely to be more an agreement in form than in fact. If the analysis of the underlying philosophy of the members of the two blocs up to this point is correct, the antagonisms and conflicts run too deep to be readily composed. The discussion which follows in this and subsequent chapters would seem to support this assessment. What is more likely is a tactical retreat by the Casablanca powers. Having made little headway with their Pan-African designs, they may find it prudent to try to reach an accommodation with the Monrovia powers leading to a truce on subversion and interference in the internal affairs of independent African states and to the acceptance of the inherited colonial boundaries subject to the possibility of peacefully negotiated revisions. As with all truces, however, which do little more than defer issues, the underlying differences remain and could manifest themselves at any time.

The sweepstake for leadership in the Pan-African movement has had implications not only for the principal contestants, Ghana and Guinea, but also for all of Africa and beyond.

Dr. Nkrumah was first in the Pan-African field and is still running hard; some would say scared. He failed in his grand design to consolidate the Pan-African grip on the new states as fast as they appeared and impose himself as the chosen leader of the movement. His most formidable opponent has been his partner in the Ghana-Guinea union, President Sékou Touré. The latter, from his formal entry into the field with the advent of Guinean independence in October 1958, has, as we have seen, espoused a social revolutionary brand of Pan-Africanism. Not only political unity was the goal, but also a drastic revamping of the social structure, using all of the powers at the disposal of the state and party and as much force, coercion, and subversion as might be required to accomplish the end. Nkrumah, although he has moved with time and events closer to Touré's revolutionary social goals, has tended to rely more on a mystique of an African personality and

African ideology, more on the naked display of military power, coercion, and subversion, and more on his own role as a charismatic leader than on doctrine to guide and shape his brand of Pan-Africanism.

Nkrumah and Touré went for the big prize offered by the accession to independence of the Belgian Congo. They picked, as we have noted, the same horse to ride—Patrice Lumumba. They fought for influence and power over the Lumumbist political party, the *Mouvement National Congolais*, and then over the Lumumba government and the various components of the coalition government. The Pan-African movement was embraced by Lumumba, and he was responsive to both Nkrumah and Touré. Their competition could tend to act in only one way, to push Lumumba further along the uncompromising path of a left-oriented centralized unitary government for the Congo.

In any event, both Nkrumah and Touré lost their play in the Congo; and only after the full import of their defeat and the full impact of the associated downfall of Lumumba sank in did they go a long way toward composing their differences and merging their respective brands of Pan-Africanism. However, the personal competition between the two leaders, as well as differences in policy and tactical nuances, persist. The crisis in Angola which persists despite the failure of the original uprising should provide another testing area for the unity or lack of it among the leading Pan-Africanists.

An important aspect of the Pan-African sweepstake is the role of the North African states. President Nasser of the United Arab Republic has definite leadership aspirations in Africa, which is one of the three areas—or circles as he calls them—for Egyptian influence, leadership, and, hopefully, dominance. In 1957, 1958, and much of 1959 he was held somewhat in check by Nkrumah's ascendency in the role of all-African leader. Since then, avoiding head-on clashes with Nkrumah, Nasser reasserted Egyptian leadership at the Casablanca bloc conference early in 1961, at the Cairo All-African Peoples' Conference later in 1961, and intermittently ever since, particularly in the early stages of the Congo crisis.

Nasser has vaguely been styled a Pan-Africanist, and in the sense of asserting a UAR leadership role in African affairs he is

Pan-Africanist. However, President Touré's open invitation to Nasser in early 1961 to join the Union of African States (Ghana, Guinea, and Mali) went begging. Could Nasser become one among many in an African union and still maintain the role Nasser envisaged for the United Arab Republic before its dissolution in the Middle East and the Muslim world? Could Nasser digest membership in an African union while still confronted with the drastic problems of unity within a new or reconstituted United Arab Republic? In fact, is Nasser interested in organic union with African states? Such a union would at a minimum create unmanageable problems of reconciliation of Nasser's dream of an Arab union with Nkrumah's of an African union, and in all likelihood it would involve serious conflicts of interest.

It is pertinent to note that in July 1961 Nasser launched "Arab socialism," not African socialism. It is also relevant to note the type of conflict which arose in Zanzibar, with the Arab-dominated party, the Zanzibar Nationalist Party, looking to Nasser, and the other principal party, the Afro-Shirazi Party, drawing its membership primarily from the African and racially mixed populations, looking to Nyerere. In the Horn of Africa, too, Nasser's support of Somalia in her conflict with Ethiopia has injected the element of North African Arab or Muslim vis-à-vis black African—"pagan," Muslim, or Christian.

Nkrumah, Touré, and Keita tend to reject the differences between the Arab North and the black South as more of the imperialist divide-and-rule strategy and to include North Africa in their concept of Pan-African union. It is not at all clear that the North Africans will be able or willing to go the Pan-African route. Certainly Nasser has not jumped at the opportunity. It will be of considerable importance to see how an independent Algeria assesses Pan-Africanism when it comes right down to the ultimate question of merging its new sovereignty into that of a larger African union. Independent Algeria has adhered to the radical nationalist bloc, and is a member of the Casablanca bloc. Will it go all the way and identify radical nationalism with Pan-Africanism? Will Maghreb—a union of North African states—be viewed as an alternative or a way station to a larger Pan-African union?

If other African states south of the Sahara are to be attracted to Pan-Africanism, will North African members be an asset or liability? Certainly exponents of *négritude*—a mystical black African cultural aspiration as well as heritage—would have difficulty reconciling it with North African Muslim and Arab culture. And, as Moroccan and Tunisian troops learned in the Congo, there are differences among Africans. Racialism is not entirely missing from the African scene, and the obvious difference between North Africans and sub-Saharan Africans was not without significance in shaping the role played by the different national contingents in the United Nations force.

In any event, friction, antagonism, and even conflict may evolve from or center around the geographical coverage implied in or asserted for Pan-Africanism.

Among the leaders of the French-speaking states the foregoing conflicts have been accentuated by personal bitterness among leaders on both sides. The attitude of President Touré toward President Houphouët-Boigny of the Ivory Coast perhaps reveals this most vividly:

> The personal activities of the President of the R.D.A. [Houphouët-Boigny] have, in fact, transformed our great freedom movement into one of the best and most servile instruments of colonialism.[15]

A possible reconciliation between these two African leaders has from time to time been rumored. A personal reconciliation, however, would not be needed as much as a policy rapprochement, and at this point it is not clear which would be more difficult to achieve.[16] This may be said too for the bitterness that has entered into Nkrumah's attacks on Prime Minister Balewa and Foreign Minister Wachuku of Nigeria, and a score of others. The policy conflicts have been augmented by personal antagonisms.

Evaluation

The three routes to stability are likely to continue to hold their attraction for the bulk of the current actors on the African scene. There may be some shifts or realignments. The Somalis are, for example, insecurely in the Monrovia bloc, and may fall out or remain in; or Morocco, which is one of the few remaining monarchies in Africa and odd man out among the radical nationalist Casablanca bloc, might shift allegiances. But by and large the struggle will center around the new states as they emerge. Thus with independence Tanganyika, Burundi, Rwanda, and Uganda have been much sought after by both blocs, and Nyasaland and Kenya which are approaching independence are also being ardently wooed. If the blocs formally merge the competition will go on but within the new body.

It is too soon to know which way or with what links an East African federation, if it came into being, would develop. Tanganyika may adopt a posture suggestive of Nigeria's. In fact an East African federation might shape up like the Federation of Nigeria rather than as a Pan-African nucleus. On the other hand, Tanganyika, which attended the second full conference of Monrovia powers at Lagos in January 1962, has not acceded to the new charter of the Inter-African and Malagasy States Organisation. Tanganyika has become increasingly active in the Pan-African Freedom Movement for East, Central and South Africa (PAFM-ECSA).[17] At various times Nyerere has suggested the possibility of Zanzibar, Rwanda and Burundi, and Northern Rhodesia joining an East African federation, and it has also been suggested that Nyasaland might adhere to such a federation; such a grouping would then assume Pan-Africanist proportions.

However, Prime Minister Banda of Nyasaland, who has spoken approvingly of Pan-Africanism, has in the past tended to identify it with Dr. Nkrumah and President Touré rather than with President Nyerere. Dr. Banda has also tended to identify himself with the radical nationalists rather than with Nyerere, whom he seems to view as more conciliatory and moderate in outlook. However, with President Nyerere adopting a more militant nationalist line this view may alter.

Even less clear is the likely route Northern and Southern Rhodesia would seek to follow in the quest for stability, and still more so, the Portuguese and Spanish territories on their accession to independence.

Antagonism and conflict are likely to continue and may even

intensify as the tides of the three movements ebb and flow. Intervention in the affairs of other African states, and even subversion of their governments, by the radical nationalist states is likely to accelerate if they find all other ways blocked or if their frustrations grow, notwithstanding any temporary truce, engendered by an apparent reconciliation and agreement on minimal points of principle, which may be reached at one time or another by states of the principal blocs. The counter-thrusts of the adherents of individual country nationalism and of Eurafricanism may grow sharper and more vigorous. The outlook would seem to be for a period of controversy, recrimination, maneuver, and even sporadic and intermittent violence. These turbulent and thrusting cross-currents are already faithfully mirrored in the African presence emerging on the world stage. African affairs have become daily fare for the agenda of the United Nations and the foreign ministries of the leading nations of the world. As the realization grows that violence anywhere on the African continent has world-wide implications, internal African rivalries become a new and important dimension of the struggle for world peace and the balance of political power in the world.

Chapter 10

AFRICAN NEUTRALISM AND THE UNITED NATIONS

Neutralism as the sought-after and proclaimed attitude of many of the new African states bears little resemblance to the traditional neutrality of Switzerland or Sweden, or that of Belgium before World War I. It does not involve withdrawal from world affairs, let alone opting out of the world, after the fashion of the Swiss, to the extent of refusing membership in the near-universal United Nations.

What then does neutralism mean when an African leader asserts that it is the foreign policy of his country?

To discover its meaning one might look first to some of the terms that have come into common usage among its practitioners to describe their African-type neutralism. Two of the most common are "positive" and "non-alignment." The first reflects an attempt to resolve the logical dilemma of all of the self-proclaimed African neutralist states. How can these states purport to be neutralist and still live in the world in which they must take daily decisions which affect one side or another in one foreign policy issue after another? How can they be members of the United Nations and vote on the regular diet of issues which regularly confront that organization? How can they reconcile neutralism with the obligations of United Nations membership imposed by the charter? Obviously they do not intend to withdraw from world affairs. Hence the term "positive neutralism" to describe the phenomenon of making decisions and taking sides on world issues and to signify generally that African neutralists will act. But, they say, they will act only in their own interests and in accordance with their own lights and never in keeping with the interests of either side in the cold war, and this position they call "non-alignment."

Thus even as a concept African neutralism comes to mean little more than non-affiliation with either the West or the Communist bloc—in essence, "Africa first." But it does not mean refraining from participation in affairs or making decisions on issues which support the position of one or the other bloc. Thus in the Congo crisis not one of the self-proclaimed neutralist African states was in fact neutral—toward the factions within the Congo, toward one another, or even toward the West or the Communist bloc.

African neutralism tends to be self-centered, self-interested, and even parochial; and its declaration of principles, as perhaps best exemplified by the vanguard neutralists, *the Casablanca bloc*, is an exercise not in idealism but in *Realpolitik*. For example, the oft-cited dedication of the African neutralists, particularly the radical nationalists among them, to the cardinal principle of neutralists, self-determination, has little to do with the principle espoused by Woodrow Wilson after World War I. For the African neutralists are concerned with the principle of self-determination only insofar as it affects African areas. They are not concerned with self-determination of Asian and European peoples held in colonial bondage by Communist China and the Soviet Union. For many African neutralists the political horizon is limited to Africa and external intrusions into Africa. Colonialism for them means only European colonialism on the African continent. And for many more, taking a principled position on self-determination would entail risks of Communist recrimination impugning their posture of neutrality. To side with the Tibetan and Hungarian anti-colonialist movement might be viewed as anti-Chinese Communist and anti-Soviet. It might even be construed as pro-Western.

The African neutralists will no more stand up and be counted for self-determination everywhere in the world than, according to their complaints, will the United States in Africa.

Even in the African context self-determination has a special singular meaning—that of agitation for independence directed only against the colonial powers. It has nothing to do with the rights of people confined within artificial geographical configurations to determine their own future once independence is in the offing or has been achieved. For the neutralists, particularly for the radical nationalist brand, such internal self-determination on the African scene is, on the one hand, a neo-colonialist plot to destroy the unity of the state or, on the other hand, an outburst of tribalism to be ruthlessly suppressed. The attempts to exercise one or another degree of self-determination of Katanga, Ashanti, Buganda, Barotseland, to name a few of the more prominent examples, are all so characterized by the African neutralists.

The Neutralist Vanguard: The Casablanca Bloc

When Ghana, Guinea, and Mali—alone among the independent African states—supported in one degree or another the Soviet troika proposal for reorganization of the United Nations Secretariat, they made explicit their lack of neutrality on the basic issue of the United Nations' role in world affairs, previously implicit in their role in the Congo. They were taking the restrictive Soviet view of the role of the United Nations. They were endorsing the extension of the veto power to the operations of the Secretariat. Thus they acted in clear opposition to the view of the West and most of the Afro-Asian world. And almost as if to dissipate any lingering doubt with respect to Ghana's lack of neutrality on this issue, the joint communiqué at the close of Dr. Nkrumah's visit to the Soviet Union in July 1961 proclaimed an "identity of opinions" of Ghana and the Soviet Union regarding the present structure of the United Nations, and called for "effective and equitable" representation on United Nations bodies of "neutralist countries [and] the Socialist states as well as the Western powers and their allies." [1]

This is the Soviet Union's line pure and simple. The acceptance of the concept that there are three and only three groups of states in the world is a Soviet-manufactured concept bearing no relationship to the realities of modern neutralism.

The very category "neutralist countries" is meaningless. This was fully revealed in the prolonged and sometimes bitter quarrel over what states should be invited to the Conference of Heads of State or Government of Non-Aligned Countries held in Belgrade in September 1961. Prime Minister Nehru of India failed in his effort to have West European states which have had a classic neutrality, such as Ireland and Sweden, invited, along with many of the non-Casablanca bloc African states. As a matter of fact, the European neutrals were too neutral for such neutralist states as Yugoslavia, the United Arab Republic, and Ghana. And most of the African states, being anti-Casablanca bloc, were apparently not neutralist in terms of the conference in the view of several of its sponsors—Tito, Nasser, and Nkrumah. Yet many of them are neutralist in the restricted African sense of non-affiliation with the Western and Communist blocs. In fact, some have been criticized as being too neutralist for rejecting affiliation with an Afro-Asian or a Pan-African bloc. The belated invitation to Tunisia to attend the Belgrade conference is most revealing. Tunisia was apparently thought to be too pro-Western to qualify as a neutralist until after the Franco-Tunisian crisis over Bizerte arose. This incident suddenly transformed Tunisia into an eligible neutralist.

It is also interesting to note that after much discussion Nigeria was invited to the Belgrade conference. The elasticity of the neutralist concept could, it seems, now accommodate Nigeria, which had been for Nkrumah, ever since the Monrovia Conference, the archetype of Eurafrica-oriented powers. Nigeria rejected the invitation in a manner which suggested that the invitation had been somehow misaddressed.

In short, African neutralism allows, and in fact requires, the taking of sides on cold-war issues. The United Nations issue is the clearest illustration that this is true of the self-styled "vanguard" of African neutralist states. It is also the case where an African state lends itself to the Communist-bloc "national liberation" movement under the guise of anti-colonialism. For, as spelled out in the important declaration of Communist bloc parties issued in Moscow in December 1960, in bloc usage "national liberation" refers only to the liberation of colonial territories under Western control, not to those under bloc control. Moreover, it covers liberation of independent African states which the Soviet Union and Ghana later denominated "neo-colonialist stooge governments," which in fact implies assistance and support to the subversion of the legally constituted governments of a large number of African states. For example, Nkrumah has referred to the twelve Brazzaville powers as "stooge governments."

Neutralism also embraces the principle of freedom to take external economic aid from any source—the West, the Communist bloc, or preferably both—so long as it is aid "without strings." The proviso "without strings" is never defined. Apparently aid from Western powers is suspect. Since its demands may be hidden, the posture toward it is one of pristine purity defending its virtue against concealed attack. If in the end aid is accepted, the implication is that the strings have been rendered powerless or cut. Aid from the Communist bloc, however, is viewed in public as without strings. Privately, many precautions are taken to ensure that the bloc demands are neutralized. The most obvious method is to get aid from the West in sufficient quantity to counter-balance Communist aid, or, better, to have Western aid well entrenched first. This has been the pattern in Ghana, the United Arab Republic, Morocco, and Mali. Only Guinea started with Communist-bloc aid, the result of a convergence of Western hesitancy to provide aid in the face of French opposition and the pro-bloc ideological position of the most radical nationalist element of the *Parti Démocratique de Guinée*, which preferred bloc aid as the clearest manifestation of Guinean independence.

Neutralism, for the vanguard neutralist states, also sanctions the receipt of any military aid as a legitimate exercise of sovereignty, whereas Western military aid to other African states is viewed as part of a neo-colonialist conspiracy to continue or reassert colonial control over the newly independent states. Thus, although Guinea, Ghana, Mali, Morocco, and the United Arab Republic receive Communist bloc military assistance, including tanks and jet aircraft in several cases, to defend their independence, if Nigeria, the Ivory Coast, and Tunisia should receive Western arms it is because they are "stooge governments" and are being used for colonialist purposes. It is permissible for Ghana and Morocco to receive Western arms, for these states are beyond suspicion of being used by the colonialists. They cannot be seduced. It is only the others who are susceptible.

To sum up, then, the vanguard neutralists are not neutral on such important cold-war issues as the role of the United Nations in world affairs, the Communist bloc's "national liberation" policy, and the question of aid posture, particularly with respect to military aid. The Casablanca bloc takes positions on cold-war issues. All that can be said for it with regard to neutralism is that it has not become openly aligned with either side in the cold war. It hardly needs to be noted that, like the all-aid-short-of-war posture in a shooting war, the all-allegiance-short-of-alignment posture in the cold-war context appears neither impartial nor neutral to the other party in the dispute.

The Other African States

Although many of the other African countries have resisted the temptation to adopt the neutralist label, some have accepted the formulation "non-alignment" or "independent" to describe their foreign policies, and all have to a degree found it convenient to strike something of a neutralist posture and to take over some of the symbols and language of neutralism.

Prime Minister Balewa of Nigeria, during his visit to the United States in July 1961, described the foreign policy of his country as non-alignment. He said: "We have a policy not of neutrality but of non-alignment. We want to side with whomever we think is right, whether Afro-Asian, Western, or Eastern Countries." [2] Nigeria would decide its policy on each issue on its merits, according to "the truth." In the Prime Minister's words: "We don't believe in one side or the other. We are on the side of truth." [3] Although the Prime Minister has been careful not to employ the word "neutralist," the Nigerian Foreign Minister,

Jaja Wachuku, has used the words "neutralist" as well as "non-alignment" to describe Nigeria's foreign policy.

The foreign policy posture of Ghana and Nigeria are worlds apart. Nigeria's role in the Congo of all-out support for the United Nations was in sharp contrast to Ghana's equivocal on-again-off-again support of the United Nations, intervention on behalf of Lumumba and then Gizenga, and participation in the Casablanca bloc's general line on the Congo issue. In fact, Nigeria's general foreign policy role in and adhesion to the Monrovia bloc is the antithesis of Ghana's with respect to the Casablanca bloc. Yet spokesmen for both states use many of the same terms to describe their foreign policies.

President Nyerere, describing Tanganyika's foreign policy as an "independent policy" came close to describing the basic Nigerian position. Fittingly, he stated his policy on a visit to Nigeria in April 1961. He said:

> The people of Africa . . . will be independent rather than being neutral or aligned with any of the existing power blocs. Neutrality is absurd when human affairs are being discussed.[4]

It is interesting to note that Mr. Nyerere refrained from using the expression "non-alignment" as well as "neutralist" to describe the Tanganyikan position. Nevertheless, it would be difficult to distinguish between the underlying basic policy of Nigeria and Tanganyika in world affairs.

Still another view on neutralism has been expressed by the President of the Upper Volta, Maurice Yaméogo, who has been a remarkable fence-straddler in internal politics and an adroit one in external affairs. He spoke from a background of experience when he denied a rumor that he proposed to lead the Upper Volta into the positive neutralist Casablanca bloc.

> If there is positive neutralism, then there must be another sort of neutralism and one can choose between them, but when one chooses one is no longer neutral. We are not acrobats in the international arena.[5]

Not only did he recognize the difference between classic neutrality and African neutralism in his cogent comment, but he also pointed out that the very act of adopting the posture of positive neutralism was inherently not neutral. Thus Yaméogo has kept one foot in the Monrovia bloc and one foot in the Casablanca bloc in a demonstration of Upper Voltan neutrality between African blocs.

Lastly, it should be noted that the Monrovia Conference of the Heads of African and Malagasy States, as it was officially referred to in its resolutions, while not committing itself to the Western or NATO blocs, did refrain from using the mystical phrases "neutralism," "non-alignment," and "uncommitted." In fact, the conferees recognized they had not been neutral with regard to the many positions they took in their resolutions, e.g., condemnation of all attempts to "weaken or undermine the authority of the United Nations." This position was the opposite of that of the Ghana-Guinea, Mali Union on the Secretariat.

The Significance of the Neutralist Label

What is the significance of the impreciseness and ambiguity of the African concept of neutralism and of its adoption as a foreign policy posture by so many of the newly independent African states?

The significance would seem to be twofold. First, the widespread adoption of the word to describe the foreign policy postures of states covering the whole political spectrum reveals a vague but pervasive feeling among the newly emergent African states that somehow they have more security, crucial to the development of political stability, by remaining formally aloof from the two major power blocs in the world. They seem to reason that both blocs will pay them the homage and respect due neutralists. India, for many, is proof of this.

Second, the label is useful as camouflage. For some states it provides a policy sanctuary from which cold-war doctrines can be advocated and interference in the internal affairs of other African states manipulated. The voice of Ghana and the voice of Cairo have from time to time done both. For other states it provides the degree of political coloration thought necessary to dis-

arm or obviate domestic and foreign radical nationalist criticism
of being pro-Western. Either way, neutralism is an important
element in total external political posture. And in all instances,
irrespective of the school, neutralism is intimately related to the
country's search for security and stability at the international
level.

Neutralism is also intimately related to the country's internal
search for stability. It gives the radical nationalists ample scope
for Pan-Africanist drives and foreign ventures with which to reinforce their hold on the imaginations of their people and divert
the nation's attention from internal problems. The neo-colonialists
and imperialists serve as substitute whipping-boys for the former
colonial powers against which the party in a one-party state can
mobilize support under its leadership. For other leaders of independent African states the adoption of a formal or nominal neutralist posture is a way of stealing the thunder of the radical nationalists among their own peoples or of stilling their voices. In Nigeria
the move toward a position less frankly pro-Western, more avow-
edly neutralist, coincides with Nigeria's emergence as a leading
African state and with the espousal by the leader of the opposition,
Chief Awolowo, of the radical nationalist line to the extent of
urging Nigerian affiliation with the Ghana-Guinea, Mali Union.
In Liberia the moves away from a generally assumed pro-United
States position toward a more neutralist posture coincide too with
Liberia's bid for a major role in African affairs (for example,
membership on the United Nations Security Council and sponsor
of the Monrovia Conference) and with the emergence of a radical
nationalist-oriented group among the younger generation of Li-
berians.

New States in the United Nations

Starting with Nkrumah in 1957, the leaders of all the new
African states have energetically sought membership in the United
Nations as the factor demonstrating to the world at large that a
sovereign state has been born. It has been only slightly less im-

portant internally as a demonstration to the population at large that its leaders have achieved recognition far and wide for their newly independent country. Thus United Nations membership has become a status symbol associated with independence, sovereignty, and national dignity. It signifies recognition by the mighty as well as the humble. It puts the new states, the former colonies, on the same footing as the former colonial masters.

United Nations membership also implies security and stability. The African view has been that the United Nations would shield its members from aggression; that it would also provide a platform for anti-colonialism and a forum in which the colonial powers could be effectively arraigned. This view has been of particular importance to the new states which have sought security and stability in a Pan-African solution. For every new African state has been for them a potential, or, it was originally assumed, automatic, candidate for affiliation in a Pan-African grouping—and the United Nations promised to be a fertile recruiting ground.

Membership in the United Nations also has opened the door to membership in the Afro-Asian bloc for those new African states seeking security and stability in an inter-state system transcending African limits, but excluding Europe. At first only the United Arab Republic, which, as part of the Arab bloc at the crossroads of Asia and Africa, had a foot in both worlds through its membership in the Arab League and its participation in the first Accra Conference of Independent African States in 1958. Pan-Africanists tend to emphasize Africa to the exclusion of the rest of the world. Thus Nkrumah dismissed Nasser's early attempts to introduce the Arab-Israeli dispute into African affairs as an intrusion of extraneous Asian problems. However, with repeated rebuffs to their Pan-Africanist maneuvers, both Ghana and Guinea, particularly the former, have moved increasingly into Afro-Asian groupings. This tendency has been reinforced by the radical nationalist acceptance or agreement with the Chinese Communist position on the nature of the threat of imperialism and neo-colonialism to Africa, with the Chinese Communist allegation that the United States is the backbone of the neo-colonialist movement, and with the doctrine of the need to use force for the success of African national liberation movements.

However, along with these benefits United Nations membership also imposes certain obligations under its charter. As good U.N. citizens who could not escape or neglect their duty, the new African states must take positions on the whole range of world problems. Therefore African neutralism in its various forms has had to be reconciled with United Nations membership.

For the radical nationalist states this has not been a difficult task since their version of neutralism not only allows but requires position-taking. It also allows bloc membership so long as it is not membership in the Western bloc or the Communist bloc. In short, although United Nations membership has impaired the ability of the radical nationalists to see African problems in splendid isolation, and as the fulcrum of international politics, it has afforded a convenient umbrella for positive neutralism.

For others the obligations of United Nations membership have been characterized by the unavoidable necessity to make decisions on a whole range of non-African problems involving cold-war considerations. With the Congo crisis came the necessity of making decisions on African problems with cold-war aspects. For these states United Nations membership has not so much disturbed their nominal or formal neutralism as exposed them to the outside world. Non-involvement in world problems—not so much from a desire to be neutral as from an isolationist urge to stay out of issues not directly concerning Africa—is no longer possible. Simultaneously, however, United Nations membership has provided a convenient rationale for the African states' decisions on world issues with cold-war overtones. It has served to strengthen their claim to a formal neutralism; they are merely fulfilling their United Nations responsibilities, not taking sides.

Of all the African states Nigeria appears to come closest to the view that the United Nations is a separate entity and individual force for law and order in world affairs, transcending its membership. Nigeria wants to strengthen the United Nations, and particularly its capacity to enforce its decisions. Prime Minister Balewa was deeply distressed by what he considered the French defiance of the Security Council decision in July 1961 on the Bizerte incident and the seeming inability of the United Nations to overcome the defiance.

President Bourguiba of Tunisia tends to view the United Nations as a most useful forum for reviewing world problems. He steadfastly supported the United Nations in the Congo crisis. He also, however, recognizes the limitations of its power and did not expect it to be able to force the French out of Bizerte. Rather, the United Nations was to provide a forum in which to embarrass the French, and the West generally, in order to render the French more amenable to negotiations and vulnerable to pressure for their withdrawal from the Bizerte naval base.

Ghana has oscillated in its attitude toward the United Nations. For some time it tended to take the present Nigerian view. In the Congo crisis Nkrumah swung from complete approval of the, admittedly changing, United Nations position to threats to withdraw his troops from the U.N. command. In the end he largely supported it. His adoption of the Soviet troika proposal, however, moved Ghana a considerable distance away from the initial Ghanaian position. The United Nations is now viewed by Ghana more as an instrument of national policy than as an independent supranational agency with its own personality.

Guinea has moved even further than Ghana from a position of reposing full faith and credit in the United Nations as the impartial monitor of world affairs and the stronghold of small nations. As a symbolic gesture of its distrust for the United Nations after the Congo affair, Guinea demanded the recall of the United Nations aid mission to Guinea. The United Nations had become in Guinean eyes a stronghold for the colonialists. President Touré recently shifted this attitude somewhat when he appealed for a United Nations investigation into the assassination of President Olympio of Togo in January 1963.

Many of the Brazzaville bloc states tend to view United Nations membership in terms of Eurafrican relations and thus frequently have supported or refrained from opposing France on such difficult African issues as Algeria and Sahara bomb tests in reciprocation for French support of their governments in the economic and defense fields.

In summing up the African approach to the United Nations it should be emphasized here that even for the radical nationalists African interest in world affairs remains Africa-focused. "Africa first" has been their guiding principle. If other countries, particularly advanced Western countries, were to adopt positions as consciously focused on their own interests they would earn opprobium throughout Africa as chauvinists, parochialists, and even imperialists. For example, if the United States were to abstain from voting in the United Nations on an issue of importance to African states on the ground that, because of conflicting interests, United States policy was to be one of "positive neutralism and non-alignment" on the issue, and went on to explain that "whatever we have done we have always placed America first," it would be roundly denounced. Yet it would be acceptable for an African state under similar circumstances on a non-African issue to abstain on the grounds of neutralism or non-alignment and Africa-first considerations. In fact, President Nkrumah announced with considerable pride to a party conference in June 1961:

> We have adhered strictly to our policy of positive neutralism and non-alignment and whatever we have done we have always placed Africa first.[6]

The African focus applies to African membership in the United Nations. Hungary, Tibet, Berlin, and so on, are beyond the African ken—counters in horse-trading deals, embarrassing subjects on which to avoid being counted. The references in the United Nations charter to self-determination of peoples is held to mean African people, or at most colonial peoples under Western control. Thus the African commitment to the United Nations, like the African commitment to neutralism, is rooted in avowed self-interest. Reflecting as it does African realities as they are assessed by African states, it is neither more nor less idealistic than the commitment of states from other areas. It covers a wide spectrum and is as varied as African neutralism; it is different for different states, and for the same states at different times.

Despite the many gradations of African commitment to the United Nations, and there have been many changes in the nature of the commitments, as a rule the new states of Africa tend to see the United Nations in a kindly light. When all is said and done, each state, large or small, and there are many small ones in Africa, has one vote and one voice in the General Assembly. The African presence in the United Nations is a disproportionately large one, and a disproportionately significant one. The prospect is for an expanding African influence vis-à-vis the developed world, and the Asian sector of the Afro-Asian world, as an automatic consequence of the impending emergence of more independent African states.

The African bloc in the United Nations is not as homogeneous as might be suggested by the foregoing statements. The votes and postures of the African states reflect their internal political situations, their attitudes toward nationalism, Pan-Africanism, and Eurafricanism, and their brand of neutralism. Nevertheless, on some issues, such as an increased African representation in United Nations organs and staff, they constitute a formidable bloc. Moreover, the large new membership from Africa has drastically affected the balance of power in the General Assembly and other bodies. At the Monrovia Conference, for example, the twenty participants agreed "to present a united front in the future to all world problems with which Africa might be faced at the U.N." [7] Twenty votes, pulling together, can certainly affect the balance of an organization with just over a hundred votes.

How much will this changing balance affect the fortunes of the West and the Communist bloc in the U.N.? There can be no question that their fortunes will be visibly affected. The Soviet Union's troika proposal reflected a Soviet awareness of the shifting balance and an attempt to tip it in its own favor. The United States can no longer assume an automatic majority in the General Assembly as it could for the most part when there were less than seventy-five members. Not only is a body of a hundred or more members likely to be more unpredictable, but there is also likely to be a considerable amount of interaction between, say, the new African states and Latin American states which will make the latter's position on a good many issues less predictable than heretofore.

In addition to these uncertainties, the United States association with the NATO powers, which has little effect by and large on Latin American countries, and only a limited one on Asian countries, has a direct and discernible effect on the African nations. To the extent that this effect is unfavorable to the United States, some of it will undoubtedly brush off on underdeveloped areas around the globe and render even more uncertain the voting disposition of the General Assembly membership. Then, more than ever, the United States will have its work cut out for it in the United Nations. It will not be enough to be right on an issue; it will also be necessary to take account of the nature of African neutralism and of special African interests. In Chapter 12 we return to the role of these special African interests, dealt with here from the point of view of African neutralism, in the wider context of the African presence at the United Nations and the impact of this presence on the world balance of power.

PART FOUR

The African Presence in World Affairs

> There should not be any hesitation, because we are at a turn of the road where our attitude will be of decisive significance, I believe, not only for the future of the United Nations Organisation but also for the future of Africa. And Africa may well in present circumstances mean the world.*
>
> DAG HAMMARSKJÖLD

* Address by the Secretary-General to the United Nations Security Council (at the onset of the Congo crisis), New York, July 22, 1960.

Chapter 11

THE AFRICAN PRESENCE AND WORLD PEACE

It may well be that the African presence in the United Nations will strengthen that organization's role in maintaining peace and stability. It may also be that outside the United Nations, as individual states, as members of intercontinental systems of states, as members of blocs, and as members of transitory *ad hoc* groupings, the African states will make significant contributions to the peace and stability of the world. These are still rather long-range possibilities to be realized as time and events permit the new massive African dimension to be reconciled with the established forces in world affairs.

There are, however, certain discernible short-range effects of the African presence which to a degree already bear on world peace and stability. These derive most directly from the African quest for political stability but are also related to the economic development focus of African states, i.e., the relative priorities assigned to internal growth and external objectives, and the use of the internal economy to achieve external goals.

Common to all of the new African states is the pressing, relentless, unremitting campaign being waged, independently or

in concert with the colonial peoples concerned, for the liberation
of the remaining colonial territories on the continent. The reaction of the colonial powers to liberation of their territories may be
conciliatory and accommodating, e.g., the British and French in
most of their African areas, or uncompromising and rejecting, e.g.,
the Portuguese and Spaniards in all of their African areas.

Sometimes the anti-colonial posture of an independent African state derives directly from the state's existence. Without conscious effort the independent state of Ghana became a symbol, an
object lesson, an attainable goal, an example to emulate, and a
dream come true for many African leaders scattered across the
continent. At other times the anti-colonial posture of the independent African states results from conscious policy decisions
which are translated into programs of action.

The Casablanca bloc has made violent anti-colonialism its
hallmark. It is an anti-colonialism that goes far beyond the espousal of national independence. It is, as we have seen, a rationale
for a Pan-Africanist thrust to achieve unity and for the radical nationalist attempt to induce social revolution. Toward the outside
world it is positive neutralist. Within Africa it is interventionist
in the affairs of states outside the bloc. The Casablanca brand of
anti-colonialism, being all these things, has led to political assessments, policies, and programs of action which, without regard to
their justification, can only have a generally disquieting and intermittently disruptive effect on world peace and stability.

For the Monrovia powers anti-colonialism has come to mean
opposition to remaining colonial régimes anywhere in Africa. It
means intervention to overthrow these régimes—a conscious exception to the Monrovia principles of non-interference and non-
intervention of one African state in the affairs of another and of
peaceful change as the way to alter existing African boundaries.
But the intervention contemplated tends to stress moral support
rather than physical violence, although material support and even
violence cannot be entirely ruled out. In the words of Dr. Azikiwe,
Governor-General of Nigeria:

My government will give all moral support to the legitimate
aspirations of dependent peoples seeking their freedom from colonial
status. . . .[1]

Prime Minister Adoula of the Republic of the Congo in a speech to the Belgrade Conference of Non-Aligned States in September 1961 also reportedly emphasized non-violent means.

[Adoula said] it was the duty of the Congo to give peaceful backing to the fight of neighboring Angola against what he termed Portuguese colonial oppression.[2]

Notwithstanding the emphasis on non-violent means the Congo government has provided one of the most active of the Angolan political movements, the Union of Populations of Angola, headed by Holden Roberto, with a base for armed forays into Angola and has lent tacit support, if not overt assistance, to the operation of rebel bands. The Congo has also provided a refuge for thousands of Angolans who carry on active political agitation against the Portuguese. It is hard to see how many other African countries can resist being drawn into more active roles in the Angolan crisis if it persists and grows in intensity, as now seems likely, notwithstanding the apparent success of the Portuguese in bringing the initial rebellion under control. For example, Dahomey occupied the small Portuguese enclave on its territory, the fort of São João Baptista de Ajuda in the coastal town of Ouida, on July 31, 1961; and Senegal broke off relations with Portugal in July 1961 over the latter's policy in Angola while at the same time it provided a refuge for anti-Portuguese Africans from neighboring Portuguese Guinea. Similarly, in North Africa Tunisia long served as a base and privileged sanctuary for the Algerian rebel forces, and from time to time was violated by French forces "in hot pursuit" of the rebels. Algeria has also been training officer cadres for the Angolan rebels and, the suggestion has been made, that it has also been providing technical advisers to the rebel units.

The Monrovia bloc does not sanction the use of anti-colonialism as a rationale for forcing African unity. It does not use anti-colonialism as an ingredient of neutralism with which to rationalize or camouflage the advocacy of Communist-bloc doctrine. And anti-colonialism does not mean a severance of European ties and links. On balance then, the Monrovia powers' version of anti-colonialism, although designed to oust the colonial powers and contributory to the instability implicit in anti-colonial agitation and movements, does not tend to be disruptive of world peace in the same way or to the same degree as the Casablanca bloc's version.

The differences in approach and in posture between the two major groupings of African states are manifest in three interacting forces, all of which are subsumed under the rubric of anti-colonialism by the Casablanca powers and rejected by the Monrovia powers. These three forces may be for convenience called "national liberation," irredentism, and militarism.

By way of explanation it should be noted that the phrase "national liberation" is used throughout this chapter in the special sense given it in Communist-bloc usage. That is, the bloc, in the same way that it has seized upon and distorted the meaning of such commonplace political terms as "democracy," "freedom," and "self-determination," has adopted the obvious and almost inevitable expression describing the independence revolution of colonial peoples—"national liberation"—and imparted to it multiple special meanings. In bloc usage the term means not only the accession to independence of colonial people but also the overthrow of the "bourgeois governments" of the newly independent states and their replacement by militant radical nationalist governments intent upon excising all Western influence in favor of a Communist-bloc orientation.

"National Liberation"

"National liberation" is a term that has increasingly crept into the language of the African radical nationalist prospectus, and in a very special way. It bears the imprint "made in Moscow" and its meaning is that imparted to it in the Communist bloc.

It is significant that, in July 1961, at the very time Dr. Nkrumah was in Moscow on a state visit, the Communist Party of the Soviet Union provided in its new draft program to be presented to the Party Congress in October the official definition of the term "national liberation." [3] President Nkrumah and the President of the Presidium of the Soviet Union, in a joint communiqué marking the conclusion of Nkrumah's visit, proclaimed their joint support of the "national liberation" doctrine for Africa. Nkrumah in the communiqué explicitly took note of the "full understanding and sympathy" of the Soviet Union for the "struggle of the peoples of Africa for their national liberation." [4] The ensuing discussion considers this doctrine as it is being put into practice in Africa by Dr. Nkrumah and his radical nationalist associates from Ghana and the Casablanca bloc generally.

Although the coincidence of the term "national liberation" in radical nationalist and Communist-bloc literature is suggestive by itself,[5] an examination of the application of the "national liberation" doctrine in Africa by Nkrumah and other radical nationalists makes unambiguously explicit the Ghanaian and radical nationalist commitment to a blend of the Soviet and Chinese Communist analyses of and prescriptions for imperialism, neo-colonialism, anti-colonialism, the role of the national bourgeoisie, etc.—in short, to Communist "national liberation" doctrine.

All African radical nationalists would take as their point of departure and uncritically accept the thesis that the African anti-colonial movements and revolutions are sweeping away colonialism. Admission or recognition of the second of the dual processes involved in achieving independence—the decolonization movement of the metropolitan countries—would be no more likely to be forthcoming from the African radical nationalists than from the Communists. The fact that most of the newly independent African states had relatively peaceful passage to independence has been submerged in a welter of polemic about the national struggles for independence which have now become institutionalized in the nationalists' folklore and commemorated by a number of victory arches. The acknowledgement of Prime Minister Balewa and President Senghor, for example, of the role of the metropolitan countries in bringing the colonial territories to independence (i.e., step-by-step preparation of the colonial territories through internal reforms, self-government, economic development plans, education of elite, and so on) has brought a torrent of criticism from the radical nationalists. Balewa, Senghor, and the others who think like them are "national bourgeoisie"—too conciliatory, too forgiving, too prone to be influenced by the "imperialists turned neo-colonialists." The approved model is that of Patrice Lumumba, who on June 30, 1961, in response to the paternalistic tone of King Baudouin's speech before the Congolese Parliament transferring sovereignty to the new Congolese government, denounced the role of the colonial power in such vitriolic terms that Baudouin was only persuaded from stalking out of the independence day ceremonies by dint of great effort and the promise of a speech by Lumumba the next day qualifying some of his more extreme indictments of the Belgian régime.

The doctrine of "stoogism" in the ideology of Dr. Nkrumah and his colleagues, the doctrine of the false majority Nkrumah spoke of in condemning the Monrovia Conference, has its counterpart in Communist ideology in somewhat more doctrinaire terms. It is a struggle for "real" independence involving the overthrow of the "pro-imperialist" or "stooge governments" imposed by the "neo-colonialists" in order to retain their "economic monopolies." The leaders of most of former French Africa and others who have brought their territories to independence relatively harmoniously and by negotiated steps are in this view fraudulent stooges. They are therefore not true representatives of the African people and are expendable. Intervention of Radio Ghana, Radio Guinea, and Radio Cairo is for the purpose of exposing these "neo-colonialist stooges." Support of disaffected émigré movements in Accra, Conakry, and Cairo is necessary to provide the nuclei for "true" liberation régimes to replace the neo-colonialists. Smuggled arms and personnel from these same bases are justifiable on the ground that they will encourage the inevitable historical process leading to the overthrow of the false leaders. In short, the rationale for subversion is as implicit in Nkrumah's rationale of "national liberation" as in its Communist counterpart.

In response the Monrovia powers have adopted as a central thesis the doctrine of non-intervention of one African state in the affairs of another. They have made it abundantly clear that they reject the Nkrumah-Touré practice of intervention and subversion, such as that against the Ahidjo government in the Republic of Cameroun.

The oft-repeated declarations of Nkrumah, Touré, and Nasser also make it clear that long after the smoke of the anti-colonial struggle has disappeared its ghost is to be invoked to explain any and every failure of their régimes, and particularly the all-important failure in each of these countries to really get off the ground with respect to solid economic development. There is thus full accord by these leaders with the view expressed in the Soviet Communist Party analysis that "imperialism . . . remains . . . the chief obstacle to the solution of national problems facing the young sovereign states."

Lastly, the view of Nkrumah and his associates which justifies collaboration with bourgeois elements to achieve independence and the subsequent liquidation of the "national bourgeoisie" as enemies of progress also has its counterpart in Communist-bloc usage of the term "national liberation." The concept provides a rationale for the left-authoritarian practice of crushing all internal opposition once it has outlived its usefulness or spent its strength on behalf of independence. (And in the process of entrenching the radical nationalist wing of an independence movement by eliminating all opposition, potential opposition to a future Communist *coup d'état* or takeover is also eliminated.) The trend toward left-authoritarianism would suggest that the African radical nationalists have to a considerable extent already put into practice the liquidation theory associated with the "national liberation" doctrine they share with the Communists.

Nigeria, as we have seen earlier, is nearly a unique phenomenon in Africa in tolerating and protecting the rights of political opposition. The right-authoritarian states tend to be non-ideological in their approach to opposition. They absorb or suppress opposition on an *ad hoc* basis as and where it arises. There does not tend to be a systematic across-the-board approach to wiping out "the national bourgeoisie" or any other class or specific leadership group on the basis of a theoretical analysis of their actual, potential, or supposed opposition to the incumbent régime.

What does the "national liberation" philosophy of the radical nationalist African states—Ghana, Guinea, Mali, the United Arab Republic, and Algeria—mean to the peace and stability of Africa and the world at large?

It can only mean controversy, conflict, and violence. Every régime in independent Africa outside the Casablanca bloc must be aware of the threat to its continued existence and, on guard to forestall both external thrust and internal subversion, that it must have force to meet force. Since national forces were non-existent or limited at the time of independence, there has been a built-in limitation on violence, and the controversy and conflict have tended to be verbal, with the violent exception of the rebellion in the Republic of Cameroun manipulated in part by Guinea. However, the arms race now getting under way holds out the likelihood of an intensification of the use of force; and even in its absence the very threat of interference and subversion has created an atmosphere of distrust and antagonism. It has stimulated the non-Casablanca bloc powers to enter the arms race in earnest.

The evolving situation constitutes a growing source of instability in Africa and a mounting threat to the peace of Africa and the world. The Congo crisis vividly demonstrated the possibilities Africa holds for world involvement. The arms race now gaining momentum must involve the outside world as supplier, trainer, and ultimately as partisan. Algeria has demonstrated the rich opportunities for external involvement through the supply of armaments or military training cadres. For example, in 1960 the then Algerian government in exile announced that it would receive "multiform" military assistance from the Soviet Union and Communist China, and intimated that such arms would arrive through the neighboring countries of Tunisia and Morocco. On the other hand, throughout the Algerian conflict a constant complaint of the Algerian government in exile was that the United States and other NATO countries were providing France with arms to put down the rebellion. Now with independence, as we have noted, Algeria is training Angolan rebel troops, which may be a precursor to additional types of assistance. Once again the complaint has been raised that the United States and other NATO countries are providing arms to Portugal to suppress the rebellion. The Casablanca bloc version of "national liberation" in combination with the universal African attitude which justifies intervention to expel the remaining colonial powers creates an outlook for convulsion, turbulence, and strife. Africa is in for violent times. If Angola is an example, the magnitude of the violence will endanger the peace of large areas of Africa and carry the threat of contagion to other areas as external forces decide, as almost inevitably they will, to play a part in forcing a decision.

Irredentism

Even if the "national liberation" doctrine had not been embraced by African radical nationalist leaders as part and parcel of their Pan-Africanist approach, the old-fashioned irredentist drives which have plagued all of the continents of the world at one time or another are present in abundance in Africa.

The colonial borders damned time and again by African nationalists in the struggle for independence have been without exception inherited by the new states. To the extent that the contentions of the nationalists were correct, and in the main they were, Africa has a series of boundaries which ignore ethnic, tribal, geographic, historic, and economic factors. And as if this were not enough, the course of African development has resulted in uneven growth. Some areas with natural resources have become islands of development in a sea of subsistence economies; those with favorable geographic locations have become the corridors of access and egress for land-locked neighbors; some have become restive enclaves in larger geographic units; and others have become sprawling giants without any unifying or homogeneous common denominators. Africa's legacy is a dozen or more natural powder kegs. It is only a matter of time before the fuses touched off by Pan-Africanist pressure ignite one or more of them.

The Sahara, as we have seen, with its newly developing oil and mineral wealth, has been a crucial issue not only between France and Algeria. It is one also between Morocco and Algeria and Tunisia and Algeria. Both Morocco and Tunisia have claims on the vast Sahara hinterland. In a North African union, a Maghreb association of Morocco, Algeria, and Tunisia, a solution might be found. Bourguiba at an early date took this possibility into account. In the absence of a Maghrebian solution the Sahara holds the potential of multiple irredentist disputes. When the Spanish Sahara and the Spanish territory of Ifni, both of which are claimed by Morocco, are added, the opportunities for controversy in this part of Africa become formidable. Finally, if Morocco's claim to the entire area occupied by the Islamic Republic of Mauritania is thrown into the calculation, Northwest Africa presents a fertile source of conflict. As Mauritania's mineral resources become increasingly apparent, the intensity of Morocco's irredentism may well increase proportionately.

In the confine of boundaries in West Africa the expansionist drives of President Nkrumah threaten to upset the *pax colonialist*. Nkrumah's most emphatic and far-reaching claims have been on his immediate neighbor to the east, the Republic of Togo. As we have already noted, nothing less than the total incorporation of Togo into Ghana has been proposed by Nkrumah as the way to unify the Ewe tribe, divided between Ghana and Togo. Nkrumah has also given notice of his interest in a tribe divided between Ghana and the Ivory Coast and has made statements about a Ghanaian hegemony in West Africa which brought forth critical responses from Prime Minister Margai of Sierra Leone, the late President Olympio of Togo, and President Houphouët-Boigny of the Ivory Coast.

When such colonial bits of West African real estate as Portuguese and Spanish Guinea, *inter alia,* come on the market, the irredentist claims to the area are likely to accentuate the rivalries already present. For example, does Senegal or Guinea have a superior claim to Portuguese Guinea when it achieves independence? Both have provided sanctuary to Portuguese Guineans, and both have a finger in the pie. The area is not likely to be viable by itself, and in any event the pressures for adhesion to one or the other neighbors are likely to be considerable.

In Equatorial Africa the fragmented Cameroons are likely to provide at least a lingering source of claims and counter-claims. Although the Northern Cameroons have voted in a United Nations plebiscite for inclusion in the Federation of Nigeria, President Ahidjo has made it clear that the last has not been heard with respect to the Federal Republic of Cameroon's claim to the area. And although the Southern Cameroons have voted in a United Nations plebiscite for union with the Republic of Cameroun there could well be difficulties in launching the new federation, with disaffected groups finding refuge across the border and setting up irredentist claims of one sort or another.

In Central Africa the Congo itself incorporates within its present geographic confines many of the problems suggested above. With independence of the Portuguese areas—Angola and Mozambique—and the Rhodesias there is likely to be a whole new set of pulls and counter-pulls, claims and counter-claims. The Bakongo tribe, divided as it is among the former French Congo, the former Belgian Congo, and Angola, has already been the source of considerable controversy in the Congo crisis. Many more such disputes are likely to be in the offing as part of the dismantling of the whole colonial structure in Central Africa.

In the Horn of Africa, Somalia has laid claims to Northern Kenya, Eastern Ethiopia, and French Somaliland. The Somali people were as badly fragmented by colonial partition as any people in Africa. Newly independent Somalia's self-appointed mission to reunite the Somalis has already led to a chain of violent incidents with Ethiopia. Raids and counter-raids, retaliation, and repression have all grown in intensity in the last year. There have also been incidents on the Kenya northern frontier.

The United Arab Republic has in the past made claims to various segments of the northern Sudan. When these claims may be reactivated, if at all, is difficult to predict. In the present atmosphere of Africa, however, they cannot be totally filed away as "closed business."

In addition to such situations as those just cited there are many latent and dormant situations which could erupt any time it becomes convenient for one or another contestant in the leadership competition in Africa to advance this or that claim. For example, the ill-defined border between Liberia and Guinea which runs through some of the richest iron ore deposits in Africa, or the divided tribe which straddles the border of Northern Rhodesia and Katanga in the heart of Africa's copper belt, could become the source of bitter dispute between independent African states.

The Pan-Africanist states have by and large created an atmosphere conducive to irredentism. In their constant agitation for larger and larger geographic units a background for territorial claims has been laid. For example, Nkrumah's claims on Togo blend with his constant Pan-African protestations and the founding of the Union of African States (Ghana, Guinea, and Mali). Morocco has found aid and comfort in the Pan-Africanist movements for its claims on Mauritania until quite recently.

The Monrovia powers have been so concerned at the outlook for irredentist conflict that they called for peaceful change of boundaries. Prime Minister Balewa of Nigeria has been particularly exercised at the dangers to African peace from this source. Time and again he has condemned the use of force and threat and called for peaceful negotiation to resolve boundary questions. In a speech to the National Press Club in Washington, D.C., during an official visit to the United States he spelled out his thinking on this point:

. . . It [is] important for the African states to recognize the existing boundaries in the continent.

All of them, on gaining independence, would like to be admitted to the United Nations as a separate country. Therefore, it is most important to recognize the existing boundaries in Africa and only agree to one country in Africa being absorbed by another country under the free will of the people of the country concerned.

It is very dangerous for one country to try to eat into the territory of any other country, however small it may be.[6]

The effects of African irredentism are bound to transcend African borders. The Monrovia powers are on record as pledged to take all such incidents to the United Nations. Even without such a pledge the extra-African implications of the individual African country and bloc associations and postures are likely to call forth outside concern and even interference. The Soviet Union's propensity to deliver ultimata or to adopt unilaterally the position of self-appointed protector ensures, if nothing else does, that there will be an external dimension to African disputes of any magnitude. When put in the context of the mounting African arms race, and the involvement if not participation of other nations in that race, external involvement in irredentist conflicts in Africa appears inevitable.

The African Arms Race

The transfer of sovereignty from the European metropoles to the new African states entails the transfer of the duty of national self-defense and maintenance of internal law and order. Sovereignty confers the right to raise and maintain armed forces for these purposes. It also makes possible the diversion of the use of these forces to other purposes. External aggression instead of national self-defense, and internal repression instead of maintenance of law and order, have been the history of armed forces the world over. On the evidence of present trends, the prospect for Africa is that various states will be as prone as other states elsewhere have been to misdirect or misuse their armed forces.

The trail-blazer and the pacemaker on the African scene for many purposes has been Kwame Nkrumah. Arms for Africa must be included among his "firsts." Ghana, with a population variously computed between six and seven million (a population smaller than that of New York City), now has an army, a navy, and a jet air force. All are expanding, all are British-trained and still have, in part, British officers, and all are under the command of the President as Commander in Chief. The army has had experience in the Congo under approximate combat conditions.

Nkrumah had proclaimed as his goal the best armed forces in Africa. Their possible mission has been a source of concern for his neighbors. None of them has armed forces of any size, and by no stretch of the imagination, Nkrumah's or anybody else's, do neighboring forces constitute a threat to Ghanaian independence, territorial integrity, or sovereignty. If the mission of Ghana's armed forces is not national defense with respect to attacks from neighbors, is it national defense with respect to attacks from further afield? National defense against whom? The imperialists, colonialists, and neo-colonialists is one answer offered by apologists for the Ghanaian military build-up. The Anglo-French invasion of Suez, the French in Algeria and Tunisia, even the Italians in Ethiopia as long ago as 1936 are all pointed to as the type of threat or contingency Ghana is preparing for. None of these carries any great conviction. Ghana would seem to have several other clearly identifiable purposes behind its policy of a military build-up.

First and foremost is Ghana's desire to play a major Pan-African role. Nkrumah is aware of the power he has derived from his relatively advantageous economic position. Ghanaian reserves, as we have seen, have provided Nkrumah with the resources for influencing decisions in many parts of Africa. Nkrumah is also aware of the power imposing armed forces would give him in influencing decisions in many parts of Africa. In retrospect, one of the key limiting factors in the role Nkrumah chose for Ghana to play in the Congo crisis was the small size of the forces at its disposal. Nkrumah and his radical nationalist colleagues have repeatedly called for, and have even taken some steps toward, the formation of an African high command.

The "national liberation" policy which Ghana has blended into its Pan-African role calls for substantial armed might in the final analysis. Intervention and subversion in independent African countries entail military assistance and technical cadres. They may even in the last resort involve armed forces. Retaliation by the African government being subverted cannot be ruled out.

Ghana's active brand of anti-colonialism, also incorporated into the country's "national liberation" policy and Pan-African role, at a minimum entails military assistance and technical cadres. It may also involve the dispatch of "volunteers" after the Chinese example in Korea: from time to time Ghanaian sources alluded to the possibility of volunteers for Algeria. It is likely too to involve serving as an arsenal and transmission belt for arms coming from further afield; as Guinea served in the Cameroun Republic rebellion and the United Arab Republic in the Congo crisis, Ghana may in the Angola situation. The sanctuary principle established in Korea may not carry over into Africa. Certainly France did not feel constrained by any such principle in North Africa.

Second among Ghana's reasons for military build-up, national prestige seems to call for commanding all of the paraphernalia of sovereignty, including armed forces. The African general and admiral seem in some areas of Africa to be as necessary as evidence of independence and national dignity as the elected African official and the Africanized civil service. The drive is to have everything everybody else has.

Third, authoritarian governmental systems have found armed forces a useful instrument for sustaining their power. It is too soon to draw conclusions about this aspect of militarism in Africa. In Egypt and the Sudan, once military *coups* were effected, the armies became the backbone of the régimes and the instruments for internal repression. In Morocco, one of the Casablanca powers, the army is an important support for the government of King Hassan II. In the Republic of the Congo (Brazzaville) President Youlou has used the army to put down the opposition. It is pertinent to note, however, that Nkrumah has sought to nullify the possibility that the armed forces could evolve as an independent focus of power—as happened in Egypt and the Sudan—by retaining professional British officers in key posts four and five years after independence. However, with the recent ousting of a large contingent of British officers from the Ghanaian army this avenue of risk may have been opened, and with the growth of the armed forces, magnified.

In any event, whatever the reasons, and all of the foregoing would seem apposite, Ghana has opened a highly competitive field which endangers not only the stability but also the peace of Africa under circumstances which create the most explosive conditions for external involvement.

Ghana has in the first instance relied on the United Kingdom for arms and training as well as staffing. Of late Ghana has, at least in its "national liberation" exercises, looked to the Communist bloc. Guinea has been Communist-bloc armed, trained and, in part, officered. The United Arab Republic is likewise bloc armed and trained. Morocco has had both Western and Communist-bloc arms and training, but the bloc presence is more recent.

The United Arab Republic has, with bloc aid, developed something of a light-arms industry, and a multiplier effect is in evidence as Nasser has provided arms to Somalia, and at one time in limited quantity to the Gizenga faction in the Congo, and may offer them to others.

The Communist bloc has held itself available as a cooperative alternative source of arms if they should not be forthcoming from the West. Touré claims that he initially turned to the bloc only after the United States "rebuffed" his request for arms. Bourguiba threatened to turn to the bloc if the United States and the United Kingdom did not provide arms he thought he needed. Lumumba turned to the bloc, too, after the United States and the United Nations refused his demands.

Thus we see the outlines and the beginnings of an arms race, involving outside cold-war sources of supply and personnel, emerging from the radical nationalist bloc of African states. The response of the rest of Africa has not been passive.

Nigeria has embarked on a program to build up its armed forces to a level commensurate with its size and its role in African affairs. Nigerian forces are being equipped and trained by the United Kingdom and Canada. According to Governor-General Azikiwe, Nigeria views its role as "resolute support of the United Nations," opposition "to all forms of aggression and coercion," and "moral support to the legitimate aspirations of dependent peoples seeking their freedom from colonial status." [7] In the context of its general foreign policy posture Nigeria's entrance into the arms race can be viewed as largely responsive to the forces—Pan-Africanism, irrendentism, and "national liberation"—which Nigeria has opposed. Sierra Leone has a defense agreement with the United Kingdom and is receiving its equipment, training, and cadres from that source. Sierra Leone, as we have noted, has also reacted sharply to Nkrumah's pretensions to oversee West Africa.

The former French territories in West and Equatorial Africa are also looking to their armed forces. With the exception of Guinea and Mali, all are looking to France for arms, training, and cadres, and all are receiving them. Every state of l'expression française in this group from Mauritania to the Chad is developing national armed forces. The Ivory Coast has kept the Ghanaian example very much in sight. Mauritania has similarly kept the Moroccan example very much in sight. As we have already seen, Ethiopia and Somalia are engaged in controversy and conflict, and Somalia is drawing arms from the United Arab Republic. Ethiopia has received its arms from the United States. Thus by and large the Monrovia powers are all going through a military build-up partly a normal concomitant of the transfer of sovereignty and partly a reaction to the Casablanca posture.

The situation is pregnant with danger. Not only is there a possibility of armed conflict but there is also a diversion of scarce human and material resources to one of the most unproductive of all national sectors. Such diversion detracts from economic development and, if of sufficient magnitude, can undercut it. National armed forces beyond the minimum needed to maintain legitimate law and order, by adversely affecting growth, contribute to internal political instability and reinforce the direct danger to African stability and peace arising from the external impact of the evolving arms race.

It is significant that the African states have recognized the threat to world peace of the nuclear arms race between the West and the Communist bloc but have hardly perceived the one gaining momentum on their own continent, where the risks of limited wars, because war there is at least conceptually susceptible to being limited, are so great. Ghana particularly has been outspoken in urging the establishment of a "nuclear-free zone" in Africa and the "removal of foreign bases" from Africa. Nkrumah has said nothing of making Africa an "arms-free zone" and the "removal of foreign arms." The first demand—a "nuclear-free zone" in Africa—has little if any meaning except with respect to French nuclear explosions in the Sahara. And the demand for removal of foreign bases refers primarily to French bases in North and West Africa, but also to United States and United Kingdom bases in Libya, and the United States communications base in Ethiopia. Although there can be no objection to these proposals if the African countries concerned agree—e.g., if the states of *l'expression française* want French bases removed—they are misleading in that they do not deal with the very real threats to the stability and peace of Africa and the world arising from other policies being vigorously pursued by the radical nationalist states or evolving generally in Africa.

As we have seen, the African presence in world affairs is a dual one. One aspect of it currently signifies for the world at large a series of restless and precipitous forces which, unless restrained, have the potential to jeopardize world peace. In fact, in the name of world peace the radical nationalist bloc in Africa has assumed a posture which threatens to endanger that very peace by unleashing a floodtide of little wars and arms contests here, there, and everywhere on the continent.

A second aspect of the African presence—if somewhat less dramatic, still currently that of the majority—brings a serious restraining influence on the radical nationalist African presence and offers an alternative course for the new states—economic growth to sustain political independence in a context of peaceful change and friendly relations. The Monrovia bloc, in adopting this posture, put itself in clear opposition to the radical nationalist Casablanca bloc.

The dual presence thus not only signifies two very different things to the outside world; it also injects, as we shall see in the following chapters, into the stream of world affairs a basic African dichotomy with all that means for the balance of political power in the world at large.

Chapter 12

THE WORLD BALANCE OF POWER

As we have already seen, an arms race in Africa will surely affect world peace; and the policies of the new states with regard to economic development will both affect their respective international roles and alter trade and other economic relations. Nevertheless, at present and for a long time to come the new African states are not likely to affect the disposition of world military and economic power. It is in the political sphere that the multiplicity of new African states will make their presence felt in the foreseeable future, with respect to the power positions of the free world, the Communist bloc, and the underdeveloped world. Already the high national birth rate on the African continent has significantly altered the world balance of political power.

Effects of the emerging African presence is being felt in four major areas of political power—Western Europe, the United States, the Communist bloc, and the Afro-Asian grouping. These areas are all considered in this chapter in the light of changes already apparent and in the offing. The manifestations in the United Nations of the shifts in power in these areas are also considered.

The African Presence and West Europe

The disappearance of the colonial relationship between the leading European colonial powers, excepting of course Portugal, and their former African territories has altered the position of the metropolitan power not simply within Africa but also, and significantly, in the world at large. Moreover, the process will continue. As the remaining dependent territories on the African continent accede to independence, and those recently independent display increasing independence psychologically and politically as well as legally, the position of the metropolitan countries will change even more.

As for Portugal, the handwriting is on the wall for those who would read it. Portugal's position in Africa has already undergone a drastic transformation; once the master colonial power in the classic tradition, Portugal has been catapulted into the role of number one colonial villain—anachronistic, despotic, and doomed. In the world at large Portugal is rapidly approaching the status of the Republic of South Africa, that of an exile from the world community. Portugal is *persona non grata* throughout the underdeveloped world, an obvious target for the Communist bloc, and an increasing embarrassment to the free world. Probably the single most important liability of the newly organized Development Assistance Committee of the Organization for Economic Cooperation and Development is Portuguese membership. It is unfortunate that this most promising of aid-coordinating bodies should at this moment in history be handicapped by the membership of a country which evokes throughout Africa bitter memories of all the predatory aspects of European colonialism.

The United Kingdom, with the demise of its African empire, is no longer the world's leading imperial power, but it occupies a new and still important position as *primus inter pares* in the new Commonwealth of Nations. The new Commonwealth now has a preponderance of Afro-Asian members, and the prospect is for more such members. The Commonwealth, the sterling area, trade

and economic ties, cultural and educational links, and a waning
military power are the instruments of the United Kingdom's continuing relationship with the former members of the Empire,
particularly those in the Afro-Asian world. The political dimension
of the relationship is new. The political control of the earlier empire days has been replaced by the informal and formal consulta-
tions of Commonwealth Prime Ministers and their ministerial associates. Ghana, the former Gold Coast, is able to establish and
pursue policies in open conflict with those of the United Kingdom
and other Commonwealth countries. So, too, are the other independent African and Asian states. In fact, notwithstanding the
United Kingdom's obvious reluctance, the new Afro-Asian balance
of power in the Commonwealth was able to force the withdrawal
of the Union of South Africa, one of the earliest members, which
subsequently became a republic, severing any remaining allegiance
to the British crown. So far has the shift in the balance of power
in the Commonwealth proceeded that Queen Elizabeth visited
Ghana as planned in early November 1961, despite serious misgivings at home about her physical safety, to say nothing of the
seeming approbation her presence would lend to a régime widely
disapproved of in the United Kingdom. The government feared
not only the reaction in Ghana, which might have gone as far as
withdrawal from the Commonwealth according to reports then
current, but even more the critical reaction likely to come from
elsewhere in Commonwealth Africa, and probably Asia, if the
Queen's visit were cancelled or deferred.

Nevertheless, despite the shift of power within the Commonwealth, the United Kingdom in its new if lesser role as first among
equals has in one important way enhanced its world power position. The Commonwealth is in many ways a more important body
than ever before. It has members in all the continents of the world
representing most if not all of the races in the world. Its membership is larger than ever before and likely to grow. The Commonwealth has provided the United Kingdom with a graceful way out
of empire and into its new role as a non-colonial power. The Commonwealth prevents the United Kingdom from being viewed as a
relatively small if highly populous European power with an important but relatively declining industrial and military potential.

On balance, then, African independence has transformed the United Kingdom from the world's leading imperial power with major holdings in Africa (even after Asia had gone its way) into a European power struggling to maintain a new, and lesser, international position through its remaining economic power and its political leadership within the new Commonwealth.

France too, with the disappearance of its empire in Africa, has lost her position as a leading imperial power but has a leading role in the Franco-African Community. France has also moved into something akin to a senior partner's role with many of the former French territories in Africa which remain on friendly and close terms with her but outside the formal structure of the Community. This Franco-African Community, the Common Market, the franc zone, trade, economic, and foreign aid ties, cultural and educational links, and military arrangements remain the principal channels of France's relations with the former French colonies in Africa. The political relationships are special and still evolving. The Community states and other friendly former French territories tend to follow French foreign policy leadership and to keep fairly close political liaison with France. On various issues the relationships have been strained. The Algerian rebellion, the Tunisian pocket-war, and French atomic explosions in the Sahara have all put to the test the political relationships. However, despite sporadic and spotty criticism the new African states of *l'expression française* have remained surprisingly steadfast in their adherence to French foreign policy positions.

Guinea, which broke entirely with France, and Mali, which retains a continuing but attenuated relationship, feel little constrained to follow the French lead in international affairs. In fact, Guinea has often seemed to feel compelled to oppose the French at every turn and has frequently been in the forefront of African countries critical of France's African policies. Lately there have been signs of a Franco-Guinean rapprochement. Notwithstanding, Guinea has come to occupy a position in former French West Africa potentially disruptive of the French interest in maintaining any sort of political hegemony in the area. In many ways the very existence of the independent break-away state of Guinea tends to act as a magnet drawing other former French territories, if not to Guinea itself, away from too intimate a relationship with France. The association of Guinea and Mali with the vigorous anti-French state of Ghana in the Union of African States has tended to accentuate the gulf between France and these two former colonies.

In North Africa the two former protectorates of Morocco and Tunisia have had an uneven relationship with France, at times openly hostile and strained, and at times apparently friendly and cooperative. The possibility of a union or association of the North African states of Morocco and Tunisia, Algeria, and France has waxed and waned. For a long time the seven-year Algerian war was the chief obstacle to the realization of President Bourguiba's concept of Maghreb. The 1961 Bizerte incident between France and Tunisia interposed another formidable obstacle at the very time when an accommodation between France and Algeria was being reached on the Evian agreement. Since then Algeria has come to independence and the Bizerte incident appears to have been conveniently lost to sight and mind. France has inaugurated a major economic aid program for Algeria and resumed the extension of significant economic aid to both Tunisia and Morocco. The climate of Franco-North African relations has thus improved markedly. Nevertheless, time would seem to have run out on the possibility of any sort of a French political union with the Maghreb states. The most that seems possible now would be an economic association of France and the three North African states linked to or under the umbrella of the Common Market.

In any event, with the exception of the French territory of Somaliland, now under increasing pressure from the independent state of Somalia, the French political presence in Africa has become one of a former colonial power having close ties with many former colonies and strained relations with others. In terms of influence the political power of France has decreased strikingly from that formerly exerted by the strong French presence in Asia and above all in Africa, and at least nominally in the Pacific and America. In the United Nations context France has in one sense enhanced its importance by drawing support from many of the new African states of *l'expression française;* but in another sense she has become vulnerable from time to time to embarrassing votes against French positions by former French African territories or protectorates. Guinea, Mali, and to a lesser extent Morocco have been actual or potential opponents on a good many issues.

France's attempt to create a formal counterpart of the Commonwealth, that is, to reorganize the Community so that France would occupy a role comparable to that of the United Kingdom in the Commonwealth, has not succeeded. The Community has gone through a drastic transformation and today has little of the Commonwealth's intangible but nonetheless real authority in the affairs of its members and the world at large.

Belgium has not only been reduced to its natural size; it has also been subjected to such pressure that its uneasy internal unity has been badly damaged, perhaps irreparably. The Congo's gaining of its independence, followed by the seemingly endless Congo crisis, has transformed Belgium from an empire with valuable African holdings into a divided nation. The violence in the Trust Territory of Ruanda and the abortive Belgian effort to establish a republic there on its own authority and without the assent of the United Nations, prior to Ruanda's accession to independence, have dealt further serious blows to the Belgian position not only in Africa but in the world at large.

The image of a neo-colonialist Belgium invading the Republic of the Congo, supporting the "secessionist state" of Katanga under President Tshombé, exploiting Katangan copper and cobalt resources, and manipulating the opposing forces in Ruanda is likely to haunt Belgian relationships with African states for at least a generation to come, notwithstanding the partial mitigation of Belgium's relatively harmonious withdrawal from her role as the United Nations trust power in Ruanda-Urundi in mid-1962 with the accession of the territories to independence as the Republic of Rwanda and the Kingdom of Burundi. And, to only a slightly lesser extent, it is likely to color Belgian relationships with most of the underdeveloped world.

Thus the relationships with Africa of the United Kingdom, France, Belgium, and Portugal, and simultaneously their political power in Africa, have undergone revolutionary transformation. Of the minor colonial powers, Italy has completely disappeared from Africa, and Spain's hold on its few remaining enclaves and bits and pieces is precarious. The political imperium has gone or is going.

A new set of political relationships has been evolving, with the United Kingdom and France enhancing their strength in the United Nations, on the one hand, through more potentially friendly votes, and exposing their flanks, on the other, through more potentially critical votes from former colonies, whether consistently or only sporadically hostile to the former metropoles.

The cultural and economic ties remain, transformed and adapted, but identifiable and significant. The revamped but still evolving cultural and economic ties are likely to influence the eventual shape and form of the new political relationships and may even provide the underpinnings for them. This is most clearly seen in the area of language and trade patterns. The Eurafrican links in these fields are likely to persist for a long time to come and provide, if nothing else, practical imperatives for evolving complementary political relationships between the metropoles and their former colonies.

The United States and Africa

For the United States, despite the absence of any history of involvement in Africa, the establishment of satisfactory relationships with the new African nations is not all clear sailing. For example, because of the United States' relationship with France the possibilities for close and friendly relations with Algeria have been rendered more difficult. The United States has also been engulfed by some of the backwash of the violence in Angola, the trouble in the Federation of Rhodesia and Nyasaland, and the racial discrimination in the Republic of South Africa. Nevertheless, for the United States it is fundamentally true, in a sense which cannot apply for the European countries, that every new African state is a potential friend. The real opportunities, even in those instances where there are complications arising from triangular situations involving Europe, Africa, and the United States, far outweigh the possible pitfalls.

In the pre-independence period in Africa, before 1957, and even in large degree until 1960, the United States tended to view

Africa as a closed continent and as the private preserve of its European friends and allies. The United States' relations with African areas tended to be limited. They were mostly confined to a traditional trading relation along the North African coast, especially with Morocco, dating back to American action against the Barbary pirates, and a special historic relation with Liberia arising from the resettlement of freed American slaves on the Liberian coast in the first half of the nineteenth century. There were a handful of investments, mostly in South Africa, a scattering of missionaries in remote corners of the huge continent, reaching as far afield as the island of Madagascar in the Indian Ocean, and a limited amount of trade, largely in minerals, with the balance of trade consistently unfavorable to the United States.

The United States was content to deal with Africa by and large through the European metropoles, and they in turn were happy to keep a direct American presence out of Africa. Thus even the Congo Basin area, which by the terms of the Act of Berlin of 1885 was to be open to all powers for trade and investment on an equal basis, largely remained a European preserve insofar as the United States was concerned. The Belgian Congo and Northern Rhodesia were thought of in American terms as Belgian and British, respectively, for practically all purposes—economic as well as political.

The revolutionary changes in political relationships between Europe and Africa implied the creation of new relationships between the United States and Africa; and since the advent of Ghana in 1957 and the ensuing thrust of African states onto the world scene, the United States has had to place Africa in an entirely new policy perspective. The United States now has an active and growing political interest in Africa, and *vice versa*. It has found many friends as well as some critics of its policies in Africa. On such vital African issues as the Congo crisis, the Angolan rebellion, and condemnation of South African apartheid, the United States has generally found itself on the same side as most African states. On other key African issues such as Algeria, the Bizerte incident, and the immediate abolition of colonialism the United States has often found itself abstaining from or opposing the position of the majority of African states. By and large the United States has found common ground with the bulk of African states—the Monrovia bloc—on most issues. And similarly it has not infrequently found itself at odds with the radical nationalist states—the Casablanca bloc—on many issues.

Thus, insofar as the free world as a whole is concerned, the diffusion of the Eurafrican links and the shift in the political balance of power occasioned by the dissolution of the European empires in Africa has been partially offset by new links between the independent African states and the United States. The African political factor, which for the West historically operated in bilateral channels stretching north and south between Africa and Europe, has become triangular, reaching from Africa to the United States and Canada as well as to Europe, with a resulting marked shift in the balance of political power within the West.

The triangular relationship has brought a new dimension to United States policy. Not only must the new African presence be taken into account in decisions on Afro-European problems; it must also be considered in formulating almost all international policies. For example, the various brands of neutralism, as we have already seen, lead to their exponents' taking or refraining from taking a variety of positions on such diverse issues as Berlin, nuclear testing, and the admission of Communist China to the United Nations. On all three of these issues African practitioners of "positive neutralism" are likely to oppose the position of the United States in the United Nations and in other contexts where these neutralists exert political power, e.g., the Belgrade Conference. Many of the Brazzaville powers—the twelve former French territories banded together in the Union of African and Malagasy States (UAM) and part of the larger Monrovia bloc—are likely to take the positions contrary to the postive neutralists. The net result may be more support than opposition for the United States on these issues. Under some circumstances, however, the opposite result may obtain. Thus, in the General Assembly debates in late 1961, on the issue of outlawing nuclear weapons and declaring Africa a "denuclearized zone" without creating a system of controls and inspection, the bulk of the African states voted affirmatively, in company with the Communist bloc, in the face of determined Western opposition to the opportunism and transparent insincerity of the Soviet Union, which had just completed a series of nuclear tests in defiance of the voluntary test-ban on nuclear explosions.

The United States is also subject to pressure, actual or potential, from the large number of new African states in many of its international actions. The United States, particularly under the Kennedy Administration has been solicitous of African and Asian opinion on such issues as the self-determination of colonial peoples and nuclear testing. There were uncontrolled exclamations of disappointment, frustration, and even anger by American spokesmen at the role of many of the self-styled uncommitted and unaligned Afro-Asian powers at the Belgrade Conference in September 1961. The United States had gone a long way to accommodate and conciliate Afro-Asian opinion in the United Nations and elsewhere on a score of issues, involving difficult decisions disturbing to the European side of the triangular relations already discussed, on general grounds of principle which such African states as Ghana, Guinea, Mali, and Morocco seemed to ignore at Belgrade. President Kennedy reacted sharply. In signing the new International Development and Security Act the President issued a statement which Senator Keating of New York later incorporated in the 1962 fiscal year appropriation act providing funds for the new "decade of development" foreign aid program. The language, although qualified in subsequent utterances and overlooked in practice where its application apparently pinched too hard (e.g., in aid to Ghana and Guinea), is now part of the total United States posture toward the Afro-Asian world:

> In the administration of these funds great attention and consideration should be given to those nations which share the view of the United States on the world crisis.[1]

The Communist Bloc and Africa

In the same way that Africa has with independence opened itself up to North American powers (and Western European

powers not previously involved with Africa) it has also opened itself up to the Communist-bloc nations, and there has been a
further shift in the political balance which obtained during the
colonial era.

The Communist states, like the United States, are largely
treading virgin territory insofar as their evolving relationships with
Africa are concerned. Outside of a limited tsarist interest in and
relationship with the ancient empire of Ethiopia, Russia had almost no contact with Africa until the recent African political up-
surge. There have, however, been limited Communist sallies into
Africa ever since the end of World War II. These have been
mostly attempts to indoctrinate and convert African students in
London and Paris to Marxism, and if possible Soviet communism.
There have also been limited attempts to penetrate French West
African trade unions through the French *Confédération Générale
de Travail* (CGT) and to penetrate here and there some of the
new African groups. Some French African political leaders have
been influenced by these attempts. In his earlier days President
Houphouët-Boigny of the Ivory Coast was influenced by Marxism,
and President Sékou Touré of Guinea still is. There has been less
evidence of Marxist influence in former British areas of Africa,
although President Nkrumah, as we have noted, has described
himself as a "Christian Marxist" and claims that he derived the
organizational tactics used in founding the Convention People's
Party in Ghana from Communist primers. Nevertheless, it is not
an overstatement to say that it was only with Guinea's accession
to independence by "secession" late in 1958 that the Soviet Union,
and thereafter the rest of the bloc, made their formal diplomatic
debut in the new Africa.

In Guinea, with the vacuum left by French withdrawal, the
Communist bloc found a warm reception on the African continent.
Ghana, since it became a republic in 1960, has been moving closer
and closer to the bloc in its political policies, internal and external, as well as in its trade and aid policies. Several other African
states have been willing to make or receive bloc overtures. By and
large the radical nationalist states have viewed bloc connections
as proof of their "neutralist" positions. All of them—Guinea,
Ghana, the United Arab Republic, Morocco, and Mali—have im-

portant economic, technical and military aid arrangements with the bloc, as well as evolving trade relations and important foreign policy links. All have been at great pains to demonstrate their anti-West "neutralism." The UAR has had its ups and downs with the bloc, particularly with respect to bloc interference in internal UAR politics and in Middle Eastern affairs. Guinea too, as we have noted, has had its difficulties with Soviet Union interference in its internal affairs. Morocco has also tended in some ways to be more restrained in its pro-bloc "neutralism" than other Casablanca bloc powers. Among Monrovia powers, Liberia in late 1961 and the Ivory Coast in January 1963 both charged Communist implication in plots against the lives of the heads of State, and intimated "foreign connections."

In any event, the same process of dilution of the Western European colonial-power political hegemony in Africa which has enhanced the role of the United States in Africa has also enlarged the Communist-bloc role in Africa. The bloc has not been slow to move in, and it now has aid programs of one type or another in at least a dozen African states ranging from the normally pro-Western "neutralist" states of Tunisia and Ethiopia to clearly pro-bloc "neutralist" states among the Casablanca group. And the Soviet Union is not the only member of the bloc to participate. With the exception of Albania and possibly Rumania, all of the European satellites are represented in Soviet-led multi-lateral aid programs in Africa. One of the side effects of the Sino-Soviet doctrinal dispute is the development of separate Communist Chinese aid programs in Africa outside the Soviet-bloc programs. The bloc presence has meant diplomatic missions, economic and technical aid personnel, military personnel in those countries receiving military assistance, trade personnel, information and cultural exchange personnel, and wandering minstrel men, ballerinas, and even Hungarian gymnasts. It has also meant many educational scholarships, travel grants, and straightout junkets for Africans in bloc countries. The whole apparatus of bloc relations is unfolding in many places in Africa.

Unlike the United States, the Soviet Union appears prepared, however, to disregard neutralist opinion and opposition, including that of the African states, whenever it suits its purposes. Thus the Soviet Union resumed nuclear testing, abandoning the voluntary, self-imposed ban of the world's atomic powers, to coincide with the meeting of "neutralist states" at Belgrade in the autumn of 1961. The Soviet Union's attitude seems to be one of self-assurance that even when it blatantly ignores world neutralist opinion many of the so-called neutralist states will through fear, favor, or faith apply a double standard which will condone or ignore Soviet transgressions. The neutralist states would probably condemn in most instances comparable acts by the United States.

This dualism with regard to actions of the Soviet Union and the United States among neutralist states speaks volumes about their basic outlook toward the leading world powers. The United States, it would seem, is not likely to react to neutralist condemnation with anything more than hurt feelings. One can hardly predict, however, just how the Soviet Union might react when sufficiently provoked. Self-proclaimed neutralist states in Africa have been no more immune than such states elsewhere in the world from using this double standard for measurement of Russian and American behavior. For example, Presidents Nkrumah and Keita of Ghana and Mali, respectively, used the double standard at the Belgrade Conference and then repaired to Moscow and Washington, respectively, to sell the Belgrade line on an impartial basis, although only the Soviet Union at that point had breached the ban on nuclear testing.

On balance, then, the Soviet Union is seeking to cultivate the favor of all neutralist states, and more widely in Africa, the favor of all the new states. She is prepared, however, to sacrifice their good opinion whenever it is deemed advantageous to do so without, apparently, any great fear that she will be unable to recoup her losses in relatively short order. The African presence in the world arena has broadened the Soviet field of action and created new Soviet opportunities. It has also created among many of the Monrovia powers a potential opposition to the Soviet Union's more ruthless power moves even though the opposition may sometimes be muted in tone. A vote against the Communist bloc in the United Nations, no matter how low-keyed the voice registering the vote, is still a nay.

The African Presence in the Afro-Asian World

In the Afro-Asian world also there is a dramatic shift in process. The African states, only eight in number in 1958, were the junior partners in the Afro-Asian bloc. But with thirty-two members at the end of 1962 and another half-dozen on the horizon, they are rapidly gaining in potential power. The African states have not yet exercised to the full their increased strength within the bloc. Asian personalities still tend to carry the greater weight, and they have in an historical sense priority claims to world recognition. Ambassador U Thant of Burma was unanimously elected Secretary-General of the United Nations, and Rajeshwan Dayal of India was at a critical time head of the United Nations operation in the Congo. Nevertheless, the African states are increasingly exerting their influence in the Afro-Asian bloc, and significantly also in African blocs.

The largest grouping of African states, the Monrovia bloc, is strictly African in composition and orientation and is likely to remain so. The more nearly it welds itself into a homogeneous group, the more likely it is to assert itself as an independent factor in the larger Afro-Asian bloc. The Casablanca bloc, which is also strictly African in composition but not in orientation, is likely because of its limited membership of six states, and because of its relatively isolated position in Africa, to seek closer contact with and integration in the larger Afro-Asian bloc or in a neutralist bloc on the order of the Belgrade Conference group, unless it achieves a reconciliation with the Monrovia bloc which checks this tendency. It was not accidental that Ghana, the United Arab Republic, Mali, Guinea, and Morocco—*all* of the Casablanca bloc powers at the time—constituted a majority of the African states at the Belgrade Conference.

The Brazzaville twelve—former French African territories —which are members of the Monrovia bloc and the Afro-Asian bloc, also have, as we have seen, strong Eurafrican ties. They have plural interests and do not in any sense operate as strictly "African-

bloc" or strictly "neutralist" states. They act in many contexts—
the African, the Afro-Asian, and the Eurafrican, to say nothing of
the world arena generally.

It may be said that the growing number of African states
has already shifted the balance of power within the Afro-Asian
bloc and, of course, within Africa itself. The accession to independence of the large number of former French territories ended
the monopoly position of the pioneer African nationalist of recent
times, Dr. Nkrumah; and with Nigerian independence an alternate
pole of attraction was supplied for many of the new states. Thus
Dr. Nkrumah could lead only the Casablanca bloc powers into
the Belgrade Conference, and the outlook is for little more success
for his efforts to merge African states other than the six Casablanca powers more tightly into Afro-Asian groupings.

The shifts within the Afro-Asian world (and within Africa
itself) have important implications not only for the political posture of the Afro-Asian bloc and for the African presence in world
affairs but also for the West and the Communist bloc. The African
presence has disrupted the façade so carefully contrived at the
Bandung Conference of a community and identity of interests
among most, if not all, Afro-Asian states. Some attitudes are
common to almost all of them, e.g., anti-colonialism and opposition to the use of nuclear weapons. Beyond this level of generality
there are distinct differences and even problems between various
Asian and African states and among African states. There are distinct differences in attitudes on such basic matters as the proper
relationship between former colonial territories and former metropoles, between Afro-Asian states and Israel. There are problems
over the role of India in Africa, over Communist China's admission to the United Nations, over the priority to be accorded various
international problems agitating world peace and stability, and
over Sino-Russian support of so-called "national liberation" movements in Africa.

Thus the absence of a monolithic Afro-Asian point of view
reflects the growing divisions within Africa itself. In practical terms
this means not only that political power is shifting toward Africa
within the Afro-Asian group, but also that the situation is fluid
within Africa itself and that both the West and the Communist

bloc have the opportunity and need to evolve new relationships with African states. Neither the West nor the Communist bloc can think any longer of winning the Afro-Asian world *en bloc*. The new states have national identities and national interests, like states anywhere else in the world. The relationships must be shaped to the individual states.

The African Presence at the United Nations

The over-all effects and the process of the shifts in the balance of world political power are perhaps most visible in the United Nations. The African presence in the United Nations has taken on massive proportions—numerically and substantively. One quarter of the membership is African, and starting in mid-1960 every session of the General Assembly and the Security Council has been confronted with a major African issue—the Congo, Algeria, Angola, Bizerte, Rwanda-Burundi, Southern Rhodesia, the Republic of South Africa, and residual colonialism. It goes without saying that the Trusteeship Council has been largely occupied with matters concerning the decolonization of African trust territories, with Togo, the Cameroons, Italian Somaliland and Tanganyika achieving independence in 1961, and Ruanda-Urundi in 1962. The Afro-Asian lobby and the more specialized standing group at the United Nations of the independent African states are in the thick of things, sponsoring resolutions, promising support, threatening opposition, and generally maneuvering for position. An African member of the Security Council has now become a recognized necessity. And in this regard the United Arab Republic, despite the fact that it votes with the African bloc in the United Nations, is thought of as a Near Eastern state rather than as an African one. Thus in 1961 and 1962, while the UAR was a member of the Security Council, first Liberia and then Ghana was viewed as the African member of the Security Council.

The large African contingent in the United Nations has had the effect of making the world conscious of the African presence. The scramble for African votes on this or that issue among the great powers has so vividly dramatized that presence that the symptom has frequently been mistaken for the cause. The new African presence is significant, as we have seen, because it has basically altered the political balance of power in the world; African votes in the United Nations are but one symptom, albeit an important one, of this altered balance of power.

The plethora of African issues on the agendas of the Security Council and the General Assembly are another symptom or manifestation of the changing political balance of power in the world. The recurrent agenda items concerning colonial crises, which we noted above, also are reflections of the changing political positions of the European metropolitan countries in Africa and beyond. The African states can now take to task—almost with impunity —their former colonial overlords and the remaining colonial powers. The Eurafrican relationship has assumed dramatically new proportions, and the United Nations is the stage on which the African states display the change with most gusto.

Perhaps the most vivid illustration of the African presence in the United Nations is the General Assembly vote of 67 to 1, in October 1961, to censure the Republic of South Africa for remarks made by the South African Minister of Foreign Affairs in the Assembly. The remarks were censured as "offensive, fictitious, and erroneous." Any objective reading of the remarks would reveal that they were no more "offensive, fictitious, and erroneous" than the Soviet charge, often repeated in the United Nations in connection with Prime Minister Lumumba's death, that Secretary General Dag Hammarskjöld was a "murderer"; but, as a leading American newspaper has noted, "no one moved for censure of such statements as 'offensive, fictitious, and erroneous.' " [2] Similarly no one has moved for censure of repeated Soviet charges that country A or B was responsible for the "murder" of the late Secretary-General.

The Republic of South Africa incident and the crisis issues on the United Nations agenda have tended to portray only one view of the volatile African presence—the direct full-face view of colonial and former colonial territories emerging on the world scene against a backdrop of violence and strife, in the Congo, Algeria, Angola, Bizerte, and Ruanda-Urundi. It is necessary to examine the profile views to get a fuller picture of the African presence in the United Nations—and, thus, in the world arena.

The case of the admission of Mauritania and Outer Mongolia to the United Nations provides a double exposure. One view exposes the willingness of large numbers of African states to engage in power politics to achieve their goals; the other view exposes the type of problem which divides African states and makes the African presence in world affairs a many-faceted one.

Morocco has laid claim to the entire territory of the Islamic Republic of Mauritania, the last of the French West African territories to achieve independence, and found support for its position among the Casablanca bloc. Mauritania turned to the other former French African territories and found support in recognition by the Brazzaville twelve, and generally among the powers which were later to constitute the Monrovia bloc. Morocco's irredentist claim to Mauritania is vague and undocumented, not unlike those of other African states to neighboring territory. Generally the Pan-Africanist states—the Casablanca powers—reject colonial boundaries and tend to support irredentist claims. And, as we have also noted, the Monrovia powers tend to accept existing geographic borders as realities which could be altered only by mutual consent of the parties.[3]

In order to exclude Mauritania from the United Nations when it applied for membership in early 1961, Morocco sought support from the Soviet Union, which voted against Mauritania's admission, much to the chagrin of most African states. Morocco's relationship with the Communist bloc became closer and closer, including enlarged economic aid and trade and the acceptance of Soviet military aid, including jet planes.

In the 1961 winter session of the United Nations the Soviet Union offered a deal. It would refrain from casting a veto on Mauritania's application if the West and Nationalist China would refrain from vetoing the admission of the Communist state of Outer Mongolia. Nationalist China balked and threatened to exercise its veto. The African states, particularly those of *l'expression française*, reacted not only against the Soviet Union, which tied together the unrelated applications of these two states in an arbitrary manner, but even more strongly against Nationalist

China, and indirectly but with effect against the United States. The African states suggested that if Nationalist China vetoed Outer Mongolia and thus precipitated a retaliatory Soviet veto of Mauritania, the African states might have to vote to recommend the admission of Communist China to the United Nations and the ouster of Nationalist China, or possibly to recognize the Communist delegation instead of the Nationalist Chinese as the rightful occupant of the Chinese seat in the United Nations.

The Soviet proposal went through. Nationalist China and the United States abstained on Outer Mongolia, and the Soviet Union on Mauritania.

Thus the factions within Africa acted on the Soviet Union and the United States on the cold-war issue of admission of states into the United Nations. The African blocs were willing to deal in power politics, using cold-war issues to gain their respective points. Morocco and her allies in the Casablanca bloc were willing to turn in the first instance to the Communist bloc to block Mauritania. The Brazzaville bloc, turning to the free world with threats of going over to the Communist bloc on the issue of Communist China's admission to the United Nations, sought free-world acquiescence to Outer Mongolia's admission, the Soviet price for Mauritania's admission. The United States was vulnerable on the question of Communist China's admission and used its good offices to dissuade Nationalist China from voting against Outer Mongolia. Thus the African states involved themselves in cold-war power politics and will now of necessity continue to influence the two-Chinas issue. Presumably the African states which forced the admission of Outer Mongolia, particularly the Brazzaville twelve, will now vote for Nationalist China, whereas the Casablanca bloc will probably vote for Communist China.[4]

In any event, the African states will increasingly affect the balance of political power in the United Nations.

Even though the Congo crisis has subsided, the problems growing out of it will persist for a long time. There will also be Angola and South Africa and probably Southern Rhodesia and Mozambique. There will also be any number of issues between African states. The African presence in all of its exposures and many facets will be in action—the crusading anti-colonialism, the pragmatic politics bargaining for advantages, and the self-interested advocacy seeking support in a dispute with a near neighbor. The forums of the United Nations are likely to echo and re-echo with the words of African statesmen in all these contexts. And the contexts all derive from shifting balances in the relationship of Africa and Europe, Africa and the United States, Africa and the Communist bloc, and Africa and Asia.

The Ongoing Shifts in the Balance of Power

As we have seen, the African presence in the world arena is dynamic, many-sided, and still evolving, and so too are its reflections and manifestations in the United Nations. The process of change in the political power relations of Africa and other areas has not come to an end. Some African territories still await independence; others have only recently achieved it and have not yet moved far enough in any direction to discern where they are headed; and still others have embarked on various routes to economic and political development and to international relationships. The international political balance of power has been affected and continues to be, and it will not strike an equilibrium for some time to come. For Africa is too volatile a factor.

What then is the outlook for the future? What are the prospects for further shifts in the balance of power? Is the pendulum poised to swing back from an anti-colonial extreme to a midway point of new relationships and institutions involving the new independent states of Africa and the old ones of Europe?

One new economic factor should be noted, the European Economic Community. In revamping its constitutional structure, originally built on colonial relationships, to accommodate the reality of African independence, it will probably become a new and important Eurafrican link. It can go some way toward compensating for the shift in the Eurafrican political balance of power. Europe has not only lost much of its political power vis-à-vis Africa; it has also lost much of the world political power it derived from its imperial position. If the EEC serves to establish

new economic relationships between Europe and Africa, or between substantial segments of both, and the prospects are promising, it may do two things. For the ties of the colonial era it may
substitute economic ties which will benefit the economic position
of both areas. It may also lay a foundation for building new political relationships which will go some way toward restoring the
diminished political power of Europe at the same time that they
enhance the power of Africa. The EEC, by creating a new community of shared interests, may at least partly redress the shift
in the balance of power away from West Europe. In the absence
of such developments there remains little question that the African
independence revolution, with its resulting drastic alteration of
the political position of European nations in Africa, will continue to affect adversely their power position in the world.

The possible association of the United Kingdom with the
Common Market emphasizes its potential importance in Eurafrican relationships. If the United Kingdom had been able to
negotiate membership or association with the EEC in a way
which would have accommodated the interests of Commonwealth
members—particularly those in Africa, and these Commonwealth
members followed the British lead, then a new configuration of
not only economic power but also of political power would have
resulted. The shift in the balance of political power away from
the United Kingdom and West Europe generally would have
been redressed. If, however, the United Kingdom adhered to the
EEC—which seemed quite possible until President de Gaulle interposed a French veto to the United Kingdom's application and
African Commonwealth countries rejected association with the
EEC, as Ghana, Nigeria and Tanganyika have announced is their
intention—then the shift of political power away from West
Europe, and particularly from the United Kingdom, insofar as
support of many former British territories is concerned, would
have been accentuated. The apparent willingness of the United
Kingdom to adhere to the Common Market under these circumstances may leave a residue of uneasiness and doubt with the
African Commonwealth members about their long-term relationship with the United Kingdom. Thus, even the failure of the
United Kingdom's bid for membership may have impaired its

relationship with some of the Commonwealth African countries.

One still uncertain political factor should also be noted: the fate of the Franco-African Community. In time the Community may evolve, particularly if the Common Market succeeds in building the new basis for the association of independent African states recently agreed on, in a way which will strengthen its hold on its members and exercise a new appeal for the former French territories outside the Community, and almost in direct proportion strengthen France's political position both in the Community and among other nations. The Community, however, is not likely to achieve the status or importance of the Commonwealth either in Africa or on a broader scale. If the Common Market does not flourish with respect to its African associates, then the outlook for the Franco-African Community is most uncertain. If the Franco-African Community does not take a new lease on life but becomes moribund, then France's political position in all areas is likely to be weakened even more. France will in any event continue to have a special interest in Africa, which could but is not likely to be frustrated in the absence of institutional channels such as the Common Market or the Franco-African Community, so long as France continues its substantial aid and trade programs in former French Africa.

Thus the political position of the two principal African colonial powers is still in transition. The Belgian position, as already noted, is likely to grow considerably weaker, although with the independence of Ruanda-Urundi, if the tide of events in the Congo changes, Belgium may be able to remove some of the tarnish from its political position. Portugal, if it persists on its present course, is likely to isolate itself in Africa and beyond, and to precipitate future shifts in political support away from West Europe and the West generally.

The very uncertainty of the European position in world politics deriving from the new, looming African presence has, as we have noted, created a fluid situation in which the United States and the Soviet Union are both finding their way.

The African presence, in its ubiquitous if varied anti-colonial embodiment, offers the Communist bloc its most attractive opportunity to realign the world's balance of political power to its own advantage. The free world would ignore this fact at its peril. Policy toward Portugal and South Africa, to say nothing of the Rhodesias, can be allowed to drift, and await the onslaught of successive crises, only at great risk to free world–African relations.

The Soviet Union will undoubtedly continue to push its campaign to identify itself with the anti-colonial philosophy of the Afro-Asian states, particularly that of the radical nationalist African states. In doing so, however, it will court the opposition of many of the Monrovia powers which have repeatedly denounced subversion and interference in their internal affairs justified as fighting neo-colonialism—the stock in trade of the Casablanca bloc and their spiritual allies, the Communist bloc, in the national liberation movement which both of them have endorsed and are sponsoring.

In the long run African states, like states anywhere, will evolve different relationships with many of the more than one hundred states in the world. Some are likely to develop pro-Communist-bloc neutralist postures and one or two may even openly become part of the Communist bloc. Many more are likely to develop pro-Western neutralist postures and remain linked with Western or free-world states through such bodies as the British Commonwealth, the Franco-African Community, and the European Economic Community. One or two may even develop a neutral status akin to the Swiss model. If the remaining vestiges of European colonialism on the continent can be liquidated during the 1960's without major violence (in new contexts or in extension of existing troubled situations), the long-run outlook in Africa is not likely to be unfavorable for the free world in the divided cold-war world.

If major violence cannot be avoided, then the outlook for the free world will be seriously clouded. The free world will be faced with the choice of risking the favorable long-term outlook for its relations with the new African states or breaking with the hold-out colonial power, Portugal, and the present government of the Republic of South Africa. The United Kingdom and France are likely to complete their decolonization in Africa, and the Spanish fragments are likely to be absorbed by the independent African states as the 1960's move along. Hopefully the departure of the United Kingdom, France, and Spain will be accomplished with a minimum of violence, although the defeat of Sir Edgar Whitehead and his party in Southern Rhodesia at the hands of Winston Field and his "white supremacy" party late in 1962 seems to point to a violent denouement of the ill-fated British attempt at a multi-racial federation of the two Rhodesias and Nyasaland. Portugal and the Republic of South Africa remain hard-core problems.

The Communist bloc will keep vigil over the decolonization process. Persistent strife or sudden violence on any scale in Africa between Europeans and Africans will provide the Communist bloc with its main chance and simultaneously jeopardize the free-world position vis-à-vis the independent African states. We can expect that, to maximize such a possibility, the Communist bloc will persistently assert a position even more anti-colonial than that of the colonial territories and their colleagues-in-arms, the independent African states. The Soviet Union will continue to press relentlessly for independence of all dependent territories *now*, always in the knowledge and hope that *now* will not be acceptable to one or another remaining colonial power, particularly the Portuguese.

Thus it can be said that there is a shift in the balance of political power in Africa, and to some degree in the world at large, between the Communist bloc and the free world. To the extent that the bloc makes political inroads in Africa, the free world sustains a setback in its political power in the area. To the extent that the bloc wins the support of new African states on cold-war issues the free world loses it, and there is a decided shift in the political balance in the world. Thus when Ghana, Guinea, and Mali sided with the Soviet Union on its "troika" proposal for reorganizing the United Nations Secretariat, the Soviet Union enlarged its support and acquired an aura of respectability deriving from the support of well-advertised small, new, neutralist states.

As one or the other African states provides the bloc with staging areas for propaganda, for contacts, and for funneling military assistance to "national liberation" movements, then too the political balance in Africa and the world is shifted away from the West. There can be little doubt that the bloc is hunting for benevolent neutrals and possible recruits on the African continent.

There is also a serious potential in the procession of independent African states for a shift in the balance of world political power away from the Soviet Union. Hardly ever in the history of the United Nations has a state (except perhaps South Africa) been so isolated as the Soviet Union was when it sustained in 1961 what was in substance a 72 to 0 vote against its position in the General Assembly on a critical vote on the Congo crisis. Even the other Communist bloc nations, under considerable African pressure, were induced to abstain in the final vote.

The Soviet Union is not likely to be so badly isolated again. However, there is a substantial possibility that on other issues the Soviet Union may find itself opposed by many of the new African states. In Guinea, as we have noted, it overplayed its hand and meddled in the internal political and trade union affairs of the country. The Soviet ambassador's ouster has been followed by a Guinean attempt to shift from its pro-bloc neutralism to a more balanced neutralism involving new relationships with France and the United States, and a dilution of its Casablanca bloc commitment.

The national interest of many, if not most independent African states should make their choice of benevolent non-alignment or *de facto* alignment pro-Western unless the West throws away the game. The new African states for the most part seek to ensure their political independence, build their economies, pursue independent foreign policies, deciding issues on their merits and in their own interests, contribute to world peace and security, and aid the peaceful and orderly accession of the remaining African colonial areas to independence. This last point is for the West a potential Achilles' heel. Portugal and South Africa can go a long way to negate the fundamental and mutually shared common interest of many African and Western states. The two hard-core states provide the best entrée for the Soviet Union in Africa by providing some basis for the Soviet's anti-colonial denunciations. They are the best insurance against an adjustment in the political balance of power favorable for the free world. Strife, violence, distraction of African energy and resources, and support for "national liberation" movements are the Soviets' best tools and the free world's greatest vulnerabilities. They will be important factors in determining where the power lies in Africa's nexus with the outside world.

In sum, the political balance in the world has been significantly affected by the outpouring of new African states. The former imperial powers have lost their colonies but may compensate in part for the loss through new evolving Eurafrican relationships and new free-world relationships between the new states and North America. The Communist bloc has gained political power, but it may sustain a comparative loss of power if the overwhelming number of new states should turn out to be pro-Western or truly neutral. The Afro-Asian world is in transition, with Africa itself now heavily tipped in favor of the Monrovia powers and against the Casablanca bloc. There undoubtably will be further shifts in the balance of power attributable to the new African states. There will also be many more political horse-trading situations, particularly in the United Nations, after the style of the Mauritania–Outer Mongolia deal in which the African states will use their numerical voting strength to influence the political balance of power on an *ad hoc* basis.

What is indisputable is that Africa is a new and important factor in the world balance of power which has not yet reached its peak impact. There are still another half-dozen or more African states in various embryonic stages. With their appearance the African presence in the world and its impact on the world balance of power will be accentuated. Herein lies a major challenge and opportunity for free-world policy, and particularly for the United States. We must forge friendly over-all relationships of a mutually beneficial nature with the new states. We must also recognize that, like states everywhere, African states have special interests on behalf of which they are ready to trade and bargain, and we must be ready to cope with this real but largely undisclosed aspect of the African personality.

Chapter 13

THE DECADE OF DEVELOPMENT

President Kennedy has said that "the 1960's can be—and must be—the crucial 'decade of development'—the period when many less-developed nations make the transition into self-sustained growth—the period in which an enlarged community of free, stable, and self-reliant nations can reduce world tensions and insecurity." [1]

The decade of the 1960's will perhaps be decisive in determining the meaning of the shifts in balance of power now under way in the world. The African presence in world affairs will develop from a potential to speculate about into a force with a direction and identity; and already some of the probable lines and limits of its evolution are becoming discernible. Its shape will be determined during the 1960's in significant part by how Africa comes to grips with its development problems. In turn, the African presence in world affairs will influence the course of internal African development.

For the free world, then, the two are inseparable—the African presence in the world arena and the internal development problems of the new African states. Thus the situation facing the free world—if the objective of the free world is, as it must be,

245

the maturing of African states into politically independent and
economically viable members of a peaceful world community—
affects the whole range of free-world policy aimed at influencing
internal African development.

Problems of Internal Development in Africa

For President Kennedy the decade of development calls for
"a united free world effort to assist the economic and social development of less-developed areas of the world." [2] The priority problems of African economic and social development, as we have
already seen, are the choice of economic growth models, modernization of agriculture, Africanization of the public and private
sectors, the push for education, determination of the appropriate
role for welfare state concepts, the quest for political stability internally, and the search for political security in the world arena.
If its goal of African development in a peaceful world is to stand
a chance of achievement, the free world must seek to influence the
solution to these problems.

The crux of the internal development problem in Africa
is found in the existence of the development nexus. Economic
systems evolve in the context of a state structure and a political
system. More often than not economies with decentralized economic decision-making and a multiplicity of individual economic
initiatives interrelate with democratic political systems characterized by a broad-based sharing of political power throughout
the society, recognition of a legal opposition, and respect for
individual and minority rights safeguarded by the rule of law,
administered by an independent judiciary. More often than not,
economies with centralized economic decision-making concentrated in government hands and with little scope for private initiatives interrelate with authoritarian political systems of the left
or right.

The converse of the foregoing propositions also tends to be
true in Africa. Democratic political structures and systems tend

to interrelate with open economies, and authoritarian structures and systems with controlled or closed economies. In the first ten chapters of the book we found that there are many degrees and variants of each type of economy and political system, and that many of the different types are to be found in different parts of Africa. The discussion also reveals the nature of the interrelation of the economic and political systems evolving in the new states of Africa.

Any free-world program of economic and technical assistance to the new states of Africa must take account of the interrelationship of economic and political factors. For example, economic development in Nigeria is likely to strengthen the federation and the multi-party political system. The regional, cultural, tribal, and economic differences in the three regions of the federation are likely to be minimized or even submerged in the growth of a national economy which puts a premium on economic performance rather than on status deriving from antecedent differences. An expanding economy would tend to break down regional and other traditional barriers and open up not only the economic life of the country but also the total social fabric. Political parties in such a changing environment are likely to shed parochial orientations and seek to represent various views and interests on a national basis. In fact signs of a political realignment—on the basis of interest rather than region or tribe—exist on the Nigerian political scene even now, at the outset of Nigeria's development effort as an independent state.

Another example will serve to demonstrate the variety of results which follow from the interrelationship of economic and political systems. Economic growth in Ghana would in the first instance tend to reinforce the authoritarian political system, which would claim, in what is now becoming an African left-authoritarian political catechism, that growth is directly and solely attributable to the authoritarian state system. The doctrine of the supremacy of the "political kingdom" would be taken as proven. President Nkrumah would renew his Pan-Africanist drive for political association of African states as the priority task of African states, for in this view internal development will follow along naturally if a strong political association within an authoritarian structure is established. The state of economic development or complementarity of the individual components of such an association becomes irrelevant in this view. All that is important is a political merger on authoritarian lines. The rest—for example, economic development—is secondary and derivative.

In the long run it is possible that a sufficient level of economic growth in some of the authoritarian African states would tend to relax the severity of the political system and relieve some of the pressures and tensions on which authoritarianism thrives. It is also possible that it would tend to cushion fears and build self-confidence, and thus relieve some of the xenophobic tendencies frequently associated with authoritarian political systems in Africa, particularly those of the left variety.

The short-run effects, however, already alluded to with respect to the likely impact of growth in Ghana, are likely to prevail in the 1960's. If Ghana's precedent to date holds true, a flourishing left-authoritarian state, disposing of more funds than it previously had, is likely to step up its military effort, its national liberation movement support, and its intra-African intrigues. Even worse would be economic stagnation and collapse. Once again, if Ghana's economic difficulties, following in part on its use of national resources for its Pan-Africanist designs, are taken as a precedent, internal tensions and troubles resulting from economic difficulties will tend to reinforce the authoritarian trend at home and the anti-Western neutralist outlook in foreign policy. The short-run effect of economic growth in authoritarian states would at least preserve the possibility of merging into a moderating long-run state of the type envisaged above, whereas short-run stagnation is likely to persevere and mean increasing authoritarianism throughout the 1960's and thereafter for an unspecified period.

Objectives of Economic and Technical Aid

In his foreign aid message to Congress President Kennedy interrelated economic growth and political change when he delineated the objective of United States' foreign aid. The President stated:

The fundamental task of our foreign aid program in the 1960's is not negatively to fight communism: Its fundamental task is to help make a historical demonstration that in the twentieth century, as in the nineteenth—in the southern half of the globe as in the north—economic growth and political democracy can develop hand in hand.[3]

What does this mean in terms of Africa? First, it means that, in the case of Nigeria, economic and technical assistance by the United States and its free-world associates should be forthcoming in ample amounts, in timely fashion, and in an order of priority best designed to facilitate economic growth and political stability. Since Nigeria stands out as an oasis of democratic development in an arid desert of authoritarian-inclined African states, the economic development of Nigeria in democratic circumstances would make a significant historical demonstration that "economic growth and political democracy can develop hand in hand" in Africa.

Second, it means that free-world assistance to many, and perhaps most, African states must be undertaken on the basis that its effect would potentially be threefold. Such aid would help develop viable economies which would create a climate and a setting in which free political institutions could develop, or, where they already exist, could grow and flourish, and in which the possibility and capacity for political democracy could develop hand in hand with economic growth.

Such aid should also support the political and economic independence of new African states, irrespective of their internal political systems—short of a clear-cut commitment to the Communist orbit or to a headlong plunge down the road to authoritarianism or totalitarianism and anti-Western neutralism. For the most part, as we have seen, African states prefer to look to the free world for the bulk of their aid; and where the situation is in fact otherwise, those states receiving Communist-bloc aid of magnitude are seeking to redress their dependency on the bloc by obtaining free-world assistance. It is obviously in the free-world interest to avoid situations creating or leading to African dependence on the bloc for aid, which, as we have noted, is intimately related with trade, barter, cultural exchange, and frequently military assistance.

Economic assistance also should help focus the attention and energy, as well as resources, on internal development and away from foreign adventures. Creating foreign diversions to distract the attention of the local population from internal difficulties is a time-honored technique of governments. Assistance could act to forestall this practice. It could also encourage the national leadership to concentrate in the first instance on meeting domestic development problems rather than taking what seems to be an easy way out—a foreign affairs diversion—even before internal difficulties arise.

As for the category of states on the authoritarian and totalitarian road but as yet without commitment to a hostile bloc, economic assistance to them implies a serious short-time risk and a long-term possibility of change for the better. The foregoing discussion of Ghana is illustrative on this point, and free-world policy with respect to these countries would revolve around judgement on two questions. One, has the new African state relinquished or is it on the verge of relinquishing its political independence outright or as a *de facto* matter? Two, has the new African state sacrificed or is it on the verge of sacrificing its objective of economic development outright or as a *de facto* matter? If both answers are "No," then it would appear to be in the free-world interest to take the calculated risk of forestalling either possibility by a reasonable amount of external assistance.

Finally, where a state has made a commitment to the Communist bloc, the question confronting the free world is whether external aid for development can serve any useful purpose in influencing the political development of the committed state in a way favorable to the free world. If the answer is "No," there would seem to be little reason to provide assistance.

President Kennedy has called for "a united free-world effort to assist the economic and social development of less-developed areas of the world." It would seem clear that the decade of development, insofar as Africa is concerned, is a challenge and an opportunity for the free world. The growing absorptive capacity of the new African states makes it clear that the foreign aid task—in men and money—exceeds the likely effort and political ability of any one state to undertake, if not its actual capacity. The political realities of Africa, with its evolving Eurafrican relations and its anti-colonial political sensitivities, and the political realities of Europe, with its changing relations with Africa and its political interests, make a solo effort by the United States impracticable. And from the United States' point of view, undertaking an exclusive role or even the dominant role in economic aid to Africa seems out of the question, both in terms of resource availability and in terms of United States relations with its European allies. The United States' national interest contemplates maximizing resources flowing to Africa for development purposes. The substitution of United States' aid for that of the former European metropoles does not confer a substantial net benefit on the recipient states or strengthen the total free-world aid posture toward the new states. The United States' relations with its European allies require that they carry a fair share of the economic aid burden to underdeveloped countries, and Africa is historically the place where a substantial European contribution has been made and logically should continue to be made. This, of course, does not relieve the United States from making a significant contribution too.

Thus the United States, in recognition of both the link between the economic and political systems in the new states of Africa and the interplay of internal development and external posture, must shape its economic and technical aid policy not only to meet the development problems of growth and stability but also to take account of the interaction. The new African states' political independence and economic development *per se* must be recognized as being in the United States' national interest and the free-world interest generally.

The United States needs to persuade its allies and friends in the free world to this point of view. This involves not only the encouragement of free-world economic and technical assistance contributions to facilitate African development but also a diplomatic initiative with the remaining colonial powers in an effort to pave the way for the peaceful and orderly accession of the remaining colonial areas of Africa to independence and, thence, development. When violence erupts the United States is confronted with the necessity of diplomatic intervention with its allies in an attempt to resolve the crisis situation.

The Angolan situation cannot be allowed to fester indefinnitely without seriously infecting all free-world relations with the new African states and with the underdeveloped world generally. The United States needs to face up to the damaging impact on its own and free-world interests of mounting violence in Angola or elsewhere in colonial Africa. Failure of the United States to act effectively, with a view to finding a formula for the peaceful liquidation of the colonial relationship, could leave such a formidable residue of ill-will against the free world in the colonial areas directly involved (and probably beyond) that the opportunity to use economic aid to facilitate the achievement of independence and to foster the economic viability of these last colonial areas in Africa would be lost. The Angolans and others in the same position would, under the circumstances, take aid from wherever they could get it and make their friends in the same quarters. The new states of Africa would also draw their conclusions, which, no matter how moderate they may turn out to be, could hardly be expected to redound to the credit of the free world.

Questions of Military Assistance

Closely related to free-world development assistance policy is the question of military assistance policy. By and large, even though the colonial heritage in Africa has been one of small armed forces and limited installations, the cost of maintaining these military establishments has been transferred in significant part, and in some instances almost entirely, from the colonial powers to the independent states. This is burden enough for the new states to carry; but that burden has been increased. Almost as a reflex action to the stimulus of independence the new states have tended to expand their ground forces and to venture into the development of types of armed forces not theretofore conceived of as necessary elements in colonial military establishments in Africa—navies and air forces. The infrastructure and equipment costs of these two new military arms on the African scene add a completely new dimension to each new African state's problem of building up and maintaining its own armed forces. No African state can bear the cost of diverting scarce resources, manpower, and capital to relatively non-productive military purposes. Morocco, for example, has for the last several years been spending twenty-five per cent of its ordinary recurrent budget on military purposes; more, that is, than its spends on agricultural development or on education.

As if this seemingly natural propensity for arms on the part of the new states were not enough, Ghana, as we pointed out earlier, by word and deed has launched an arms race in West Africa. At the outset Ghana was content to rely on British personnel to staff senior posts in its armed forces and to train Ghanaians, and on British equipment and supplies. Predictably, as part of the Ghanaian posture of "positive neutralism" the British presence has been markedly watered-down, and a series of moves has been made toward the Soviet Union and the Communist bloc generally. In 1961 Ghana sent substantial numbers of Ghanaians to the Soviet Union for officer training and started to receive substantial quantities of bloc military equipment and supplies. There is good reason to believe that a significant part of the equipment and supplies is earmarked for stockpiling for later shipment to other places on the continent in connection with the national liberation objective shared by Ghana with the Soviet Union.

All of Ghana's near neighbors—the Ivory Coast, Sierra Leone, and Togo—have, as we have already noted, expressed concern over the Ghanaian military build-up. The Ivory Coast has been expanding its forces with French assistance, and to a lesser degree financially straitened Sierra Leone has been doing so with British assistance. Togo has been looking to other African states and has been relying on a defense agreement with France for support in face of the Ghanaian build-up. Nigeria, somewhat further from Ghana but near enough to be concerned with Ghana's developing jet air force and the threat to Nigerian prestige in African affairs posed by superior Ghanaian armed forces, has been reacting with a build-up of its own with British assistance and more recently with assistance from Canada.

Other African states have been expanding their armed forces. Morocco, the United Arab Republic, Guinea, and Mali have been doing so with Communist-bloc military assistance, most of the former French and British territories with military assistance from their former metropoles, and Ethiopia and Liberia with military assistance from the United States.

The diversion of energy and attention from economic development to military build-ups, the channeling of scarce human and material resources into military purposes—armed forces, installations, and even, in the United Arab Republic, into industrial capacity—and the growing role of the military in the new states of Africa can only cause considerable concern to the free world. Given the interaction between economic and political systems and their development, anything which impairs the one will tend to impair the other. Diversion of energy and resources from economic growth to military purposes can only adversely affect the pace and pattern of growth, and indirectly the support a growing economy tends to impart to political stability. In addition, if the experience of the peripheral African states in the northeast corner of the continent—the United Arab Republic and the Sudan—is an indication of what growing military forces is likely to mean, then there is cause for concern about the direct impact of such forces on the political structure and system.

Some might argue that military forces are an acceptable and even a preferable alternative to corrupt and squabbling politicians; that the military is likely to bring order out of chaos and even be the instrument of social revolution. This may be; but even to the extent it is, the armed forces are an extra-parliamentary or extra-constitutional force in this role and must disrupt the existing political structure and system and replace it with something else. Certainly a policy calculated to induce military take-overs is hardly consistent with a policy to encourage economic growth in democratic circumstances, to demonstrate that growth and democracy "go hand in hand." The shabby affair in Togo, leading to the assassination of President Olympio in January 1963, and the abortive military coup in Liberia shortly thereafter, along with the involvement of a military clique in an attempted take-over and assassination of President Bourguiba in Tunisia in December 1962, all illustrate vividly the myopic nature of a policy to build up military forces in nascent African states as a technique for inducing growth or ensuring stability.

The results to date in the two African countries so far subjected to military take-overs have hardly been unequivocal testimonials to the benefits alleged to flow from such action. One of the two states, the United Arab Republic, has demonstrated the ease with which a military régime can turn outward for adventure and diversion at the expense of internal growth and development. Moreover, the authoritarian nature of the two African military régimes, in the United Arab Republic and the Sudan, suggests both the ease and the danger of changes in fundamental orientation of the two states by shifts in the policies of a handful of military personalities. The uneven nature of United Arab Republic policy illustrates how readily it can be shifted to reflect the nature of the relations between Nasser and Khrushchev at any particular moment. The break-up of the original United Arab Republic by Syria's withdrawal following a military coup, and the subsequent dissolution of the federal link tying Yemen to the UAR, hardly provide a testimonial to the stability of political structures and systems built on a military base and manned, in large part, by military personalities.

The potentially disruptive and unsettling effect of the mounting arms race in Africa is already discernible. The state initiating the build-up wastes resources and suffers artificially induced fears and tensions necessary to justify or rationalize the build-up; and those states which feel that the arms expansion is directed at them are also seriously affected. The threatened states not only encumber their economic development with retaliatory arms efforts; they also experience fears and tensions which affect their political stability. The resultant atmosphere is adverse for all concerned—the new states of Africa and the free world—and to their shared interest in the evolution of politically independent and stable African states with growing economies.

The free world must face up to the need for a coordinated policy on military assistance to African states. First, an agreed policy to avoid competition among free-world states is imperative. If the United Kingdom supplies arms to an African state in the face of a United States refusal, or *vice versa,* the free world is defeating its own purposes. It involves the possible anomaly of United States assistance to a NATO ally which in turn agrees to provide military assistance to an African state despite United States refusal to do so.

An absence of agreed free-world policy also leads to a situation, now existing in West Africa, of leading NATO allies supplying military equipment to African countries potentially hostile to one another. British aid to Ghana, French aid to the Ivory Coast, and United States aid to Liberia make an impressive demonstration of the *cul-de-sac* that the individual arms policies of free-world states lead to. They also lead to the anomaly of one free-world state providing arms to both sides of a hostile African situation in an attempt to preclude assistance from other free-world states, e.g., British assistance to Ghana on the one hand and to Sierra Leone and Nigeria on the other. Canada too is in the position of providing military training to Ghanaian and Nigerian armed forces.

Second, an agreed free-world policy is necessary to complement and buttress the shared free-world interest in the emergence and evolution of independent African states with viable economies, and one would hope in a unified free-world effort to facilitate both independence and development.

Third, agreed policy is urgently required to meet the growing Communist offers of military assistance. Military aid has become a common feature of the bloc presence in Africa—in the United Arab Republic, Morocco, Guinea, Mali, and most recently Ghana. The problem for the free world is a dual one: how to prevent arms build-ups in Africa and at the same time to avoid creating a supply vacuum in which African states frustrated in their military objectives by refusals of free-world aid turn to the Communist bloc.

The obvious first course of action—in view of the national interest of free-world states in the internal development of the new African states—is to check and obviate an arms race in Africa by seeking agreement of the African states and the cold-war antagonists. A United Nations resolution to make Africa a demilitarized zone—rather than merely the "denuclearized zone" piously proclaimed in the General Assembly's 1961 resolution—supported by all the African states would have to command the support of the free world and the Communist bloc. A resolution which classified and limited the categories and volume of arms which could be supplied to African states for maintaining internal law and order, for policing borders to enforce customs and immigration regulations, and for discharging commitments to the United Nations would go a long way toward removing armed forces in Africa from the prestige race, the Pan-African sweepstake, and the irredentist movements confronting the continent. A system of reporting, observation, and inspection would probably suffice to ensure enforcement of an agreed limit on arms shipments to Africa. Other controls could be developed if experience suggests that they are needed. If agreement within the United Nations is not practicable, an alternative approach might be direct agreement among all the major powers and African states to achieve the objectives outlined above.

If an agreement including the Communist bloc should prove beyond reach, then a free-world attempt to reach agreement with the African states would be in order, aiming at a moratorium on all arms except those needed essentially for internal law and order, and a limitation on those. Recent statements by President Senghor of Senegal and Foreign Minister Wachuku of Nigeria suggest that leading African statesmen are concerned with the mounting arms competition in Africa. They would probably prefer a United Nations resolution or big-power agreement with African states as a course of action. Failing either of these, they might sponsor an all-African agreement regulating arms shipments to Africa which free-world states could accede to.

Finally, if all these possibilities fail, the free world still needs to formulate an agreed policy on arms for Africa and continuing consultation and coordination of activity in the arms field. Only thus can the free world act to limit the adverse impact of excessive armament and still avoid opening a ready road into the military forces of the new states for the Communist bloc to travel.

Political Association and Union in Africa

Intimately related to policy on economic and military assistance to the new African states is policy toward larger units—
associations, federations, confederations, unions, and so on. The
history of the ill-fated Federation of Mali and the original United
Arab Republic would suggest that ill-conceived and ill-timed political unions do not provide the political security and stability its
members seek or the economic viability its members tend to assume
automatically accompanies such groupings. Both political associations were the work of independent states. The stormy history of
the Federation of Rhodesia and Nyasaland, created by colonial fiat
with European settler approval, points to much the same conclusions.

The seemingly stillborn Union of African States—Ghana,
Guinea, and Mali—would also seem to suggest that time and
space are dimensions that cannot be ignored in founding a successful political union of independent states merging their sovereign identities. The original Ghana-Guinea "nucleus of a union"
and the more recent Union of African states came into being
before there were any bases for union—cultural, social, economic,
or physical—other than political expediency and perhaps common
ideology, and even the existence of the latter is not entirely certain.

Unions arranged or negotiated before common interests and
bonds exist are questionable gambles. The struggle of component
parts for political ascendency at the center neither leads to political stability nor aids economic growth. Time, energy, and resources are lost in the internecine struggle for political advantage.
Similarly, failure to consider economic compatability, a common
practice in Pan-African movements, not only imposes a burden on
economic growth but also sets the stage for political conflict as
the members compete for resources—particularly those of the
wealthier member or members. Spreading limited resources too
thinly over a large area not only fails to induce over-all develop-

ment; it also compromises the possibility for achieving "islands of development" and the accumulation of capital which at a later date could be made more widely available.[4]

The Monrovia powers, as we have seen, have made it an article of faith to concentrate on internal development and to view political associations as a possibility for some time in the future when mutual interests and common bases for a political merger and superstructure may exist. The Casablanca powers are generally committed to political union as a precondition for African development. The distinction between the two approaches is manifest and important.

The free world needs to take account of the two approaches and formulate policy to accommodate them. Obviously the decisions about size are for the African states. The free world must be able to respond effectively to both the Monrovia-type and Casablanca-type approaches. It should be clear though that it is in the free-world interest to facilitate and support the development of federations, such as the Nigerian, which appear well-conceived and -timed. The Federation of Nigeria, with its pre-independence experience, with the historical growth of links among the components parts under British rule, and with its shared interests, appears a most promising political union. It is too soon to assess the new Cameroon federation. An association in East Africa based on the common services of the earlier colonial East Africa High Commission seems a real possibility. For the rest, many of the benefits of size for economic purposes—enlarged markets, free trade areas, common tariffs, free movement of labor and capital, regional power, telecommunication, and transportation grids—could be achieved by customs unions, trade agreements, and other arrangements short of political merger. Many of these features can be building blocks toward a solid political union and provide a fund of experience with which to build such a union.

In any event, it behooves the free-world states to formulate policy attuned to African aspirations and needs but still compatible with the political and economic realities of the area. It should not be assumed that large size *per se* is advantageous either for political stability or for economic development. To the extent that the free world has a measure of influence in this matter of size of states and groups of states it should be carefully exercised in light of the interests and links which exist or are absent in the proposed constellation of states. The 1960's will probably witness sustained and persistent efforts at bloc-building and political association-building in Africa. These two objectives are likely to be intimately interwoven with efforts of the new states to achieve stability and growth. As we have seen, some will try the route of large-unit development and others internal development of their own countries. Either way though, inevitably, the opportunities for internal development will be affected, hampered, or enhanced. The development nexus will be stretched to a union or confined to individual states. The interrelationship of political and economic systems will continue to be the focal point of African internal development, and it will continue to affect its outward posture.

In Conclusion

It is in the broad contexts of economic and social development, maintenance of military forces, and political evolution, particularly toward regional groupings, unions, federations, and associations, that the free world will meet the major African policy issues of the 1960's. This book has dealt with many problem areas in these contexts, seeking to give substance to the problems in order to demonstrate their complexity and interrelationships and to identify the elements that should be considered in the formulation of free-world policy responses to the crucial African issues. It would be presumptuous for an individual at this point, as well as an exercise beyond the scope of this book, to attempt to formulate detailed policy proposals to meet these fundamental and still evolving policy issues growing out of the ongoing African political revolution. Instead we have attempted to provide the ingredients for policy: the identification of the major problem areas, an appreciation of the context out of which they grow, recognition of the interplay of forces internally and between internal development and the external pressures on the world scene, and sketching in general lines for policy action at various points in the book, particularly in this concluding chapter.

If the decade of the 1960's is to be a decade of development as conceived of by President Kennedy, a decade of development compatible with free-world interests, then the free world must evolve suitable and interrelated policies on the complex of African development issues we have identified and considered. If the free world is to act in timely fashion—and time is of the essence—then the burden is on the United States to initiate policy proposals on the range of issues involved in the economic and social development, the achievement of political stability, and the physical security of the vast and explosive African continent. The United States is the only major free-world state which has not had colonial ties in Africa. The disengagement of the colonial powers, now well along, is still to be completely accomplished. The United States, then, must propose bold policies for the free world in these basic policy areas and help too to dispose quickly of the problems arising from remaining colonial ties. If this is done, there is a solid hope of seeing the 1960's evolve into a decade of development for the new states of Africa, and of seeing the African presence in world affairs become increasingly a force for world peace.

An important first step has been taken. The United States has given impetus to the concept by inducing the General Assembly to declare the 1960's the decade of development. The General Assembly's resolution of December 1961 sets as the goal for the end of the ten-year period "an annual growth rate of at least 5 per cent" in the underdeveloped countries of the world. The General Secretary of the United Nations, U Thant, has termed the resolution "perhaps as significant in its potentialities as any resolution ever adopted by the United Nations." [5]

The stage is set; it now remains to breathe life into the performance, to translate words into deeds, to bring to fruition some of the great promises we are holding out for the 1960's to the new African states. We have seen that the way is fraught with dangers, that the new states see their problems in very different lights, and that the European powers principally concerned also see the challenges Africa projects onto the world scene in many different ways. As the principal free-world nation our leadership role is undeniable. Thus the new African presence in world affairs coincides with our own presence in the international arena in the role of leader of the free world. The significance of this meeting cannot be overestimated, either with regard to the interests of the United States and the free world or to the interests of the new Africa.

Appendix I.

AFRICAN STATES IN ORDER OF ACCESSION TO INDEPENDENCE
(as of March 31, 1963)

Appendix I.

Country (Capital)	Area (Sq. Miles)[a]	Population (1961 Est.) [b]	Date of Proclamation of Independence
1. Ethiopia (Addis Ababa)	457,148	22,000,000 (1960)	Empire is consolidation of earlier independent kingdoms dating from ancient times
2. Liberia (Monrovia)	42,989	1,085,000 (1960)	July 26, 1847
3. Republic of South Africa (Cape Town)	472,236	16,122,000	May 31, 1910
4. United Arab Republic (Egypt) (Cairo)	386,000	26,578,000	February 28, 1922
5. Libya (Tripoli and Benghazi)	679,182	1,216,000	December 24, 1951
6. Sudan (Khartoum)	967,248	12,109,000	January 1, 1956
7. Morocco (Rabat)	171,260	11,925,000	March 2, 1956
8. Tunisia (Tunis)	48,319	4,168,000 (1960)	March 20, 1956
9. Ghana (Accra)	91,820	6,943,000	March 6, 1957
10. Guinea (Conakry)	94,901	3,000,000 (1960)	October 2, 1958
11. Federal Republic of Cameroon (Yaoundé)	183,521	4,097,000 (1960)	January 1, 1960
12. Togo (Lomé)	21,848	1,480,000	April 27, 1960
13. Senegal (Dakar)	76,104	2,980,000	June 20, 1960
14. Mali (Bamako)	464,752	4,100,000 (1960)	June 20, 1960
15. Malagasy Republic (Tananarive)	227,740	5,577,000	June 26, 1960
16. Republic of Congo (Léopoldville)	905,328	14,150,000 (1960)	June 30, 1960

Type of Government [c]	Designation of Head of State & Head of Government (when it is separate office)	Special Notes
Empire (see Special Notes)	Emperor; Prime Minister	With the exception of the Italian occupation 1936–1941, Ethiopia has been an independent country. Eritrea, former Italian colony, was federated with Ethiopia by the U.N. on September 15, 1952; in 1962 it was totally integrated into the Empire.
Republic	President	
Kingdom; Federation (until April 27, 1963)	King; Prime Minister	Three former Italian colonies—Cyrenaica, Tripolitania, and Fezzan—were organized into a federation and brought to independence by the U.N.
Republic	President	The Union of South Africa became a Republic on May 31, 1961.
Republic	President	Egypt and Syria formed U.A.R. on February 21, 1958, and Syria broke away on October 1, 1961.
Republic	President	
Kingdom	King; Prime Minister	Spanish Morocco became independent and part of the Kingdom April 7, 1956.
Republic	President	
Republic	President	Ghana became a republic on July 1, 1960.
Republic	President	Guinea achieved independence on September 28, 1958 when it voted "no" in the plebiscite on the constitution of the Fifth French Republic.
Republic; Federation	President	Former Southern Cameroons federated with the Cameroun Republic on October 1, 1961.
Republic	President	Former British Trust Territory of Togo came to independence March 6, 1959, as part of Ghana.
Republic (see Special Notes)	President	Senegal broke away from the Federation of Mali on August 20, 1960.
Republic (see Special Notes)	President	The former French Soudan retained the name Mali after the dissolution of the Federation of Mali.
Republic	President	
Republic (see Special Notes)	President	The U Thant constitution for the Congo which is the basis for the reintegration of Katanga has been described as "federal" in character.

Appendix I. (Continued)

Country (Capital)	Area (Sq. Miles) [a]	Population (1961 Est.) [b]	Date of Proclamation of Independence
17. Somali Republic (Mogadiscio)	246,137	2,030,000	July 1, 1960
18. Dahomey (Porto Novo)	44,684	2,050,000	August 1, 1960
19. Niger (Niamey)	458,874	2,870,000 (1960)	August 3, 1960
20. Upper Volta (Ouagadougou)	105,841	4,400,000	August 5, 1960
21. Ivory Coast (Abidjan)	124,471	3,300,000	August 7, 1960
22. Chad (Fort Lamy)	495,624	2,680,000	August 11, 1960
23. Central African Republic (Bangui)	238,162	1,227,000 (1960)	August 13, 1960
24. Republic of Congo (Brazzaville)	132,012	795,000 (1958)	August 15, 1960
25. Gabon (Libreville)	103,062	440,000 (1960)	August 17, 1960
26. Federation of Nigeria (Lagos)	356,576	35,752,000	October 1, 1960
27. Mauritania (Nouakchott)	419,121	740,000 (1960)	November 28, 1960
28. Sierra Leone (Freetown)	27,918	2,470,000 (1960)	April 27, 1961
29. Tanganyika (Dar-es-Salaam)	361,706	9,404,000	December 9, 1961
30. Burundi (Usumbura)	10,000	2,500,000	July 1, 1962
31. Rwanda (Kigali)	11,000	3,000,000	July 1, 1962
32. Algeria (Algiers)	919,352	11,020,000 (1960)	July 3, 1962
33. Uganda (Entebbe)	93,957	6,845,000	October 9, 1962

Type of Government [e]	Designation of Head of State & Head of Government (when it is separate office)	Special Notes
Republic	President; Prime Minister	British Somaliland achieved independence June 26, 1960 and joined with the Italian Trust Territory on July 1, 1960 as part of Somali Republic.
Republic	President	
Republic	President	Title President of Council exists but is merged with office of President.
Republic	President	See Special Notes for Niger (19)
Republic	President	
Republic	President	Title of Prime Minister exists but is merged with office of President.
Republic	President	
Republic	President	See Special Notes for Chad (22).
Republic	President	See Special Notes for Chad (22).
Dominion; Federation	Governor-General; Prime Minister	Former Northern Cameroons joined the Federation of Nigeria as part of the Northern Region on June 1, 1961.
Islamic Republic	President	
Dominion	Governor-General; Prime Minister	Queen Elizabeth of England is Queen here too; also in Nigeria and Uganda.
Republic	President	Tanganyika became a Republic on December 9, 1962.
Kingdom	Mwami; Prime Minister	The Belgian Trust Territory of Ruanda-Urundi came to independence as the two states of Rwanda and Burundi. This was the last U.N. Trust Territory in Africa, with the exception of South-West Africa, whose status is presently before the International Court of Justice for decision.
Republic	Premier	
Republic	Premier	The Saharan "Departments" have come to independence along with the "Department" of Algeria as one state.
Dominion (see Special Notes)	Governor-General; Prime Minister	The Kingdom of Buganda and 3 smaller kingdoms have special "federal" links with the rest of the country.

ᵃ Area in square miles calculated from km² figures (1 km² = 0.386 sq. mi.) given in United Nations, *Statistical Yearbook, 1961,* New York, 1962, except for Burundi (30) and Rwanda (31), from *The New York Times,* August 1, 1961 (combined U.N. figure is 20,910 sq. mi.).

ᵇ Unless otherwise stated figures are for mid-1961. If given, estimates are those in United Nations, *Monthly Bulletin of Statistics,* July 1962. Exceptions are Ethiopia (1), Liberia (2), Mauritania (27), from *FAO Africa Survey,* Rome, 1962, p. 16; Republic of Congo (24), as of January 1, 1959, from United Nations *Demographic Yearbook, 1960,* New York, 1961; and Burundi (30) and Rwanda (31), from *The New York Times,* August 1, 1962 (for which the United Nations gives a combined 1961 population of 4,980,000).

ᶜ Unless otherwise indicated, all African states have unitary governmental structures.

Appendix II.

MEMBERSHIP OF INDEPENDENT AFRICAN STATES IN REGIONAL AND INTERNATIONAL GROUPINGS
(as of March 31, 1963)

Country (In Order of Accession to Independence)	African						Eur-african		Currency Area		Other		
	Inter-African and Malagasy States Organisation (Monrovia Bloc)	Union of African and Malagasy States (Brazzaville Bloc)	Casablanca Bloc	Union of African States	Conseil de l'Entente	Equatorial Africa Customs Union	Associated Countries of EEC	Franco-African Community	Sterling Area	Franc Zone	Commonwealth	Arab League	Participants in Belgrade Conference of Non-Aligned States (September 1961) †
Independent before 1960													
Ethiopia	x												x
Liberia	x								5				
Republic of South Africa													
United Arab Republic (Egypt)			x									x	x
Libya	2								6			x	
Sudan									6			x	x
Morocco			x							7		x	x
Tunisia	2									8		x	x
Ghana			x	x					x		x		x
Guinea			x	x						9			x
Independent before 1962													
Federal Republic of Cameroon	x	x					x	x		x *			
Togo	x							x		x **			
Senegal	x	x						x	x	x **			
Mali			x	x				x		10			x
Malagasy Republic	x	x						x	x	x			
Republic of Congo (Léopoldville)	x							x					x
Somali Republic	³							x					x
Dahomey	x	x				x		x		x **			

	African						Eur-african		Currency Area		Other		
Country Independent before 1962	Inter-African and Malagasy States Organisation (Monrovia Bloc)	Union of African and Malagasy States (Brazzaville Bloc)	Casablanca Bloc	Union of African States	Conseil de l'Entente	Equatorial Africa Customs Union	Associated Countries of EEC	Franco-African Community	Sterling Area	Franc Zone	Commonwealth	Arab League	Participants in Belgrade Conference of Non-Aligned States (September 1961).†
Niger	x	x			x		x			x **			
Upper Volta	x	x			x		x			x **			
Ivory Coast	x	x			x		x			x **			
Chad	x	x				x	x	x		x *			
Central African Republic	x	x				x	x	x		x *			
Republic of Congo (Brazzaville)	x	x				x	x	x		x *			
Gabon	x	x				x	x	x		x *			
Federation of Nigeria	x								x		x		
Mauritania	x	x					x			x **			
Sierra Leon	x								x		x		
Tanganyika	⁴								x		x		
Independent during 1962													
Burundi							x						
Rwanda							x						
Algeria			x							10		x	x
Uganda									x		x		

271

NOTES TO APPENDIX II

Note: Membership in the United Nations and associated institutions is omitted in view of the universal nature of these organizations, and the tendency of African States to join all of them. Membership in non-official organizations of individuals or groups is also omitted, e.g., Afro-Asian Solidarity Council, as beyond the scope of this table.

* *Member of La Banque Centrale des États d l'Afrique Centrale.*

** *Member of La Banque Centrale des États de l'Afrique de l'Ouest;* all of the members of the Bank, with the exception of Togo, have a common currency; there is a fixed parity, however, between the currency of Togo and the other Bank members.

† The "Belgrade Conference" is the only conference included because more than any other conference, which has not resulted in a formal organization, it provides insight into the nature of African world politics, and is referred to at various points in the text in keeping with this judgment.

[1] Withdrew from the Commonwealth during 1961. [2] Original member of the Monrovia bloc; withdrew in January 1962. [3] Original member of the Monrovia bloc; failed to initial the Charter of the Inter-African and Malagasy States Organizations in December 1962. [4] Became independent after the Monrovia bloc was formed; attended the bloc's meeting in January 1962, but failed to initial the Charter in December 1962. [5] Uses United States Dollars as currency. [6] Not member of sterling area, but has special sterling transfer association. [7] Not member franc zone since 1959, but close special relationship. [8] A "nominal" member of the franc zone, whose actual relationship with the zone is not very different from that of Morocco. [9] Withdrew from franc zone after achieving independence. [10] A member of franc zone with special relationship which is less inclusive than that of other African franc zone members, e.g., Mali is not a member of *La Banque Centrale des États de l'Afrique de l'Ouest,* and Algeria has more latitude in foreign exchange transactions.

Notes

NOTES

Note to *Preface*

1. Arnold Rivkin, *Africa and the West: Elements of Free-World Policy*, Frederick A. Praeger, New York, and Thames and Hudson, London, 1962.

Notes to *Chapter 1*

1. Quoted in *Africa Report*, Vol. 6, No. 11 (December 1961), p. 17.
2. Quoted in *West Africa* (London), No. 2325, December 23, 1961, p. 4122; see Chapter 8 for a particularly ironic application of this doctrine.
3. Kwame Nkrumah, *I Speak of Freedom*, Frederick A. Praeger, New York, 1961, pp. x–xi.
4. Nnamdi Azikiwe, *ZIK*, Cambridge University Press, Cambridge, 1961, pp. 72–73.

Notes to *Chapter 2*

1. Hon. Zanna Bukar Dipcharima, Federal Minister of Commerce and Industry, quoted in *Federal Nigeria*, Vol. IV, Nos. 1–3 (January–March 1961), p. 11.
2. Kwame Nkrumah, *I Speak of Freedom*, Frederick A. Praeger, New York, 1961, pp. 218–222.
3. *Ibid.*, pp. 167–168.
4. *Ibid.*, p. 201.
5. Statement by President William V. S. Tubman at Press Conference in New York, October 17, 1961, quoted in Embassy of Liberia, *Press Release* (unnumbered), October 18, 1961.

6. Government of Liberia, advertisement in the *New York Times,*
January 9, 1962.
7. Ursula K. Hicks, *Development from Below,* Oxford University Press,
London, 1961, pp. 5–9.
8. Ursula K. Hicks and others, *Federalism and Economic Growth in
Underdeveloped Countries,* Oxford University Press, New York, 1961, pp.
14–15.

NOTES to *Chapter 3*

1. Program of the Communist Party of the Soviet Union adopted at its
22nd Congress in October 1961.
2. Mamadou Dia, *L'Économie Africaine,* Presses Universitaires de
France, Paris, 1957, p. 82. All translations in the book from French to English by the present author unless otherwise indicated.
3. Charter of the Union of African States, published in *Ghana Today*
(London), Vol. 5, No. 11 (July 19, 1961), pp. 8–9.
4. Sékou Touré, *Toward Full Re-Africanisation* [rev. English ed.],
Présence Africaine, Paris, 1959, p. 39.
5. See Léopold Sédar Senghor, *African Socialism* [English ed.], American Society of African Culture, New York, 1959, p. 38.
6. Touré, *op. cit.,* p. 64.
7. *Ibid.,* pp. 64–65.
8. *Ibid.,* p. 38.
9. *New York Times,* December 28, 1961 and February 9, 1962.
10. Speech by President Nkrumah at the opening of the U.S. Exhibition in Ghana, November 27, 1961; published in Ghana Information Services, *Ghana* (New York), Press Release No. 169, November 29, 1961.
11. Kwame Nkrumah, "Toward the Future," President's Session Address to Parliament, July 4, 1961, reprinted as Supplement with *Ghana Today*
(London), July 19, 1961, p. 8.
12. Touré, *op. cit.,* p. 14.
13. Senghor, *op. cit.,* p. 29.
14. As quoted in *West Africa* (London), No. 2307, August 19, 1961,
p. 903.

NOTES to *Chapter 4*

1. *Economic Survey of Nigeria, 1959,* Nigeria Government Printer,
Lagos (1959), p. 22.
2. European Economic Community Commission, *Report on the Economic Situation in the Countries of the Community,* Brussels, September 1958,
p. 585.
3. The percentage figures in this and the preceding paragraph are from
United Nations, *Economic Survey of Africa Since 1950,* New York, 1959,
Ch. 3.
4. Speech by Dr. Nkrumah, published as Foreword to *Ghana, Second
Development Plan, 1959–64,* Government Printer, Accra, 1959, p. iii.
5. Kwame Nkrumah, *I Speak of Freedom,* Frederick A. Praeger, New
York, 1961, p. 191.

6. *Economic Survey of Africa Since 1950, op. cit.*, p. 44.

7. *Ibid.*, p. 50.

8. United Nations, *Enlargement of the Exchange Economy in Tropical Africa*, New York, 1954, pp. 9–13.

9. *Economic Survey of Africa Since 1950, op. cit.*, p. 41.

10. International Labour Office, *African Labour Survey*, Geneva, 1958, p. 111.

11. Pierre-Bernard Cousté, *L'Association des Pays d'Outre Mer à la Communauté Économique Européenne*, Librairies Techniques, Paris, 1959, p. 88; Léopold Sédar Senghor, in his book *African Socialism* (American Society of African Culture, New York, 1959), estimates that "peasants . . . constitute more than 90 per cent of the population" of African countries (p. 38); and the United Nations, *Economic Survey of Africa Since 1950, op. cit.* (p. 49), speculates that: "It is probable that in all African countries, with the exception of the Union of South Africa, the majority of the economically active Africans are engaged, intermittently or permanently, in traditional agriculture."

12. Jacques Lefebvre, *Structures Économiques du Congo Belge et du Ruanda-Urundi*, Editions du Treurenberg, Brussels, 1955, p. 53.

13. The projected expenditures in agriculture and industry during the new plan period (1962–1968) are, in the Western Region, at more than 40 per cent, compared to 20 per cent in the period beginning in 1955; in the Northern Region, more than 30 per cent, compared with 15 per cent during the earlier period; and in the Eastern Region, about 40 per cent, compared to 14 per cent in the preceding period.

14. For the most part the statistics on the allocation of planned expenditures for agriculture and industry in the development plans of African areas have been drawn from the *United Nations Economic Survey of Africa Since 1950, op. cit.*, p. 245.

15. Minister of the Congo and Ruanda-Urundi, Auguste De Schrijver, in a radio address on October 16, 1959; reprinted in full (in French) in Centre de Recherche et d'Information Socio-Politiques, *Congo 1959*, Brussels, 1960.

16. East Africa Royal Commission, *Report*, 1953–1955 (Cmnd. 9475), HMSO, London, pp. 65–66.

17. *Ibid.*, p. 66; also p. 67 viz. the quoted passage from the Food Shortage Commission of Enquiry, 1943, "*We recommend that such exportable surplus* [of maize] *should be kept as small as possible and that the future policy of the Colony* [Kenya] *should be not to encourage the production of maize for export*"; and p. 69, "The basic problem of East Africa is not the achievement of security at the expense of economic efficiency and mobility. Attempts to cushion off producers from the world markets . . . weaken the general economy . . . because they mis-apply . . . resources [and] inhibit the economic expansion. . . ."

18. The pertinent paragraph of the Groundnut Scheme declared: "No significant increase in the present output of oilseeds can be achieved, however, by the existing methods of present production. Nothing but the most highly mechanised agricultural methods, on a vast scale never previously envisaged, will result in any appreciable amelioration of the present disastrous food position." "A Plan for the Mechanized Production of Groundnuts in East and

Central Africa" (Cmnd. 7030), HMSO, February 1947, p. 18, quoted in S. Herbert Frankel, *The Economic Impact on Under-Developed Societies*, Basil Blackwell, Oxford, 1953, p. 145.

19. *Ibid.*, p. 152.

20. Bankole Timothy, *Kwame Nkrumah*, George Allen & Unwin, London, 1955, p. 174, and Nkrumah, *I Speak of Freedom*, *op. cit.*, p. 25. See also George Padmore, *The Gold Coast Revolution*, Dobson, London, 1953, pp. 224–225.

21. Nyasaland Commission of Inquiry *Report* (Cmnd. 814), HMSO, London, p. 19.

22. *Ibid.*

23. John F. V. Phillips, *Agriculture and Ecology in Africa*, Faber and Faber, London, 1960, pp. 369–375.

24. There can be little doubt that one hoped-for result of the European Economic Community insofar as France is concerned is the solution of the *surprix* problem. By lowering the protection somewhat on agricultural commodities, principally coffee, flowing from former French African territories to France, and by opening the markets of these African areas to the EEC countries in return for broadening the area of protection for the primary products of these African territories to include the six Common Market countries, France hopes to lighten the load on its own resources by sharing the burden with its EEC partners, particularly West Germany, and by increasing the earnings of the African territories so that they can finance some of their own development, or at least meet ordinary budget deficits now defrayed by France.

In addition, the $571 million Overseas Development Fund, largely earmarked to flow to former French Africa over a 5-year period, 1958–1962, is designed to speed the development of former French Africa, particularly in the social overhead field and to a lesser extent directly in the productive sectors of the economies. The new Convention of Association provides for another $500 million for the five-year period, 1963–1967, for the eighteen African Associated States, of which a majority will go once again to the former French territories. The bulk of the special $230 million agricultural diversity and productivity fund is also largely destined for the former French territories.

25. International Bank for Reconstruction and Development, *The Economic Development of Nigeria*, John Hopkins Press, Baltimore, 1955, pp. 193–194.

26. P. de Schlippe and B. L. Batwell, "Preliminary Studies of the Nayangware System of Agriculture," *Africa* (London), Vol. XXV, No. 4 (1955), p. 334.

27. Quoted in *The Economist* (London), August 12, 1961, pp. 638–640.

28. *Ibid.*

29. *Ibid.*

Notes to Chapter 5

1. *The Nigerianisation of the Civil Service* (The Phillipson-Adebo Report), Federal Government Printer, Lagos, 1953, p. 8.

2. Parliamentary Committee on the Nigerianisation of the Federal Public Service, *Final Report* (Sessional Paper No. 6 of 1959), Nigeria Government Printer, Lagos, 1959, p. 2, quoting from the Federal Malayanisation Commission, *Report* (Sessional Paper No. 65 of 1956), Kuala Lumpaur, Malaya, 1956.

3. *Ibid.*, pp. 63–64.

4. Sékou Touré, *Toward Full Re-Africanisation* (rev. English ed.), Présence Africaine, Paris, 1959, p. 40.

5. Parliamentary Committee on Nigerianisation *Final Report, op. cit.*, p. 64.

6. *Ibid.*, p. 58.

7. Commission on Post-Certificate and Higher Education in Nigeria, *Report*, Nigeria Government Printer, Lagos, 1960, p. 64.

8. "Statement of Policy of the Government of the Federation on the Nigerianisation of the Federal Public Service and the Higher Training of Nigerians, 1955–60" (Sessional Paper No. 4 of 1956), Lagos, 1956, p. 2, quoted in Parliamentary Committee on Nigerianisation *Final Report, op. cit.*, p. 3.

9. *Ibid.*, pp. 60–61.

10. *Ibid.*, p. 59.

11. *Ibid.*, p. 3.

12. In the Northern Region of Nigeria the program is one of not merely Nigerianization but "Northernization" of the public service, to replace not only expatriates but Nigerians from the Eastern and Western Regions in the public service of the Northern Region.

13. All statistics quoted in this paragraph are the latest available for 1959 and are for the Western, Eastern, and Northern Regions as of April 30, April 1, and October 1, respectively. The statistics are cited in Annex III, IV and V of Kenneth Younger, *The Public Service in New States*, Oxford University Press, London, 1960, pp. 107–108.

14. "The British in Nigeria," *West Africa* (London), No. 2257, September 3, 1960, p. 986.

15. Tom Stacey, "Non-Alignment Is British Advice to Nigeria," *The Sunday Times* (London), October 2, 1960.

16. *The Times* (London), October 6, 1960.

17. *Ibid.*

18. "Localization" has also been declared to be the policy for Kenya and the East Africa High Commission, which administered certain joint services in Uganda, Kenya, and Tanganyika. With the independence of Tanganyika in December, 1961, it was reconstituted as the East African Common Services Organization but continues to perform essentially the same functions.

19. If it were possible to make a selection of the hard-core crucial civil service posts from the 355 key ones, there is no question but that in these the percentage of expatriates would exceed 42 per cent quite significantly.

20. Ministère de l'Information de la République de Guinée, "Quelques Aspects du Problème des Cadres en République de Guinée," paper included in *Problèmes des Cadres dans les Pays Tropicaux et Subtropicaux*, Institut International des Civilisations Différentes (INCIDI), Brussels, 1961, pp. 71–81.

21. It is interesting to note in this connection that when, for example,

"foreigners brought new trades to England in the sixteenth and seventeenth centuries, the patents of monopoly which they were granted often included the condition that the foreigner must train a number of Englishmen in his craft within a stipulated period." W. Arthur Lewis, *The Theory of Economic Growth*, George Allen & Unwin, London, 1955, p. 197.

22. *Ibid.*

23. L. R. Darracq, "Le Problème des Cadres en Côte d'Ivoire," in INCIDI, *op. cit.*, p. 88.

24. See *Ibid.*, p. 73.

25. Félix Eboué, "Circulaire Générale sur la politique Indigène en Afrique Équatoriale Française," Brazzaville, November 8, 1941, p. 26, quoted in Jacques Denis, *Le Phénomène Urbain en Afrique Centrale*, Académie Royale des Sciences Coloniales, Brussels, 1958, p. 267.

26. David Howarth, "Kariba: The Epic of the Dam," Pt. 3, *The Sunday Times* (London), March 6, 1960.

27. Denis, *op. cit.*, p. 264.

28. See, for example, Walter Birmingham, "An Index of Real Wages of the Unskilled Labourer in Accra, 1939–1959," *The Economic Bulletin* (Accra), Vol. 4, No. 3 (March 1960), particularly p. 4: "Unfortunately for the manual workers, the Korsah Award was part of a general wage salary increase which gave everyone substantially more to spend on a basis roughly proportionate to their existing rate of pay. . . . Inflation voided the gains which came from the award."

29. East Africa Royal Commission, *Report*, 1953–1955 (Cmnd. 9475), HMSO, London, 1955, p. 160.

30. Governor Pétillion is quoted to this effect, in Denis, *op. cit.*, p. 266.

31. The Belgian authorities in the Congo attempted to distinguish between *chomeur*, i.e., unemployed persons discharged from their jobs and unable to find other work, and *non-emploi*, i.e., unemployed persons who have never held wage-paying jobs who have been attracted to urban centers in large part by the apparent affluence of relatives and friends settled there. It is the latter group the Belgian administration particularly attempted to repatriate to tribal areas, especially after the 1957 commodity price break, and then again after the 1959 Leopoldville riots. See Commission Parlementaire Chargée de Faire une Enquête sur les Evénements Qui Se Sont Produits à Léopoldville en Janvier 1959, *Rapport*, March 27, 1959 (Chamber of Representatives, Document 100 [1958–59] No. 3).

32. *Review of Salaries and Wages*, Report by the Commission appointed by the Governments of the Federation, the Northern Region, the Eastern Region, and the Southern Cameroons, Nigeria Government Printer, Lagos, 1959, p. 3.

33. Léopold Sédar Senghor, *African Socialism*, American Society of African Culture, New York, 1959, pp. 38–39.

34. "Policy for Independent Nigeria," *West Africa* (London), No. 2262, October 8, 1960, p. 1129.

35. Senghor, *op. cit.*, p. 38.

36. Kenneth Younger, *The Public Service in New States*, Oxford University Press, London, 1960, p. 68.

37. *Ibid.*, p. 70.

38. Georges Fischer, *L'Indépendance de la Guinée*, Présence Africaine,

Paris, 1960, as quoted by Georges Gayet in "La Formation des Cadres Africains dans la Communauté Franco-Africaine," in INCIDI, *op. cit.*, p. 148.

39. Léopold Sédar Senghor, then President of the Federal Assembly of Mali, speaking of the Parti Fédéral Africain in a broadcast April 15, 1960, as quoted by Georges Gayet in *ibid.*, p. 151.

40. INCIDI, "Conclusions of the 32nd Study Session," *ibid.*, p. 662.

NOTES to *Chapter 6*

1. The Director of Native Education of Southern Rhodesia, as quoted in Franklin Parker, *African Development and Education in Southern Rhodesia*, Ohio State University Press, Columbus, 1960, pp. ix–x.

2. K. M. Panikkar, *The Afro-Asian States and Their Problems*, Allen & Unwin, London, 1959, pp. 65–66.

3. *Ibid.*, p. 65.

4. *Education in the United Kingdom Dependencies* (COI Pamphlet No. 4), HMSO, London, 1959, pp. 2–3.

5. National Academy of Sciences, *Recommendations for Strengthening Science and Technology in Selected Areas of Africa South of the Sahara*, Washington, D.C., July 1959, p. 7.

6. For example, in East Africa it has been estimated to exceed 40 per cent (East Africa Royal Commission, *Report, 1953–1955* [Cmnd. 9475], HMSO, London, 1955), and in the Western Region of Nigeria it has been said to be as high as 48 per cent. (The latest census in the Western Region, 1952, put the figure at 48 per cent for those "under 14 years of age.") This compares with 20 per cent of the population for this age group in the United Kingdom.

7. See, for example, J. C. de Graft-Johnson, *An Introduction to the African Economy*, Asia Publishing House, Bombay, 1959, p. 21, for this estimate made in the African context.

8. Conference of African States on the Development of Education in Africa, *Final Report*, UNESCO, Paris, 1961, Chapter I, p. 3. (The conference was sponsored jointly by UNESCO and the U.N. Economic Commission for Africa.)

9. W. Arthur Lewis, "Problems of New States," an address to the International Conference on Science in the Advancement of New States, Rehovoth, Israel, August 15, 1960, p. 6 (mimeographed).

10. Conference of African States on Education, *Final Report, op.cit.*, Chapter II, p. 10.

11. *Ibid.*, Chapter III, p. 11.

12. Kwame Nkrumah, *I Speak of Freedom*, Frederick A. Praeger, New York, 1961, pp. 242–243.

13. *Final Report*, Conference of African States on Education, *op. cit.*, Chapter V, p. 37.

14. Commission on Post-Certificate and Higher Education in Nigeria, *Report*, Nigeria Government Printer, Lagos, 1960, pp. 45–46.

15. Lewis, *op. cit.*, p. 6.

16. L. Paye, "Educating for Citizenship," in *Panorama*, Vol. 1, No. 4 (Winter, 1959), p. 12. M. Paye was Rector of the University of Dakar when he wrote this article.

17. See *Africa Digest* (London), Vol. IX, No. 2 (October 1961), p. 65.

18. Sékou Touré, *Toward Full Re-Africanisation* [rev. English ed.], Présence Africaine, Paris, 1959, pp. 62–63.

19. Conference of African States on Education, *Final Report, op. cit.*, Chapter I, p. 6.

NOTES to *Chapter* 7

1. I. M. D. Little, A *Critique of Welfare Economics* [2nd ed.], Oxford University Press, London, 1960, p. 259.

2. "It is . . . a misfortune for a backward country to have a government which is committed to *laissez-faire*. . . . This has been the misfortune of the British Colonial Empire in the nineteenth and twentieth centuries." W. Arthur Lewis, *The Theory of Economic Growth*, George Allen & Unwin, London, 1955, pp. 412–413.

3. C.E.L.P.U.F., Conférence plenière, January 10, 1957, *Le Développement des Pays Économiquement Arriérés et le Problèmes Posés à la France*, quoted in Pierre-Bernard Cousté, *L'Association des Pays d'Outre-Mer à la Communauté Économique Européenne*, Librairies Techniques, Paris, 1959, p. 225.

4. P. de Calan, "Note Sur l'exposé de M. Bertrand de Jouvenel," *Ibid.*, p. 226.

5. Sékou Touré, *Toward Full Re-Africanisation* [rev. English ed.], Présence Africaine, Paris, 1959, pp. 95–96.

NOTES to *Chapter* 8

1. The federal structure in the Federation of Rhodesia and Nyasaland was imposed by the British Government in 1953 on three colonial territories without any constitutional change in their colonial status. The two other cases of federalism are really both examples of consolidating independent or near-independent states rather than conscious creation of federal states in colonial areas which were then brought to independence. The ill-fated Federation of Mali is a special case where two "autonomous states" in the original Franco-African Community sought and achieved independence from France as a federal state. The federation broke up in mid-1960, several months after accession to independence. Finally, the Federal Republic of Cameroon brought together late in 1961 the independent state, the Republic of Cameroun, and the trust territory of the Southern Cameroons, which opted in a plebiscite earlier that year to join the Republic.

2. P. F. Gonidec, *Constitutions des États de la Communauté*, Paris, 1959, p. 73, quoted in Ursula K. Hicks and others, *Federalism and Economic Growth in Underdeveloped Countries*, Oxford University Press, New York, 1961, p. 32n.

3. Convocation address at University of Nigeria, Nsukka, as quoted in the *Daily Times* (Lagos), November 20, 1961.

4. For practical purposes, in the federations of Mali and Cameroon the transformations had occurred in the individual states before federation.

5. Ghanaian translation of the cable of August 14, 1960, Tshombé

to Nkrumah, published in *Correspondence between Osagyefo, Dr. Kwame Nkrumah, and Leaders of the Republic of the Congo on the Congo Situation,* Government Printer, Accra, p. 11.

6. As recently as February 1963, the Federation of Rhodesia and Nyasaland was still establishing precedents in this field for the member territories, two of which, Nyasaland and Northern Rhodesia, are on the verge of independence. Dr. Terrence Ranger, a lecturer in the University College of Rhodesia and Nyasaland, who was in disfavor with the federation government for his membership in the barred Zinbabwe African People's Union, *inter alia,* was expelled from the Federation. This moved *The Times* (London, February 21, 1963) to editorialize as follows: "In what way is the expulsion of Dr. Ranger different from expulsions by the new African governments, and by South Africa? The Federal Government sets no higher standard, apparently, than any other state in Africa devoted to tribal conformity." It is not so long ago that metropolitan powers themselves used the same instrumentalities to rid the colonies of "troublemakers," home-grown or from abroad.

7. K. C. Wheare, *Federal Government,* London, 1953, p. 48.

8. F. G. Carnell, "Political Implications of Federalism," in Ursula K. Hicks and others, *Federalism and Economic Growth,* Oxford University Press, New York, 1961, p. 24.

9. It is interesting to note that President Nkrumah's announcement of his intention to accede to the office of General Secretary of the CPP coincided with a state visit of President Tito, who occupies the dual position of state and party leader in Yugoslavia.

10. Some of those arrested during this period still remain in preventive detention at the time this book goes to press, although President Nkrumah in several executive acts has released about 300 of the people detained under the Preventive Detention Act.

11. As quoted in *West Africa* (London), No. 2303, July 22, 1961, p. 799.

12. The new external broadcasting system which started operation during the summer of 1961 has been built at an announced cost of 700,000 pounds. The "voice of Ghana" will speak in English, French, Hausa, Arabic, Spanish, and Swahili.

13. See *Guinée: Prélude à l'Indépendance,* Présence Africaine, Paris, 1958, p. 175.

14. The governmental crisis in the Western Region, which started with a split in the Action Group between the wings supporting Premier Akintola and Chief Awolowo, led the federal government in June 1962 to declare a state of emergency in the Region and to supersede the regional government with a Federal Administrator for the balance of 1962. Many issues in the crisis, including this use of constitutional authority by the federal government, have been and are being contested in the courts. A major court ruling found in favor of Chief Akintola, who in January 1963 (along with the federal government's termination of the state of emergency) was reinstated as Premier heading a coalition government of his newly organized United People's Party, based on his wing of the Action Group, and the NCNC, former opposition party in the Western Region. The remaining wing of the Action Group continues to support its party leader, Chief Awolowo, and con-

stitutes the *de facto* opposition. The governmental crisis has been complicated by the hearings of the federally-appointed Coker Commission into corruption in the Western Region government and its findings implicating Chief
Awolowo and vindicating Chief Akintola, and by the indictment and trial
of Chief Awolowo, still *sub judice*, on charges of conspiring to overthrow the
federal government by force. Chief Awolowo is conducting his own defense
which contends that the charges, together with all the other elements of the
regional crisis, are part of a conspiracy to destroy the Action Group and
his leadership thereof. Hence, the critical importance of a fair trial and honest
elections and the reaction of the electorate to the welter of charges and
countercharges. The termination of the emergency in the time period promised, the general lack of violence, and the recourse to the courts by all parties
to the dispute and the performance of the courts to date, are all on the plus
side with respect to Nigeria's ability to weather the storm and its democratic
system to survive this severe test so early in its existence.

15. After being released, Mr. Stevens, leader of the All People's Congress, was soon rearrested and convicted of "sedition, libel, and conspiracy
against the Prime Minister." He was sentenced in June 1961 to six months'
imprisonment. Since then Mr. Stevens' convictions were quashed by the Court
of Appeals of Sierra Leone on the ground that there was insufficient evidence
to support the conviction. The Rule of Law operated as an effective safeguard
for the political opposition in Sierra Leone in a way all too rare in Africa.

16. *New York Times*, September 17, 1958.

Notes to Chapter 9

1. *Ghanaian Times* (Accra), May 16, 1961.

2. Quoted in American Universities Field Staff, *Reports Service*, West
Africa Series, Vol. IV, No. 5 (General), p. 6.

3. *Ibid.*, pp. 6–7.

4. *Ibid.*, p. 17.

5. Ghana: The Autobiography of Kwame Nkrumah, Thomas Nelson
and Sons, Edinburgh, 1957, p. 53.

6. République de Guinée, *La Planification Économique*, Conakry, 1960,
p. 279. See also the preface of Aimé. Cesaire in Sékou Touré, *L'Expérience
Guinéenne et L'Unité Africaine*, Présence Africaine, Paris, 1958, pp. 5–7:
"What is happening in Guinea today is not only determining the fate of
Guinea, but the fate of Africa."

7. Text of Joint Communiqué by President Nkrumah of Ghana and
President Brezhnev of the Soviet Union, July 24, 1961, published by Ghana
Information Services, *Ghana* (New York), Press Release No. 156, July 28,
1961.

8. Interview on BBC television, reported by *West Africa* (London),
No. 2304, July 29, 1961, p. 827.

9. As reported *ibid.*, p. 841.

10. *Ibid.*

11. As reported in the *Ghanaian Times* (Accra), May 5, 1961.

12. *Ibid.*

13. Text of Joint Communiqué by President Nkrumah of Ghana and
President Brezhnev of the Soviet Union, *loc. cit.*

14. *Ibid.*

15. Sékou Touré, *Guinée Prélude à l'Indépendance*, Présence Africaine, Paris, 1958, p. 164.

16. As part of the attempt to attract Guinea back into the fold of former French African territories, as part of a possible larger reconciliation of the Monrovia and Cavablanca blocs, President Houphouët-Boigny paid a state visit to Guinea in November 1962. The joint communiqué at the end of the visit, which "affirm[s] their faith in African unity," says little more about reconciling basic policy differences. However, at the conclusion of the visit President Touré declared: "Our differences are definitely buried and on their ashes have begun the immortal flowers of fraternity and solidarity of our people in the magnificent garden of African unity." Joint Communiqué and President Touré's statement quoted in *African Diary* (Delhi), Vol. II, No. 47, November 17–23, 1962, p. 858.

17. PAFMECSA has been primarily an organization of unofficial nationalist movements. Prior to February 1962, when Ethiopia and Somalia adhered, only Tanganyika provided official participation.

NOTES to *Chapter* 10

1. Published by Ghana Information Services, *Ghana* (New York), Press Release No. 156, July 28, 1961.

2. *New York Times*, August 1, 1961.

3. *Ibid.*, July 31, 1961.

4. *The Times* (London), April 1961.

5. As quoted in *West Africa* (London), No. 2303, July 22, 1961, p. 799.

6. *Ghana Today* (London), Vol. 5, No. 9 (June 21, 1961), p. 1.

7. Quoted in American Universities Field Staff, *Reports Service*, West Africa Series, Vol. IV, No. 5 (General), p. 20.

NOTES to *Chapter* 11

1. From an address to the Federal Parliament of Nigeria on March 29, 1961; quoted in *Federal Nigeria*, Vol. IV, Nos. 1–2 (January–March 1961), p. 1.

2. *New York Times*, September 6, 1961.

3. Excerpts from the Program (draft) of the Communist Party of the Soviet Union, quoted in the *New York Times*, August 1, 1961:

"(1) A powerful wave of national-liberation revolutions is sweeping away the colonial system and undermining the foundations of imperialism.

"(2) But the struggle is not yet over. . . . The peoples of those formally independent countries that in reality depend on foreign monopolies politically and economically are rising to fight against imperialism and reactionary pro-imperialist regimes.

"(3) Imperialism . . . remains the chief enemy, and the chief obstacle to the solution of the national problems facing the young sovereign states. . . .

"(4) The national bourgeoisie is dual in character. In modern conditions the national bourgeoisie . . . is objectively interested in accomplishing the basic tasks of an anti-imperialist and anti-feudal revolution. Its progressive role and its ability to participate . . . are . . . not yet spent.

"But as the contradictions between the working people and the propertied classes grow and the class struggle inside the country becomes more aggravated, the national bourgeoisie shows an increasing inclination to compromise with imperialism and domestic reaction."

4. Text of Joint Communiqué by President Nkrumah of Ghana and President Brezhnev of the Soviet Union, July 24, 1961, published by Ghana Information Services, *Ghana* (New York), Press Release No. 156, July 28, 1961.

5. It is pertinent to note that in the joint communiqué issued by the Chairman of the People's Republic of China and President Nkrumah on the occasion of the latter's visit to Communist China the term "national liberation" is used and the meaning assigned is about the same as the definition provided in the Soviet Communist Party program. For example, the communiqué declares: "In the present struggle to safeguard world peace, the national liberation movement in Asia, Africa, and Latin America has become an extremely important force." The communiqué uses the phrases "semi-colonial peoples" and "new colonialism" as euphemisms for the inhabitants of states with "stooge governments" imposed by "neo-colonialists." These excerpts from the communiqué are taken from the text as printed in the *Peking Review* (Peking), Vol. IV, No. 34 (August 25, 1961), pp. 5–6.

6. As quoted in *West Africa* (London), No. 2305, August 5, 1961, p. 869.

7. *Op. cit.* (note 1).

Notes to *Chapter* 12

1. Public Law 87-329, Section 112, 87th Congress, 2d Sess., September 30, 1961.

2. Editorial, *New York Herald Tribune*, October 12, 1961.

3. The Congo crises raise other questions which cut across these general tendencies. Here the Casablanca powers find the colonial boundaries have a sanctity which must be defended against secessionist Katanga, aided and abetted by neo-colonialists. The Brazzaville twelve, however, have tended to sympathize with, even if they have not openly supported, the "self-determination" drive of Katanga and its attempt to alter the colonial boundaries by withdrawing from the Congo.

4. It is interesting to note that at the end of 1962 ten of the twelve Brazzaville bloc or Union of African and Malagasy States recognized Nationalist China, and the remaining two members, Ivory Coast and Niger, recognized neither Nationalist nor Communist China, whereas the six Casablanca bloc members recognized Communist China. Nigeria and Sierra Leone recognized neither one.

Notes to *Chapter* 13

1. The President's Message to the Congress, "New Program for Foreign Aid," March 22, 1961.

2. *Ibid.*

3. *Ibid.*

4. See the author's article, "The Problems of Nation-Building: Problems and Preconditions," *International Affairs*, vol. XVI, No. 2 (1962), especially pp. 132–136, for a fuller discussion of the problems involved in building international political unions in underdeveloped areas, with particular emphasis on Africa.

5. *New York Times*, January 19, 1962.

INDEX